REVISE AQA GCSE (9–1)
Design and Technology
REVISION GUIDE

Series Consultant: Harry Smith

Author: Mark Wellington

Also available to support your revision:

Revise GCSE Study Skills Guide   9781447967071

The **Revise GCSE Study Skills Guide** is full of tried-and-trusted hints and tips for how to learn more effectively. It gives you techniques to help you achieve your best — throughout your GCSE studies and beyond!

Revise GCSE Revision Planner   9781447967828

The **Revise GCSE Revision Planner** helps you to plan and organise your time, step-by-step, throughout your GCSE revision. Use this book and wall chart to mastermind your revision.

For the full range of Pearson revision titles across KS2, KS3, GCSE, Functional Skills, AS/A Level and BTEC visit:
www.pearsonschools.co.uk/revise

Contents

1-to-1 page match with the Design and Technology Revision Workbook ISBN 9781292191577

A small bit of small print
AQA publishes Sample Assessment Material and the Specification on its website. This is the official content and this book should be used in conjunction with it. The questions have been written to help you practise every topic in the book. Remember: the real exam questions may not look like this.

Industry

You need to understand the impact of new and emerging technologies in the workplace.

The workplace, automation and robotics

Automation is the use of control systems including those for design and manufacture, such as computer numerically controlled (CNC) equipment, quality control and robotics.
👍 Reduced labour costs, improved productivity and a faster time to market.
👍 Greater precision, greater control, consistency and quality.
👍 Flexible production as CNC machinery can be quickly reprogrammed.
👍 Greater job opportunities for engineers.
👎 High cost of buying, installing and repairing systems, risk of power failure and system errors.

Robotics is the use of machines to carry out complex tasks such as locating parts on an assembly line and welding car body parts.
👍 Ideal for tasks that are repetitive, require accuracy, or are hazardous.
👍 Can carry extremely heavy loads without tiring or lacking concentration.
👍 Can be programmed to do different tasks, and increase productivity.
👎 Cannot replace human judgement when making complex decisions.
👎 May lead to fewer jobs for people.

Buildings and the place of work

As new technologies emerge, companies need to adapt the place of work in a variety of ways:

- More flexible building design to improve performance and speed of product to market.
- Automation and remote working, such as driverless vehicles managed centrally.
- Smaller factory units needed as the automated ordering of materials (JIT) reduces storage space.
- Automated Storage and Retrieval Systems (ASRS) may eliminate the use of manual handling.

Automation will change the place of work for most young people by the time they enter the workplace.

Just in time (JIT) is a strategy which increases efficiency by only accepting goods when they are needed in production, saving money on storage and levels of stock held.

Tools and equipment

Existing tools and equipment need to be adapted:

- Multi-purpose equipment can increase operational flexibility.
- Equipment will be organised into flexible manufacturing cells to respond to changes in demand.
- Tools will be increasingly automated to improve safety, and speed of manufacture.

Worked example

Describe **three** advantages of a company becoming more automated. **(3 marks)**

Storage space would be reduced.

Production would be more flexible and respond to demand.

There would be less human error and potential for injuries would be reduced.

Now try this

1 Explain **three** advantages to a manufacturer for changing the design of the workplace to include more robot technology. **(6 marks)**

2 Explain **two** disadvantages to the worker when a company decides to include more robot technology in production. **(4 marks)**

1

Enterprise

Enterprises are important to the economy as they employ a large number of people. Companies need to take advantage of new and emerging technologies to help develop their enterprises. They also need to ensure that they work ethically.

Crowdfunding

Crowdfunding is a good way for businesses to get **start-up** financial assistance for an enterprise. Funding comes from a large number of people. Online platforms coordinate and administer the fundraising.

Sources of crowdfunding:

- **Donation:** Money is given but not returned.
- **Debt:** Investors hope to receive their money back, sometimes with interest.
- **Equity:** Investors have the opportunity for a share in the business.

> An **enterprise** is an individual or business that shows initiative and takes a risk in setting up and running new ventures.

Virtual marketing and retail

The internet has enabled new enterprises to reach a wider potential client-base. All companies will now have a significant **virtual presence**. Marketing activities often use social networking sites to attract more customers.

An online presence has pros and cons:

- 👍 increased sales
- 👍 relatively cheap to set up and run
- 👎 sometimes complicated / difficult to navigate
- 👎 spam emails to advertise products are often not popular with customers.

Fairtrade

As enterprises develop around the world the needs of the workers, such as working conditions and pay, should not be overlooked.

The Fairtrade Foundation protects the rights of farmers in developing countries. It guarantees that they receive **fair prices** for commodities such as coffee, cocoa and tea.

Customers are often prepared to pay more for products that have met minimum social, economic and environmental requirements.

Worked example

Give **two** reasons why virtual marketing and retail can result in increased sales for a retailer.

(2 marks)

Customers can review products in the comfort of their home. The manufacturer can display a much wider range of products as there is no need for physical floor space.

Make sure your reasons are different. Don't say the same thing in two different ways.

Co-operatives

A co-operative is an enterprise that is jointly owned and democratically controlled by its members.

Members can be employees, producers or consumers of the products and have a close interest in the success of the enterprise.

They will benefit from using a wide range of media, communications, computer technology, goods and services to make them efficient and profitable.

Co-operatives:

- 👍 can increase purchasing and marketing power
- 👍 are easy to form with limited liability
- 👎 often have limited resources or funding
- 👎 can be hard to manage efficiently, which can reduce motivation.

Now try this

1 Give the name of the organisation that protects the rights of farmers in developing countries.

(1 mark)

2 Virtual marketing is used by companies to increase customer knowledge of their products in order to increase sales. Give **two** disadvantages to a company using virtual marketing. **(2 marks)**

Sustainability

Sustainability is meeting the needs of the present without compromising the needs of future generations. New technologies are helping to protect our environment and develop non-finite resources.

1 Finite resources

A finite resource is **non-renewable** or cannot be replenished at a sufficient rate to fulfil demand and will eventually run out. For example:

- fossil fuels used in the production of plastics
- metal ores and minerals within the Earth's crust.

New and emerging technologies are critical in the development of alternative materials to reduce the consumption of finite resources.

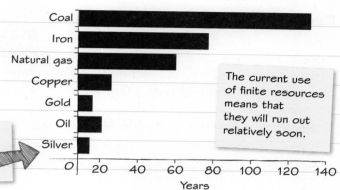

The current use of finite resources means that they will run out relatively soon.

2 Non-finite resources

A non-finite resource can be **replenished** through natural methods and can sustain the level of demand. For example:

- plants or algae are produced to manufacture fuels such as biodiesel
- oils from plants are used to produce environmentally-friendly plastics
- managed timber is used for building and furniture construction.

Worked example

Explain **two** reasons why finite resources will eventually run out. **(4 marks)**

Finite resources took millions of years to form, so cannot be replenished in a timescale that will be useful for us. It will also be more difficult to extract the resources as they will either be in deposits that cannot be reached or are too expensive to extract.

3 Disposal of waste

Any waste generated in manufacturing is expensive to dispose of and can pollute rivers, harm habitats and cause global warming.

Companies need to act responsibly and use a **Life Cycle Assessment** with the aim of minimising waste and to keep the amount of waste going into landfill to a minimum.

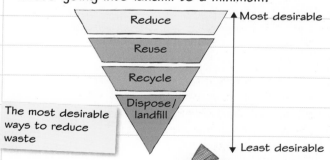

The most desirable ways to reduce waste

Strategies to minimise waste disposal

☑ **Reduce** the amount of waste produced, for example reducing packaging and size of products, improving quality control, and sending emails instead of letters.

☑ **Reuse** products or materials that would otherwise become waste, for example using re-fillable ink cartridges.

☑ **Recycle** materials to reduce the amount of new raw materials required, for example recycling plastic and glass bottles.

☑ **Recover** waste generated in factories, for example using waste heat energy to heat the factory.

Life Cycle Assessment (LCA) is a way to measure and analyse the environmental impacts of **a product at every stage of its life** (from cradle to grave).

For more on ecological impact see pages 100 and 101

Now try this

A company that manufactures kettles wants to reduce the amount of waste that has to be disposed of or that goes into landfill. Explain **four** ways that a manufacturer could reduce the amount of waste. **(8 marks)**

3

Core technical principles
New and emerging technologies
All materials

Had a look ☑ Nearly there ☐ Nailed it! ☐

People

You need to understand why products are developed and how the nature of job roles is changing.

Technology push and market pull

The development of new products can be driven in two ways:

Technology push

Research and development departments use new technologies to manufacture products where there was no existing consumer demand. Products which were impossible to produce previously can now be made due to the development of:

- new materials with improved properties
- new and improved manufacturing processes, making products more affordable
- advanced technology.

The development of Apple products, such as the iPad®, is a good example of technology push as new products are developed regularly to make people want to buy them.

Market pull

Consumer demand can dictate how fast a product develops. There are several reasons:

- Consumers desire new and improved products.
- Manufacturers want to secure a larger part of the market.
- Manufacturers must respond to market trends.
- Competitors introduce improved or new products.

The development of the digital camera is a good example of market pull. There was demand to reduce the size of a camera and increase the number of images stored. So large, bulky cameras have evolved into compact digital cameras, and then to cameras integrated into mobile phones with images stored in the cloud.

Changing job roles

Some estimates predict that two-thirds of children who are about to begin their education will have jobs that do not yet exist. Job roles are already changing due to an increase in computer technology and artificial intelligence.

- Some offices are now connected through virtual connections (conferencing) and mobile communication allows for home working or working while travelling.
- Companies will need people with technological skills who can respond quickly to change.
- People will need to become skilled in new technology such as in the film industry where CGI animation is increasingly used and automation is threatening the jobs of the less skilled.

Employers are helping universities, colleges and schools to develop courses which give students the right skills to succeed at work – now and in the future.

Worked example

Identify which of the following correctly describes 'market pull'. **(1 mark)**

A A point of sale display at the entrance to a supermarket. ◯

B There is a public demand for a product to be designed and made. ⬤

C A material that resists a stretching force. ◯

D Advertising displayed on the side of a bus. ◯

For multiple choice questions you should shade in **one** lozenge.

Now try this

 1 Describe **two** characteristics of technology push. **(2 marks)**

 2 Explain **two** reasons how the development of the iPad® has been the result of technology push. **(4 marks)**

Had a look ☐ Nearly there ☐ Nailed it! ☐

Core technical principles
New and emerging technologies
All materials

Culture

Fashion and trends, faiths and beliefs can affect product development.

Fashion

Fashion is defined as the dominant style in a given time period. Fashion affects areas of society including clothing, makeup or furniture.

- Fashions come and go relatively quickly, so new manufacturing technologies allow manufacturers to respond quickly to the latest fashion.
- Mobile communication and social media mean that the latest fashions can be found more easily and different brands are more accessible.
- Manufacturers can manage sales, marketing trends and stock more easily with **Product Data Management** (PDM), helping them analyse what is in or out of fashion in real time.

Product Data Management (PDM) is a computerised system accessible to all. It is used to manage all data about the design and manufacture of a product.

Trends

Trends reflect the general direction or development towards something new or different.

- Technology can help companies to predict trends, helping them to respond quickly.
- Trends may have different **lead times**, so companies must have flexible manufacturing systems.

Lead time is the amount of time it takes for a company to deliver a product to market from the start of the design process.

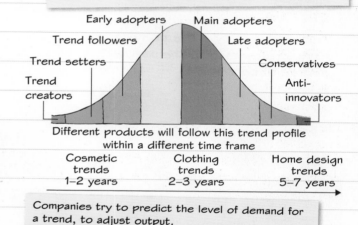

Different products will follow this trend profile within a different time frame

| Cosmetic trends 1–2 years | Clothing trends 2–3 years | Home design trends 5–7 years |

Companies try to predict the level of demand for a trend, to adjust output.

Faiths and beliefs

People from different cultures may have very different faiths and beliefs (which can be based on factors like religion, politics, vegetarianism, age or gender). People follow the rules of these faiths and beliefs as it is their measure of what they feel is right or wrong. Manufacturers must be careful to research their market to ensure that:

- their products do not give offensive images or messages
- their products do not use materials which are against the market's beliefs
- they are aware of their workers' needs such as breaks for worship or particular clothing requirements.

Culture

Culture is the shared general beliefs or customs of a specific group of people.

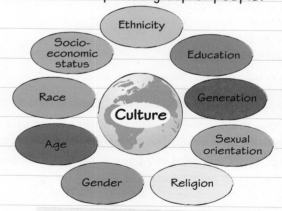

A culture can be any group of people that shares specific beliefs or faiths.

Worked example

Explain what is meant by the term 'culture' with regard to people. **(2 marks)**

Culture is the shared general beliefs or customs of a specific group of people based on faiths, beliefs, age or gender.

Now try this

Describe **three** ways the level of demand for a product will change as a trend develops. **(3 marks)**

Society

This section explores how inclusive design attempts to develop products that have a positive impact and maximise the number of potential users. There are three areas to consider.

① Design for the disabled

The one billion people around the world living with disabilities can benefit from technology to help them live a long, healthy, independent and engaging life. This includes designs for:

- assistive technology, which covers small devices such as pencil grips and text-to-speech readers to larger lifting devices and all-terrain wheelchairs that can scale uneven surfaces
- prosthetic limb technology where the electrical activity in the body can be harnessed, providing the user with a new degree of control.

② Design for the elderly

The average age of the population is increasing due to the age structure (1960s baby boom) and rising life expectancy. It is important that we address the needs of this sector of the population so that elderly people have a purpose and sense of wellbeing. This includes designs for:

- communication and accessible social media or monitoring devices
- mobility including transportation for short distances
- independence with mechanical / electronic aids for normal activities at home or away from home.

The use of **prosthetics** is improving at a rapid pace, as demonstrated with the range of cutting-edge technologies used by Paralympians.

A **prosthetic** is any artificial body part, such as a limb, a heart, or retinal implant.

Worked example

Explain **two** ways in which new and emerging technologies are improving independence of the elderly. **(4 marks)**

Mobile communications are improving the independence of the elderly because they have much greater access to social media and the internet, helping them to feel less isolated as they can communicate if needed. Mobility aids such as scooters or walkers allow elderly people who are less physically able to go out independently.

③ Design for different religious groups

Designers must consult with members of religious groups to consider their beliefs and to ensure that the design is suitable as otherwise they could lose potential customers.

- Some manufacturers will have a range of designs for a product that addresses the needs for each group and will not standardise the needs of religious groups.
- Technology can aid religious groups through improved communication. For example, followers of individual faiths can download prayer schedules or have a digital call to prayer.

The simple use of the wrong wording, colour or certain animal products in designs may offend some religions but will be acceptable in others.

Now try this

Explain **two** ways in which new and emerging technologies are allowing individuals who are blind to enter the workplace.
(4 marks)

Had a look ☐   Nearly there ☐   Nailed it! ☐

Core technical
principles

New and emerging
technologies

All materials

Environment

New products can have both positive and negative impacts on the environment.

Continuous improvement

Technological change is continuously improving quality, efficiency and processes involved in product design and reducing costs and environmental impact. This may include changes to:

- information services
- manufacturing systems (machinery)
- manufacturing scheduling (flow)
- product redesign
- materials technology.

👍 Improved products can have reduced carbon footprint.

👎 Early replacement of existing products, leading to increased use of transport, finite resources and landfill.

Efficient working

Efficiency is the ratio of time it takes to make a unit against the theoretical time needed to do it. Improvements in efficiency will save on cost and energy used. This can be achieved by developing:

- lean manufacturing
- just in time (JIT) production
- improved transport infrastructure
- redesigned factory layout
- better quality assurance and control systems.

See page 8 for more on lean manufacturing and JIT production.

👍 Fewer mistakes, lower costs, less stock and storage, products made to order.

👎 Relies on efficient supply chains, as breaks in supply chain affect production.

This factory is designed to maximise flow, reduce waste and improve productivity.

Effective factories

An **effective factory** should:
- utilise floor space
- reduce material handling
- reduce bottlenecks
- ensure work flows in a logical order
- reduce hazards to workers
- provide sufficient space / capacity.

Pollution

Pollution is the release of contaminating substances into the natural environment. As new technologies develop, companies will carry out Life Cycle Assessments (LCAs) to find ways to reduce pollution, which would include:

1. using renewable energy sources to reduce carbon dioxide released into the atmosphere
2. ensuring that its waste can be reduced, reused or disposed of easily
3. making production energy efficient.

Governments can also help by providing regulations including a carbon tax or subsidies to encourage companies to use alternative energy resources.

Global warming

Increases in global manufacturing are also increasing the carbon emissions from burning fossil fuels, causing the Earth's surface temperature to rise. This is global warming. Effects of global warming may include:

- rise in sea levels
- more unpredictable weather / storms
- widespread extinction of some species
- massive crop failure.

Renewable energy sources have been developed to slow down global warming.

Now try this

Explain **three** ways that a manufacturer can make improvements to efficiencies in its business.   (6 marks)

Production techniques and systems

New technologies are changing the way we make products in the factory system.

Computer Aided Design (CAD)

CAD combines software and hardware to create, develop, modify, test, communicate and record design information.

👍 CAD designs can be shared electronically.

👍 Ideas are tested, evaluated and modified on screen.

👍 Parts can be expanded for detail and complex calculations carried out.

👍 Processes are simulated, reducing the expense of producing prototypes.

👎 Workers need retraining.

👎 There is a risk that electronic files can be lost or sent to the wrong place.

Computer Aided Manufacture (CAM)

CAM uses computer software and hardware to translate CAD models into manufacturing instructions for **Computer Numerical Controlled (CNC)** machine tools.

👍 CAM offers greater reliability and quality as well as flexible production and improved productivity.

👍 Machine tools are faster, more accurate and can be quickly reprogrammed and linked to demand.

👍 Costs are reduced.

👍 Workers are guarded from potentially dangerous processes.

👎 Morale may be affected due to less human involvement and fewer 'machine minding' job roles.

👎 High set-up costs.

Lean manufacturing

This is a method to eliminate waste in a manufacturing system in key areas.

👍 Minimal storage, as stock materials are delivered just when needed and products are made only to order.

👍 Production is carefully set up to eliminate delays and reduce material / component movement.

👍 Rigorous quality assurance systems are established.

👍 Labour is used efficiently.

Flexible Manufacturing Systems (FMS)

FMS systems deliver high value products quickly, for example cars with various customer options. They can respond quickly to changes in demand or supply. Machinery is grouped together to be more efficient and may be handled by computer systems. Systems are effective, and close relationships with suppliers, manufacturers and retailers allow fast delivery

Just in time (JIT)

Just in time (JIT) helps companies meet quality orders quickly, and minimise time and resources using Information and Communications Technology (ICT). New stock is only ordered when needed, which means no over-ordering, better use of space and increased efficiency.

👍 Materials / components are in the right place at the right time.

👍 Storage costs are reduced as stock is not stored unnecessarily.

👍 Small batches of products can be produced cost-effectively.

👎 A break in the supply chain may cause delays.

Worked example

Describe **three** key characteristics of lean manufacturing. **(3 marks)**

The layout of the factory should be designed to minimise the movement of materials. Products will not be made unless an order has been placed. Staff deployment and use will be analysed to ensure they are used efficiently.

Now try this

 Just in time (JIT) manufacturing is a strategy to increase productivity.

Describe **three** characteristics of JIT that could lead to increased productivity. **(3 marks)**

Critical evaluation

External factors may influence design decisions.

Planned obsolescence

Some products are designed to have a specific, often short, life span.

Companies may **plan** for their products to become **obsolete** in a certain timeframe by:

- choosing appropriate parts to suit the predicted life span
- deciding on the frequency of upgrading elements of the design or a full re-launch
- launching new products using new technologies, or to meet new trends, to maintain their market share.

👍 Obsolescence increases demand by encouraging purchasers to buy again sooner.

👍 Companies can use cheaper components, which need only last as long as the planned life of the product.

👎 Consumers may complain about having to buy more regularly.

Changing mobile phone designs.

Design for maintenance

Designers need to consider whether they would want their products to be repaired by the user at a much lower cost than it could be replaced.

👍 The product has an extended life span, which is perceived to save customers money.

👍 The idea of saving money improves the reputation of the business.

👎 Technical support is expensive.

👎 The company must carry stock for repairs which takes up valuable storage space.

👎 Consumers will not want to buy new products.

👎 Home repair may lead to safety issues.

Ethics

Companies must act fairly and honestly. They **must not**:

- exploit host countries, workers or suppliers
- damage the environment, so they need to use sustainable materials, reduce energy consumption and manage any impact from waste
- forget to look at the needs of the end user and the impact of the products.

The environment

Companies must balance the demand for new products against the needs of the environment, and will use a Life Cycle Assessment (LCA) to review:

- materials processing, separation and use
- energy consumption and emissions (pollution)
- wastes and by-products of manufacturing
- transport for production distribution and use
- packaging, construction and disposal.

Worked example

1　Using an example, explain the term 'obsolescence'.　**(2 marks)**

Obsolescence is a product such as a games console that has been designed with a specific or shortened life span.

2　Explain **one** way in which a mobile phone demonstrates the concept of obsolescence.
(2 marks)

Mobile phones become obsolete because technology used is quickly replaced by the next model which is already in development. Newer versions include more features, applications and memory than was available on previous versions.

Now try this

 1　Describe **four** ways in which a manufacturing company can evaluate the environmental impact of its production and distribution of an existing product.　**(4 marks)**

 2　Explain **two** reasons why a company will not design a product to be easily repaired.
(4 marks)

Fossil fuels

Power can be generated from fossil fuels. They are **non-renewable** and will **eventually run out** as they were formed millions of years ago and cannot be replenished. Here are three examples of fossil fuels.

1 Coal

Coal is converted into useful energy in a power station by burning the coal to create heat. The heat is then used to turn water into steam to power a turbine.

The heat from burning coal can also provide a heat source for smaller applications, such as in the home.

> Power stations burn fossil fuels, such as coal to produce electricity.

👍 A large amount of electrical energy can be created from coal which is a reliable and stable form of energy.

👍 Power stations are efficient at converting energy and cost-effective once set up.

👎 A large amount of pollution is produced, such as carbon dioxide, arsenic and sulphur.

👎 The extraction of coal has environmental impacts on the landscape.

2 Gas (natural)

Natural gas is found deep underground and is combustible. Like coal, gas can be burned in a power station to create heat energy that will power a turbine to create electricity.

Natural gas can also be used in the home for cooking and heating.

👍 Large amounts of electrical energy can be created from gas, which is a reliable and stable form of energy.

👍 Cost-effective to extract as it is a ready-made fuel, and needs less processing and is cleaner than coal and oil.

👎 Pollution is produced, such as carbon monoxide / dioxide, nitrogen and sulphur dioxide gas.

👎 Extraction of gas will have an impact on the environment through emissions or damage to the countryside when **fracking**.

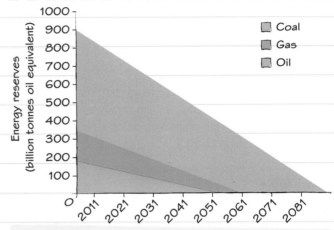

> Some sources state that fossil fuel energy reserves are predicted to run out in the future with current usage.

> **Fracking** is a way of extracting natural gas from rocks (called shale) below the Earth's surface by injecting liquid at high pressure to force out the gas or oil.

3 Oil

Oil is processed to provide different energy sources, such as petrol, diesel and paraffin.
It can be used in power plants and for smaller factory and domestic use.

> Crude oil is also a key contributor to the manufacture of plastic.

👍 Power stations are efficient at converting the energy from oil and are cost-effective once set up.

👍 A convenient source of power as the energy supply (petrol, diesel) is more portable, for example, in vehicles.

👎 Oil processing factories produce a large amount of pollutants.

👎 Impact of environmental disasters is high.

Now try this

 1 Fossil fuels will run out in the future. Describe **two** ways in which the use of fossil fuels could be reduced. **(2 marks)**

 2 Explain **two** environmental impacts of using coal as a power source. **(4 marks)**

> When asked about replacing a fossil fuel you should always consider renewable energy sources and new technology.

See page 12 for more on renewable energy

Nuclear power

Nuclear energy is energy that is stored in atoms of **uranium** and released in a reactor by fission, in the form of heat energy.

Producing nuclear energy

1 Heat energy from nuclear fission produces steam to drive a turbine.

2 The turbine then drives a generator (producing electricity).

3 A kilogram of uranium contains two to three million times the energy equivalent of oil or coal.

4 Wind farms require up to 360 times as much land area to produce the energy equivalent of a nuclear energy facility.

UK nominated sites for new nuclear power stations

● Site acquired for development
● Nominated site

Nuclear plants serving the UK are all located near the coast so that there is a large water supply.

Advantages of nuclear power

👍 No need for a large amount of space to generate energy.

👍 Does not produce carbon emissions or contribute to global warming or acid rain.

👍 Reliable and not dependent on weather.

👍 Low volume of waste produced so there is less pollution from the transport.

👍 Nuclear power reduces demand for finite resources, such as oil.

Disadvantages of nuclear power

👎 Risk of nuclear accidents, which could be disastrous.

👎 Disposal of nuclear waste is very expensive and takes a long time to decay.

👎 High levels of security are required due to the threat of terrorism.

👎 Decommissioning nuclear plants safely is costly as there is a high risk of contamination.

👎 Construction, operation and decommissioning of the reactor may harm the environment.

The damaged Fukushima nuclear power plant in 2011, which was hit by a tsunami, resulting in a harmful radiation leak.

Worked example

Give **two** reasons why a government would invest in nuclear power.   **(2 marks)**

A government would invest in nuclear power as it produces less harmful emissions than fossil fuels and it produces much more energy than all other energy sources.

When comparing nuclear fuel, it can be compared to both fossil fuels and renewable sources of energy.

Now try this

 1 Explain **one** reason why coastal areas are good locations for building a nuclear power plant.   **(2 marks)**

 2 Explain **three** risks of using nuclear energy as an energy source.   **(6 marks)**

Think about the potential hazards of obtaining, processing, storing and disposing of nuclear energy and the running of the power plant.

Had a look ☐   Nearly there ☐   Nailed it! ☐

Renewable energy

Renewable energy resources can be regenerated. They are used to make electricity without directly producing carbon emissions. They can be expensive to set up, but once these costs are paid for, the energy is very low cost.

Wind

Wind turbines create electricity through a generator and are located in areas where there is likely to be a consistent breeze.

👍 They can be used in remote areas.

👎 They can be unsightly or impede shipping if at sea.

👎 The amount of wind can be unpredictable.

Tidal

The movement of tidal water is harnessed to generate electricity. Artificial barrages can be constructed across tidal rivers and bays.

👍 Large amounts of power are available and tides are predictable.

👎 Barrages across estuaries cause ecological damage.

👎 Only available in coastal areas.

Hydro-electrical

Water is generally held in a reservoir and the release of the water will drive a turbine.

👍 Large amounts of power are available on demand.

👎 It is expensive to set up, and the construction of dams may harm the environment.

Solar

Solar power can be converted directly into electrical energy (photovoltaics) or the thermal power from the sun can be used to heat fluids or produce steam to drive turbines.

👍 They can provide homes with their own power supply.

👎 Effectiveness depends on location and sunlight available (cloud, length of day).

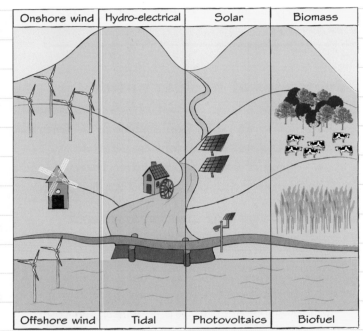

Biomass

Energy can be obtained from landfill gas from organisms, crops or alcohol fuels. Crops can also be grown to manufacture biodiesel (biofuel). Biomass also includes waste or wood, which is burned.

👍 Material that is generally regarded as waste can be used and is carbon neutral.

👎 Some greenhouse gases such as methane are produced and it is less efficient as large areas of land are needed to generate enough material.

👎 Growing biomass requires large amounts of water.

👎 The change in land use can lead to deforestation if not managed correctly.

Now try this

You must consider the positive benefits of solar power and the potential difficulties that the manufacturing company may have to overcome.

A small manufacturing company in the north of England intends to adopt a green approach to its energy needs. Evaluate the use of solar power as a suitable energy source.   **(6 marks)**

Energy and storage systems

Energy storage is vital in an increasingly technological world. All systems that rely on electrical power to work will need to be supplied with that power. You need to know about national energy storage systems and portable systems such as batteries and cells.

Kinetic pumped storage systems

- On a national level, we are moving away from fossil fuels.
- Renewable power sources such as solar and wind are not always reliable.
- Kinetic pumped storage systems help to create a more flexible and reliable grid system.

Batteries and cells

- Batteries and cells use chemical energy to make electricity.
- They have two terminals, one positive (+) and one negative (-). A chemical reaction produces electrons that collect at the negative terminal and when connected in a circuit will flow to the positive terminal.
- The circuit is completed by adding a 'load', which is the device that needs power.

How kinetic pumped storage systems work

The system is based on the hydro-electric dam and has two reservoirs (upper and lower).

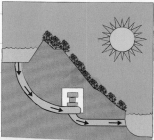 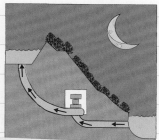

1 During the day, the potential energy in the form of water is held in the dam and flows down the slope, creating kinetic energy to spin a turbine.

2 When demand is low (night), excess electricity is used to pump water from the lower dam back up to the main reservoir to top up the water available to generate power.

Alkaline (primary) batteries

These batteries are supplied fully charged and create power by an electrochemical reaction between two materials, such as zinc and manganese dioxide.

👍 Compared to re-chargeable batteries, they have higher energy, longer shelf life and more environmentally-friendly when disposed of.

👎 Only used until the charge has been drained.

Rechargeable batteries

These batteries can be recharged many times. There is also an electrochemical reaction between two materials, most commonly lithium-ion (Li-ion) and nickel-cadmium (NiCd).

👍 Can be used many times, cost more to purchase but cheaper in the long run, produce less waste.

👎 Initial cost is higher than primary batteries.

Button　　　Phone

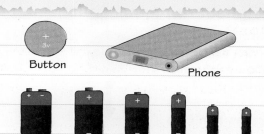

9v　D　C　AA　AAA　AAAA

Batteries come in a range of standard sizes and shapes to suit particular products, such as mobile phones and laptops.

When answering an 'evaluate' question, you must look at the advantages and disadvantages to give a balanced view.

Now try this

Batteries are a convenient portable power supply for a range of products. Evaluate the use of an alkaline battery over a nickel-cadmium rechargeable battery for powering a pocket torch.

(4 marks)

Modern materials

Modern materials are those that have been developed through the invention of new and improved processes (for example **graphene, metal foams** and **titanium**), or that can be altered to perform a particular function (such as **liquid crystal displays, nanomaterials** and **coated metals**).

Graphene

Graphene is the lightest known compound. It:
👍 is stiff and strong (200 times stronger than steel)
👍 is thin (1 atom thick)
👍 conducts electricity and heat.

Uses include aircraft parts, artificial joints and sports equipment.

Graphene could improve the performance of the products it is used in.

You need to be able to describe the modern material, identify the improved properties and explain how they could be used.

Liquid crystal displays (LCDs)

The liquid crystals respond to electrical input from an electrode to block or allow a back light to shine through and generate various colours to form images on the screen.
👍 It is compact, low energy use, has a sharp image and is bright.
👎 There is a restricted viewing angle.

Uses include TV screens, watches, and computers.

ON liquid crystals block different parts of the light source

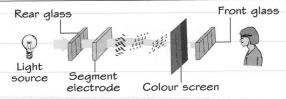

Rear glass   Front glass
Light source   Segment electrode   Colour screen

Liquid crystals can be used to generate full colour display by regulating the three primary colours.

Nanomaterials

Nanomaterials are less than 1–100 nanometres thick. One nanometer is one-billionth of a metre. Nanomaterials are used as thin films or surface coatings, such as self-cleaning glass or insulation.

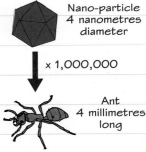

Nano-particle 4 nanometres diameter

x 1,000,000

Ant 4 millimetres long

👍 Nanomaterials improve the properties of materials (increased strength, conductivity, hardness, waterproofing, fire retardance).

Metal foams

Metal foams are made of a base metal (often aluminium) with gas-filled pores added to increase the volume of the metal. They:
👍 have high porosity and strength
👍 have good thermal conductivity
👍 are light, with good energy absorption.

Uses include impact absorbing features in vehicles.

Titanium

Titanium is a lightweight metal with low density. It:
👍 is corrosion resistant
👍 has a good strength to weight ratio
👍 is stiff and tough.

Uses include aircraft parts and artificial joints.

Coated metals

Metals can be coated with other materials to protect them, improve performance or for aesthetic reasons. Examples of coatings are:
👍 **zinc (galvanising)** protects steel from rusting
👍 **Teflon (PTFE)** provides non-stick coating for kitchen pans.

 Worked example

Explain **one** reason why steel fencing is often coated with zinc.   **(2 marks)**

The zinc coating will protect the steel as it will not allow the steel to be affected by moisture and rusting.

 Now try this

Explain **three** reasons why titanium is a suitable material for manufacturing some parts of a modern helicopter engine.   **(6 marks)**

Always relate the properties to the specific need of the product. If it is used for an engine part, it must not negatively impact on the function of the helicopter and reduce efficiency.

Smart materials

These materials have properties that respond to external stimuli and change in a controlled manner.

Shape memory alloys

Metallic alloys such as Nitinol can be bent. Heat will make the alloy return to its original shape. Nitinol is programmed (heated to 540°C) and when deformed will reform at 70°C (hot water). Different alloys will have different trigger temperatures depending on the composition of the alloy. Shape memory alloys:

👍 save space and require fewer parts

👎 are expensive

👎 wear out after time.

Shape memory alloy tubes can be compressed and inserted into arteries by surgeons. The tubes return to their original shape and hold arteries open.

Worked example

Explain how shape memory alloys can be used in dental braces.   **(2 marks)**

Dental braces are wires that can be fixed to teeth in order to straighten them. The shape memory alloy will create a constant force on the teeth as it tries to return to its original shape, helping to straighten the teeth.

Thermochromic pigments

Powder pigments are added to other materials, such as polymers and paints. These pigments change colour due to temperature changes. The change can be reversible or permanent to show that a certain temperature has been reached.

Use of these pigments can:

👍 improve safety

👍 detect and indicate change

👎 decay over time.

Uses include thermometers in fish tanks.

A non-toxic thermochromic pigment changes colour when hot liquid is poured in.

Worked example

Explain how thermochromic pigments can be used as a forehead thermometer.   **(2 marks)**

Different pigments could be designed to change colour at specified temperatures to indicate the temperature of a patient when placed on the skin.

You need to describe the stimuli (e.g. heat, temperature, UV light) and the resulting change in the material (movement, colour, shape).

Photochromic pigments or particles

Pigments in the form of compounds are added to other materials such as polymers and paints. The pigments change colour due to exposure to ultraviolet rays. The change in colour is reversed when the stimulus is removed. These pigments:

👍 can help create multi-use products

👎 can be slow to react and expensive.

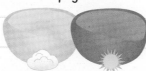

Photochromic lenses have particles that darken in sunlight to add protection.

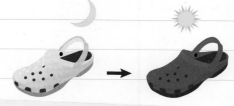

Photochromic pigments change the colour of these shoes in sunlight which indicates the level of UV light a child may be exposed to.

Now try this

What is the definition of a smart material?   **(1 mark)**

A A material made from a combination of materials. ◯

B A material that can feed back electronic information. ◯

C A material that responds to external stimuli. ◯

D A material that is a mixture of two or more materials. ◯

Composite materials

Composite materials are produced by combining two or more different materials to create a material that has enhanced properties.

Glass reinforced plastic (GRP)

Plastic is reinforced with strands or woven fibres of glass and is built up in layers.
Uses include canoes, car bodies or rigid pond liners.

👍 It has a good strength to weight ratio and is rigid.

👍 It is cheaper than carbon fibres.

👍 It can be coloured with resins.

Carbon fibre reinforced plastic (CRP)

Plastic is reinforced with strands or woven fibres of carbon and is built up in layers.
Uses include racing car parts and body armour.

👍 It has an excellent strength to weight ratio.

👍 It is very rigid, with a greater rigidity than glass fibres.

Glass reinforced plastic (GRP) being formed into a mould for a car spoiler.

Carbon fibre reinforced plastic (CRP) is used for safety in the body of a Formula 1 car.

When working with glass or carbon reinforced materials, care must be taken not to breathe in the fumes or dust. The fibres can cause respiratory issues.

Plywood

Plywood is a manufactured board formed from layers of veneers bonded together by glue, so it forms a flat sheet.

👍 It is stable in all directions.

👍 It is available in large sheets.

Each layer is 90 degrees

Veneers of wood bonded together with glue

Always an odd number of layers

Plywood comes in a range of thicknesses, for instance, 3 mm, 6 mm, 9 mm. 'Ply' tells you the number of layers in the board.

Worked example

Explain **two** reasons why carbon fibre is a suitable material for the manufacture of propeller blades.
(4 marks)

Carbon fibre has a good strength to weight ratio for use in an aeroplane as it must be strong enough to withstand strong forces, but also light to help it fly. It is also rigid and therefore has good impact resistance in case it is hit by any airborne debris.

You should always think about the intended purpose of the product when assessing the use of a particular material.

Now try this

1 Draw a labelled diagram to show the construction of (3 ply) plywood.
(3 marks)

2 Describe **two** reasons why glass reinforced plastic (GRP) would be used in preference to carbon fibre reinforced plastic (CRP) for the manufacture of a kayak.
(2 marks)

Technical textiles

Fibres of special materials can be spun to make enhanced fabrics. All technical textiles need a base fibre (cotton, wool, polyester, nylon), which is then woven, knitted, sewn, cut or braided with the strands.

Conductive fabrics

These fabrics (also known as e-textiles) include conductive materials (often carbon, titanium, nickel, or copper) strands that are woven, knitted, sewn, cut or braided into the fabric. They can conduct electricity and connect electronic components and can be used in clothing to incorporating lights or controls, or in athletic garments with heart rate monitors.

Conductive fibres can be woven into fabric and connected to lights.

Fire resistant fabrics

These fabrics are based on **aramid** fibres, which are heat resistant. They are used when there is a need for a higher level of insulation and for materials to resist fire for a set period of time; for example home furnishings and specialist clothing, such as welding overalls.

Fire resistant fabrics can give added protection in extreme situations.

Microfibres incorporating micro encapsulation

Microfibres are synthetic fibres less than one denier thick. Denier is the weight of fabric. A single strand of silk is one denier.

Micro encapsulation is when solid substances such as cosmetics or medicines are encapsulated in tiny thin-walled bubbles of natural or synthetic materials. The textiles may contain small soluble particles, and may be used for adding therapeutic fragrance or medication into clothing, or for climate control garments. One example is clothing for athletes that contains silver ion, which is antibacterial, odour resistant and temperature regulated.

Kevlar

Kevlar has a very high strength to weight ratio, and it is flexible and not affected by moisture. It can be used as a replacement for steel and spun into ropes for mooring boats or woven into clothing.

Kevlar sewn into bullet and stab proof vests provides additional protection.

Soluble means that the particles can be dissolved and released in water.

Now try this

Fire resistant fabrics used in the home have to be tested and pass stringent safety regulations. Products using these fabrics must show the fire resistant symbol.

1 Explain the term 'fire resistant' in fabrics.
   (2 marks)

2 Explain **one** way that the use of microfibres incorporating micro encapsulation can be used to improve the treatment of burns.
   (2 marks)

Think of how medication could be applied.

Worked example

Explain **two** reasons why Kevlar would be used in gardening gloves.   **(4 marks)**

Kevlar is strong, which protects hands from machinery that has sharp cutting blades and from the sharp spikes on thorns and brambles. Kevlar is also flexible and lightweight, so it does not constrict the gardener when working.

Remember that there is a difference between fire resistant and fire proof.

Systems approach to designing

A systems approach is a method to break down the stages of a process into a **series of steps**. This enables designers to develop systems without going into the detail of each stage.

Systems approach

Systems have three sections: input, process and output. They are connected together to give the desired function.

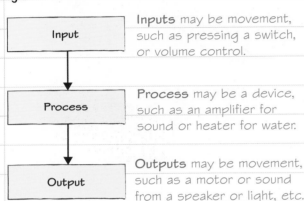

Inputs may be movement, such as pressing a switch, or volume control.

Process may be a device, such as an amplifier for sound or heater for water.

Outputs may be movement, such as a motor or sound from a speaker or light, etc.

Flow charts

Systems can be represented in the form of a flow chart. A flow chart uses graphical representations to show a sequence of operations or actions in a complex system. The sequence follows a logical order and decisions are made using yes or no questions.

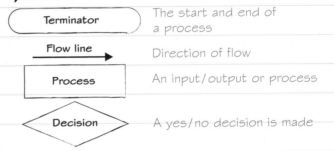

Terminator — The start and end of a process

Flow line — Direction of flow

Process — An input/output or process

Decision — A yes/no decision is made

Open loop flow chart

Open loop is when the output **IS NOT measured** or fed back into the decisions made in the system.

In this simple heating system:

- the heating system is switched on
- the boiler heats the water
- the hot water heats the radiators.

This continues until the heating system is physically switched off.

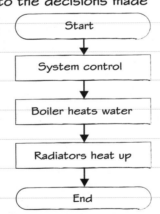

Closed loop flow chart

Closed loop is when the output **IS measured** or there is **feedback** into the decisions made in the system. Decisions are automatically made.

In this temperature controlled heating system:

- the heating system is switched on
- the boiler heats the water
- the hot water heats the radiators
- a heat sensor (thermostat) measures the temperature and feeds back to switch the system on or off.

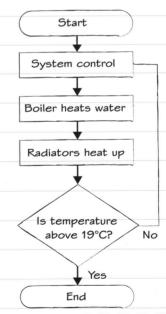

Worked example

In the flow chart shown in Figure 1, calculate how many times the process box would be acted upon.
(2 marks)

$$\frac{50}{2} = 25$$

25 times

Figure 1

Now try this

With the aid of notes or sketches, design a closed loop flow chart system for an outside light that switches on when it is dark at night and turns off again when it is light in the morning.
(4 marks)

Electronic systems – inputs

An electronic system is the physical connection of components that uses a signal in the form of electrical energy from an **input**, which is **processed** to operate an **output** device. You need to know about **four input devices**.

Light sensor (photoelectric devices)

The electrical resistance in a light sensor (known as a **light dependent resistor (LDR)**) alters in response to changes in light, and gives a signal to the system. Light sensors have **high resistance** when dark and **low resistance** in light.

Light sensor and graphical symbol

Electrical resistance is a measure of how easy or difficult it is for electric current to pass through a wire or component. Resistance is measured in units of ohms (Ω).

Temperature sensor (thermistor)

The electrical resistance in a temperature sensor (thermistor) changes in response to **changes in temperature** and gives a required signal.

Temperature sensors have **high resistance** when cold and **low resistance** when hot.

Temperature sensor and graphical symbol.

Pressure sensors

Pressure sensors can be in the form of switches that are on or off or gauges that have a change in **resistance** when there is an **applied pressure or force**. In an electronic circuit, the pressure sensor will be able to sense a force and give a required signal.

A commercial pressure switch (and the graphical symbol for a normally open (NO) pressure switch), which can be used under carpets as a burglar alarm.

NO or **N**ormally **O**pen means that the circuit is not connected (open) and requires pressure to make the circuit complete (closed).

Switches

Switches are devices that are used to make or break an electrical connection in a circuit. There are many types of switches such as push, rotary, toggle or slide. Switches can be used in a number of ways:

 A toggle switch (latched or 'single throw') has on and off positions and comes in a variety of shapes, such as light switches.

 A push to make switch (PTM) which is Normally Open (NO) is used on door bells or keys on a keyboard.

 A push to break switch (PTB) which is Normally Closed (NC) is used on fire alarms and control systems.

This diagram represents a switch connected in a simple circuit to operate a light.

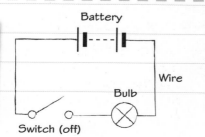

Battery

Wire

Bulb

Switch (off)

Now try this

1 Describe how the resistance in a light dependent resistor (LDR) changes in different levels of light. **(2 marks)**

2 Explain a suitable application for a pressure sensor. **(2 marks)**

Electronic systems – processes

Microcontrollers are a single chip micro-computer component you can use for **processing** in a circuit.

Microcontrollers

Microcontrollers make decisions and determine an output. They can be programmed using machine code (a programming language based on 0 and 1), but in schools a simpler programming language called **BASIC** is used.

The program is written on a computer and transferred to a microcontroller, which is used to control an output such as a counter.

PICs

Programmable interface controllers (PICs) are microcontrollers that can be programmed and used as counters, timers or for making decisions and give greater flexibility or functionality to projects. They are inexpensive and are used in a wide range of commercial products such as cars, washing machines, remote controls or microwave ovens.

👍 The size of the circuit (board) can be reduced and functionality increased.

👎 Often more expensive than a dedicated integrated circuit (IC).

Timers

The 555 timer chip

Timing can be carried out by integrated circuits (IC) such as the 555 timer, which produces single (**monostable**) or multiple (**astable**) pulses.

Counters like the 4026 decade counter can be used to count the number of pulses produced by a timer or from devices such as pressure pads.

Monostable devices produce a single output pulse that is either on or off. Uses include an alarm sensor system that operates an audible alarm once the sensor is triggered.

Astable devices give an oscillating output that moves between off and on. Uses include flashing light as an output to an alarm system.

Decision making – logic gates and truth tables

A **logic gate** is used for making a decision in a circuit. Most logic gates have two inputs that give a single output.

AND gate	OR gate	NOT gate
A —⟩ Q, B	A —⟩ Q, B	A —▷o— Q
For an output at Q there must be an input at both A **AND** B.	For an output at Q there must be an input at either one of A **OR** B **or at both of them**.	There is an output at Q only if there is **NOT** an input at A.

Truth tables will have two binary inputs that can be either of two conditions – low (0) or high (1). The result is a single output value of low (0) or high (1).

AND gate			OR gate			NOT gate	
A	B	Q	A	B	Q	A	Q
0	0	0	0	0	0	0	1
0	1	0	0	1	1	1	0
1	0	0	1	0	1		
1	1	1	1	1	1		

There is an output at Q only if there are inputs at A **AND** B.

There is an output at Q if there is an input at A **OR** B or at both of them.

There is an output at Q only if there is **NOT** an input at A.

Now try this

Explain **two** reasons programmable microcontrollers are used in home appliances.   **(4 marks)**

Electronic systems – outputs

Electronic systems have three sections: input, process and output. The input is processed into an electronic signal, which drives the output device.

1 Speakers

Speakers change electrical pulses into a recognised audible sound.

The current flows into a coil and creates an electromagnet, which creates movement. This movement is transferred to a cone that then creates the sound waves.

Cone

Coil

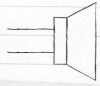
A speaker and its graphical symbol

2 Buzzers

Buzzers convert electric current into an audible buzz, normally used as an alarm. Electromagnets are switched on and off repeatedly to vibrate a metal disk between two magnetic poles.

A buzzer and its graphical symbol

3 Lamp

Lamps give off light. Typical filament lamps have a thin wire (often coiled). The filament is made from metal, such as tungsten. This provides resistance, which makes the filament heat up as the electric current passes through. As the filament heats up it produces light.

A bulb and its graphical symbol

Worked example

Draw a diagram to show how a lamp and a buzzer can be used as an output, in a simple circuit that is operated by a single switch.   **(4 marks)**

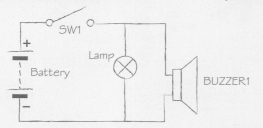

4 Light-emitting diode (LED)

An LED is a component that gives off light. LEDs come in a range of colours. They are increasingly replacing bulbs in cars and torches because they have low power consumption and are long lasting. LEDs are normally grouped in a cluster to provide good levels of light and can still work when one of the LED fails.

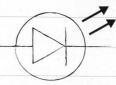
LEDs and the graphical symbol

LEDs can be directly wired into a circuit. The positive (+) side is called the anode and the negative (−) side is called the cathode.

The use of electromagnets is a good way of creating movement from an electronic pulse as it can attract or repel any magnetic materials when required.

Now try this

1 Explain how an electronic buzzer creates an audible sound from an electric current.   **(2 marks)**

2 Explain **two** reasons why light-emitting diodes (LEDs) may be used in preference to a filament bulb.   **(4 marks)**

Had a look ☐   Nearly there ☐   Nailed it! ☐

Types of movement

All mechanisms involve some kind of movement. There are four basic types of movement.

① Linear

Motion in a straight line, for example a train moving along a track or a lift travelling up in a high-rise building.

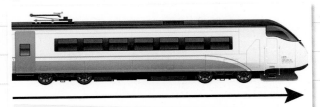

A train is an example of linear motion.

② Reciprocating

Motion that moves backwards and forwards in a straight line, for example the blade on a workshop jigsaw or a piston in a car engine.

A jigsaw blade uses reciprocating motion.

③ Rotary

Motion that goes around a central point, for example a wheel on a bicycle or a fan blade.

A bicycle wheel has rotary motion.

④ Oscillating

Motion that swings backward and forwards in an arc from a central point, for example a pendulum on a clock or a child on a swing.

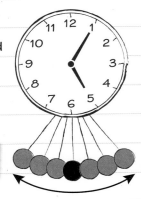

The pendulum on a clock has an oscillating motion.

Worked example

There are four types of movement. Name the correct kind of movement in the following examples.   **(3 marks)**

1 Needle on sewing machine

Reciprocating

2 Child on a straight slide

Linear

3 Gear wheel

Rotary

Human movement

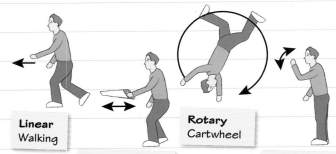

Linear Walking

Reciprocating Using a tenon saw

Rotary Cartwheel

Oscillating Waving your hand

Now try this

The diagram shown in Figure 1 shows a child's swing. Name the kind of movement demonstrated by the swing.   **(1 mark)**

A Linear ⬭

B Reciprocating ⬭

C Rotary ⬭

D Oscillating ⬭

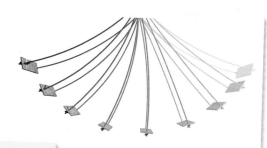

Figure 1

Levers

① First order

This lever is used to lift greater loads but the effort has to move a greater distance than the load. The load and effort are on opposite sides of the pivot.

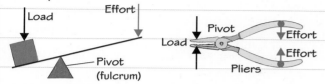

② Second order

This lever is also used to lift greater loads with the effort moving a greater distance than the load. The load and effort are on the same side of the pivot.

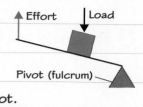

③ Third order

The effort in this lever is more than is applied to the load. This is used for precision work.

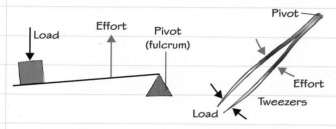

Parts of a lever

There are three parts to every lever.

✓ The **effort**, which is the amount of force put in by the user (**input**).

✓ The **pivot (fulcrum)** which is the point at which the lever pivots.

✓ The **load**, which is the **force** exerted by the load (**output**).

When a lever is balanced: **LEARN IT!**

Force × Distance of = Force × Distance of
Load (from   Effort (from
pivot)   pivot)

🖩 Maths skills Mechanical advantage (MA)

Mechanical advantage is the load divided by the amount of effort needed.

$$MA = \frac{load}{effort}$$ **LEARN IT!**

Here, a worker can lift a load of 300N by putting in an effort of 100N.

$$MA = \frac{300}{100} = 3$$

300 N   100 N

This can also be expressed as a ratio: 3:1. The load is three times the input force. This also means that the input will move further than the load (**velocity ratio**).

First and second order levers provide MA **greater than 1**. The MA of third order levers is **less than 1**.

Worked example 🖩 Maths skills

Figure 1 shows a lever used to lift a load. Calculate the velocity ratio.   **(2 marks)**

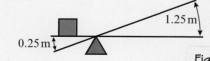

Figure 1

$$VR = \frac{1.25}{0.25} = 5$$

Here the velocity ratio is 5 or 5 : 1, which means that the effort has to move five times further than the load is being raised.

🖩 Maths skills Velocity ratio (VR)

Velocity ratio is the distance the effort moves divided by the distance the load moves.

$$VR = \frac{Distance\ moved\ by\ effort}{Distance\ moved\ by\ load}$$ **LEARN IT!**

Now try this

Calculate the mechanical advantage of the first order lever shown in Figure 2.   **(2 marks)**

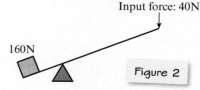

Input force: 40N

160N

Figure 2

Linkages

Systems where one or more levers are joined together are known as linkages. You can revise levers and how they work on page 23. You need to know about three types of linkage.

1 Reverse motion

This linkage uses a single lever to convert movement in one direction to movement in the **opposite direction** as used in a gear lever mechanism in a car.

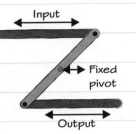
Input / Fixed pivot / Output

3 Bell crank

A fixed angle lever converts motion through that angle to allow an input force to be transmitted around a corner, as used on a brake mechanism on a bicycle.

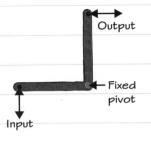
Output / Fixed pivot / Input

2 Push / pull

This linkage uses two levers to convert movement in one direction to movement in the **same direction** as used on windscreen wiper mechanisms on a car.

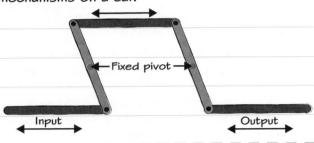
Fixed pivot / Input / Output

Pivot / Input / Output

Bell cranks are used on bicycles to allow the remote operation of brakes connected by a cable to the handlebars.

Worked example

Maths skills

The diagram shows a reverse motion linkage with a fixed pivot at **P**. The distance **BP** is 30 cm and the distance **PC** is 10 cm.

A / B / P / 30 cm / 10 cm / C / D

If point **D** moves 5 cm right, how far would point **A** move to the left. **(1 mark)**

A 5 cm ☐
B 10 cm ☐
C 15 cm ●
D 20 cm ☐

Changing forces

The output motion of a linkage can change in three ways:
- ✓ Direction
- ✓ Distance
- ✓ Force

Maths skills You can use ratios to work out the output motion of a linkage. Point B is **three times** the distance from the pivot, so point B will move three times as far as point C. The force exerted at D will also be a third less than at point A.

Now try this

The diagram on the right shows a bell crank, which is part of a brake caliper on a bicycle. An upward motion is applied at **A**.

Describe **three** ways in which the motion at **B** will be different to the motion at **A**. **(3 marks)**

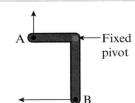
A / Fixed pivot / B

Core technical principles
New and emerging technologies
All materials

Simple gear trains 1

A gear is a toothed wheel fixed to a shaft that can mesh (connect) with other gears to produce changes in the speed of a drive mechanism.

Gears

A **spur gear** is a rotating wheel that has teeth and can mesh with a second spur gear.

The **driver gear** provides the input movement, which is transmitted to the other gear – the **driven gear**.

A **simple gear train** is when two spur gears are meshed and are fixed on parallel shafts.

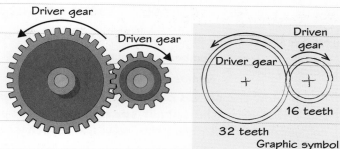
Driver gear
Driven gear
Driver gear
Driven gear
32 teeth
16 teeth
Graphic symbol

> Gears have an advantage over pulley systems because the meshing of the gears prevents any slip so that greater forces can be applied.

> When two spur gears are connected, the **direction of rotation is reversed.**

> See page 30 for more on pulleys.

Idler gear

To make the driven gear rotate in the same direction, an **idler gear** has to be used.

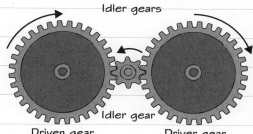
Idler gears
Idler gear
Driven gear   Driver gear

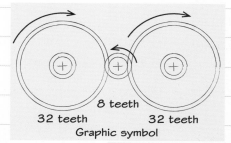
8 teeth
32 teeth   32 teeth
Graphic symbol

> An idler gear does not change the output speed.

Compound gear train

The speed change in simple gear trains is limited to the number of teeth on the two gears and space available for the gear system. It is possible to combine a number of simple gear trains to achieve higher speed changes. This is called a compound gear train.

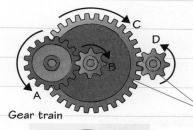
C
D
B
A
Gear train
Two gears on one shaft

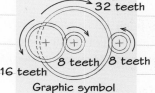
32 teeth
8 teeth 8 teeth
16 teeth
Graphic symbol

> The middle gears can change the speed and direction of rotation.

Now try this

Figure 1 shows a simple gear train that is used to drive the paper rollers in a printer. Explain **one** reason that an idler gear is used.   **(2 marks)**

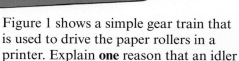
Idler gears
Idler gear
Driven gear   Driver gear

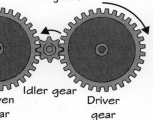
8 teeth
32 teeth   32 teeth
Graphic symbol

Figure 1

Simple gear trains 2

You need to be able to calculate velocity ratio and output speed for simple gear trains.

🖩 Maths skills   Velocity ratio (VR) and output speed

Gears of different sizes will rotate at different speeds. This is the **velocity ratio** (VR).

$$\text{Velocity ratio} = \frac{\text{Number of teeth on driven gear}}{\text{Number of teeth on driver gear}}$$ **LEARN IT!**

If you know the speed of the driver gear (the **input speed**), you can calculate the speed of the driven gear (the **output speed**). For compound gear trains the overall velocity ratio is calculated by multiplying the individual velocity ratios for each simple gear train.

$$\text{Output speed} = \frac{\text{Input speed}}{\text{Velocity ratio}}$$ **LEARN IT!**

The speed of rotation is expressed in **RPM** (revolutions per minute – how often the gear can rotate around the shaft in one minute).

Worked example 🖩 Maths skills

The diagram shows a driver gear with 80 teeth and a driven gear with 20 teeth.

Figure 1

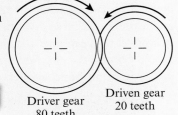

Driver gear 80 teeth   Driven gear 20 teeth

1 Calculate the velocity ratio of the gear system. **(3 marks)**

$$\text{Velocity ratio} = \frac{\text{Number of teeth on driven gear}}{\text{Number of teeth on driver gear}}$$
$$= \frac{20}{80} = \frac{1}{4} = 1:4$$

2 The input speed of the gear is 1200 revolutions per minute (RPM). What is the speed of the driven gear? **(3 marks)**

$$\text{Output speed} = \frac{\text{Input speed}}{\text{Velocity ratio}}$$
$$= \frac{1200}{\frac{1}{4}} = 1200 \times 4$$
$$= 4800 \text{ RPM}$$

Worked example 🖩 Maths skills

The driver gear in the compound gear train shown in Figure 2 is rotating at 250 RPM. Gear A is the driver gear. Calculate the velocity ratio of the gear system. **(2 marks)**

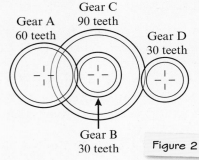

Gear C 90 teeth

Gear A 60 teeth

Gear D 30 teeth

Gear B 30 teeth   Figure 2

Total velocity ratio of the gear system = VR of Gear A to Gear B x VR of Gear C to Gear D

VR of Gear A to B = 1 : 2

VR of Gear C to D = 1 : 3

Total VR = 1 : 2 x 1 : 3 ($\frac{1}{2} \times \frac{1}{3}$) = 1 : 6

This means that, for every revolution of the driver gear, the driven gear will rotate six times.

Now try this

Figure 3 shows a simple gear train which has an input/driver gear with 44 teeth and is rotating at 100 RPM. The idler gear has 22 teeth and the output/driven gear has 10 teeth.

Calculate the following:

1 The velocity ratio of the gear system. **(2 marks)**

2 The rotational speed of the output gear. **(2 marks)**

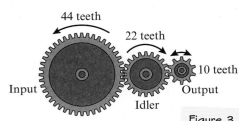

44 teeth

22 teeth

10 teeth

Input   Idler   Output

Figure 3

Specialist gears 1

You need to know about alternative types of gear system such as bevel gears and worm & wormwheels.

1 Bevel gears

These can transmit **rotary motion through 90 degrees**. The calculations for velocity ratio and output speed for bevel gears are the same as normal spur gears.

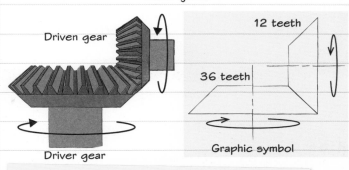

Bevel gears

Driven gear

Driver gear

12 teeth

36 teeth

Graphic symbol

Examples of bevel gears are found in hand drills and in a differential gearbox in a car.

Bevel gears can have different numbers of teeth to provide different velocity ratios and output speeds.

When bevel gears have the same number of teeth they are called mitre gears; they still turn through 90 degrees but the output and input speeds are equal.

2 Worm and worm wheel

A worm and worm wheel (or worm gear) is used to make large reductions in speed. The gear wheel (worm wheel) meshes with the worm, which is the driver. Examples of a worm and worm wheel are found on security gates and in a winch mechanism as it prevents any load fallback.

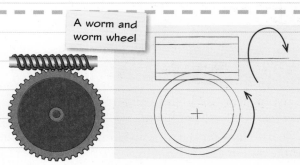

A worm and worm wheel

Calculating velocity ratio: worm and worm wheel

Maths skills

$$\text{Velocity ratio} = \frac{\text{Number of teeth on driven gear}}{\text{Number of teeth on driver gear}}$$

LEARN IT!

This formula is the same as for simple gears. However, the worm has only one tooth – one whole revolution of the worm results in the worm wheel moving forward by only one tooth. So the number of teeth on the driver wheel will always be 1.

Worked example

A worm gear has 30 teeth. Calculate the velocity ratio of the gear system. **(2 marks)**

$$\frac{\text{Number of teeth on driven gear}}{\text{Number of teeth on driver gear}} = \frac{30}{1}$$

$$= 30 \text{ or } 30:1$$

In this example the worm will rotate 30 times to turn the worm gear one full revolution.

Now try this

The bevel gear system shown above has an input speed of 3,000 RPM. Calculate the output speed. **(1 mark)**

A   1000 RPM ☐

B   3000 RPM ☐

C   6000 RPM ☐

D   9000 RPM ☐

Specialist gears 2

You need to know about alternative types of gear system such as the rack and pinion.

③ Rack and pinion

A gear wheel and a rack change **rotary motion to linear motion** and the other way around.
Examples of a rack and pinion are found in pillar drills and in a car steering system.

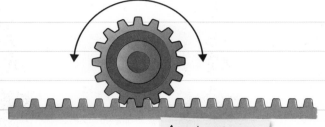

A rack and pinion

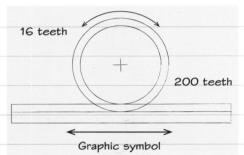

16 teeth

200 teeth

Graphic symbol

Calculating movement: rack and pinion

 Maths skills

Distance moved by rack = $\dfrac{\text{Teeth on pinion gear}}{\text{Teeth per metre (TPM) on rack}}$

LEARN IT!

 Worked example

A pinion gear has 50 teeth and it is meshed with a rack that has 400 teeth per metre.

Calculate how far the rack will move for one revolution of the pinion gear.   **(2 marks)**

Distance moved by rack = $\dfrac{50}{400}$ = 0.125m or 12.5cm

One revolution of the pinion is 50 teeth, so the rack will also move 50 teeth.

 Now try this

The pinion gear in Figure 1 has 80 teeth and is meshed with a rack which has 500 teeth per metre.
Calculate how far the rack will move for two revolutions of the pinion gear.   **(2 marks)**

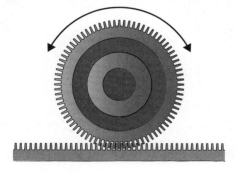

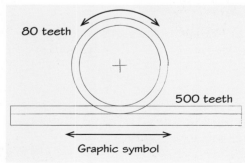

80 teeth

500 teeth

Graphic symbol

Figure 1

Cams and followers

Cams are mechanisms used for converting **rotary motion into reciprocating motion**. Cams can be shaped differently and attached to a rotating camshaft to provide different outputs that are transmitted to a **follower** held against it.

Types of cam

1 Pear shaped cam

The follower remains stable for about half of the cycle and rises and falls in the second half. For example, the camshaft in a car to open and close valves.

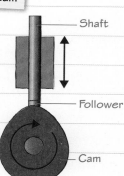

Shaft

Follower

Cam

2 Eccentric cam

The follower gradually rises and falls in a smooth continuous movement. For example, steam engines and in the fuel pump in cars.

3 Drop (snail) cam

The follower gradually rises and falls in a sudden movement. For example, devices needing a sudden drop like a shaping machine (hammer).

Worked example

A children's toy is to be designed with a cam mechanism that will slowly open the mouth of a figure but then will close shut quickly. Name the type of cam that will achieve this action.

(1 mark)

A Pear ⭕
B Eccentric ⭕
C Rotary ⭕
D Drop ⬤

Movement from a cam and follower:

1 **Rise:** Moves the follower up

2 **Fall:** Moves the follower down

3 **Dwell:** Follower remains stationary

4 **Stroke:** Range of movement of follower

5 **Rotation:** Movement of cam

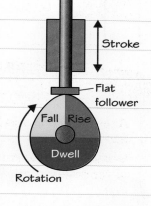

Stroke

Flat follower

Fall | Rise

Dwell

Rotation

Types of follower

Flat

👍 Greater load carrying capabilities

👎 Increased friction

👎 Less accurate

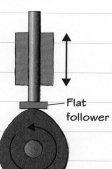

Flat follower

Knife edge

👍 Greater accuracy

👎 Wears quickly

👎 Large side thrust

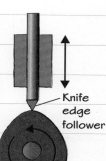

Knife edge follower

Roller

👍 Reduced friction

👍 Runs at high speed

👎 More complex

👎 Higher cost

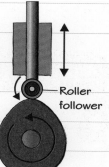

Roller follower

You must always use both labels and sketches if the question asks you to, as sometimes the labels (or notes) can improve your answer if your diagram is not clear.

Now try this

Using notes and sketches, draw a labelled diagram of an eccentric cam and appropriate follower showing all areas of movement. **(5 marks)**

Pulleys and belts

Pulleys and belts are used to transmit **rotary motion** from a driver shaft to a driven shaft.

Pulleys

A pulley is a wheel with a shaped groove. The belt fits in the groove connecting two pulleys and motion is transferred by friction.

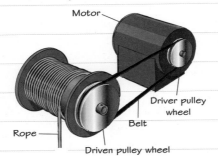

A pulley system

In a **pulley system**, two pulley wheels on separate shafts are connected by a belt. The motion and force are transmitted from the **driver pulley** to the **driven pulley**. The speed, direction and force of rotation can be changed.

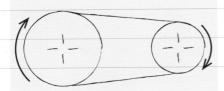

Schematic diagram of a pulley system

Belts

Round – efficient, can be crossed to change direction.

V-belt – reduces slippage by wedging into the pulley wheel.

Flat – good grip at speed due to large surface area, can be crossed to change direction.

Toothed – no slippage as belt fits into teeth of pulley, but this could pose a safety risk if anything is trapped.

📓 Maths skills **Velocity ratio and output speed**

$$\text{Velocity ratio} = \frac{\text{Driven pulley diameter}}{\text{Driver pulley diameter}}$$

LEARN IT!

$$\text{Output speed} = \frac{\text{Input speed}}{\text{Velocity ratio}}$$

LEARN IT!

In this configuration, the driver pulley and driven pulley both rotate in the **same direction. Cross belts** can be used if you need to **reverse** the direction of rotation.

The symbol Ø refers to the diameter of a circle or in this case a pulley.

Worked example

Figure 1 shows a pulley system.

Driver Ø 90 mm

Driven Ø 30 mm

Figure 1

1 Work out the velocity ratio in Figure 1.
(2 marks)

$$\text{Velocity ratio} = \frac{\text{Driven pulley diameter}}{\text{Driver pulley diameter}}$$
$$= \frac{30}{90} = \frac{1}{3} \text{ or } 1:3$$

2 The input speed is 1200 revolutions per minute (RPM). What is the speed of the driven pulley?
(2 marks)

$$\text{Output speed} = \frac{\text{Input speed}}{\text{Velocity ratio}}$$
$$= \frac{1200}{\frac{1}{3}} = 3600 \text{ RPM}$$

Now try this

In the pulley system in Figure 2 the user requires an output speed of 3200 RPM.

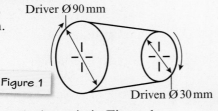

Driver Ø 80 mm

Output speed 3200 RPM

Driven Ø 20 mm

Calculate: Figure 2

a The velocity ratio **(2 marks)**

b The input speed **(2 marks)**

Papers and boards

Paper and boards are made from fine cellulose fibres and are classified by weight or construction.

Paper

To make paper, chips of wood are processed using chemicals to make a pulp. This is filtered and moved through rollers to remove the water and flatten the paper. Most papers can be recycled.

Paper thickness is measured in **grams per square metre (gsm)** (how much one square metre of the paper will weigh). Standard size paper ranges from A10 (smallest) to A0 (largest). A5 is half the size of A4.

Bleed proof 120–150 gsm	Takes colour well, thin grades, similar to cartridge paper but with a smooth surface. Low cost. Used for presentation work.
Cartridge 120–150 gsm	Slight texture on surface, creamy white colour. Used for drawing, takes paint well, medium cost.
Grid 80–100 gsm	Has a grid printed on the surface, which helps with constructing drawings. Low cost. Lines usually metric. Used for working drawings.
Layout 50 gsm	Thin, translucent with smooth surface, can be used to trace. Generally low cost. Used for preparing ideas or tracing.
Tracing 60–90 gsm	Transparent, smooth surface, hard, ink absorption is slow, strength allows for erasing mistakes. Used for tracing or working drawings. Good quality can be expensive.

Board

Board (or cardboard) is generally thicker and heavier (more than 220 gsm), or made from more layers, than paper. Board thickness is measured in **microns**: one micron is one thousandth of a millimetre. Board can be **laminated** to other materials to create different properties for specific purposes. Most board can be recycled but layers may need to be separated.

Corrugated card (fairly cheap)	Corrugated paper sandwiched between two outer layers. Excellent impact resistance, absorbs shock, strength for weight. Used for packaging as it provides protection.
Duplex board (medium cost)	Made up of two layers, making it tough and thin and often water resistant. It is white so it can be printed on. Used for pharmaceutical packaging and paper plates.
Foil-lined board (higher cost)	The board has a foil coating laminated onto one surface. Gives the board resistance to moisture. Used for food packaging and cartons.
Foam core board (medium cost)	Rigid polystyrene foam sandwiched between two outer layers. White, very light, flat and rigid. Used for models and mounting work.
Inkjet card (medium cost)	Treated so that it can absorb the inkjet and can move through the printer. Used for high quality printing.
Solid white board (higher cost)	Entirely made from the wood pulp and is bleached white. It makes an excellent printing surface and is strong and rigid. Used for display packaging, cosmetics, etc.

Worked example

Explain **two** benefits of using corrugated card for the outer packaging of a television.   **(5 marks)**

Corrugated card provides protection to the television, preventing damage if dropped. It is also lightweight, so it does not add significantly to the weight of the television when carried.

Now try this

1 Describe the difference between paper and board.   **(1 mark)**

2 Name the paper size that is twice the size of A3.   **(1 mark)**

3 How is the thickness of paper measured?   **(1 mark)**

Natural timbers

Hardwoods

These trees:
- have broad leaves and its seeds are found in a fruit
- are usually deciduous, so lose their leaves in winter
- grow slowly, often taking over 100 years to be big enough to use for timber
- were common in Britain, but most natural forests were cut down a long time ago.

Seasoning reduces the moisture content of the timber so that it can be more easily worked and is stable in use.

Mahogany

👍 Strong, durable, good workability with uniform structure.
👎 Very rare tropical wood, expensive
✅ Good for quality furniture.

Beech

👍 Strong and tough, close grained, does not splinter easily.
👎 Expensive.
✅ Good for kitchen implements, toys, chair legs.

Ash

👍 Strong, durable, flexible, attractive grain, light in colour and fairly straight.
👎 Expensive
✅ Good for furniture, baseball bats.

Oak

👍 Strong and durable and heavy.
👎 Expensive, corrodes iron.
✅ Good for furniture and barrels. Previously used for building houses.

Balsa

👍 Lightweight, soft and easy to cut.
👎 Too weak for construction work.
✅ Good for model construction or floats in old boats.

Bark
Cambium
Pith
Heartwood
Annual ring
Sapwood

Cross section of tree showing the main features.

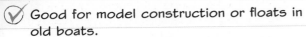

Softwoods

These trees:
- have needle-like leaves and are usually evergreen, so they have leaves on all year and seeds in a cone (coniferous)
- are planted for timber, grow quickly, ready to be used for timber after about 30 years, a lot cheaper than hardwood timber.

Larch

👍 Harder and tougher than most conifers, heartwood resins act as preservatives.
👎 May twist in humidity.
✅ Good for outdoor use, for example cladding.

Pine

👍 Quite strong and easy to work, lightweight and generally cheaper, attractive grain.
👎 Can warp and split.
✅ Good for interior construction.

Spruce

👍 Straight, even grain, small knots, quite strong.
👎 Little resistance to damp and rot.
✅ Good for indoor use, furniture, joists with preservatives.

Worked example

A toy train for a young child will be constructed using beech. Give **two** reasons why beech is suitable for this. **(2 marks)**

Beech does not splinter easily, making it safe for young children, even if chewed. Beech is strong so it can withstand rough use without breaking.

Some 'hardwoods' can be quite soft, like balsa.

Now try this

State **three** methods of identifying whether a tree is a hardwood rather than a softwood tree. **(3 marks)**

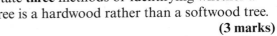

Manufactured boards

Manufactured boards are man-made to specific dimensions by using cheaper timber, offcuts, chips or fibres. This means that they will have different properties to the original timber.

Features

👍 Made into large sheets with uniform thickness and strength, dimensionally stable.

👍 Available in thin sections that would be stronger than natural timber of the same dimensions.

👎 Exposed edges will need treatment and flat surfaces usually need covering with veneer or laminate.

> All can be made water and fire resistant by using different adhesives.

Manufacturing process

1 Wood is processed into chips or particles.

2 The particles are mixed with an adhesive (formaldehyde resin).

3 The mixture is compressed into shape with rollers and heated to cure the adhesive.

4 Boards are trimmed to standard sizes.

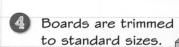

Medium density fibreboard (MDF)

Wood fibres mixed with adhesive (formaldehyde) then formed together under heat and pressure.

👍 Dense, very smooth flat surface that can be easily machined and painted.

👍 Cheap as it is made from waste wood.

👎 Heavy, fine dust produced when cut and sanded, which requires extraction / ventilation.

Chipboard

Flakes, chips or strands of timber are coated in adhesive resin (formaldehyde) and pressed into shape.

👍 Flat and stiff.

👍 Cheap as it is made from waste wood.

👎 Poor resistance to moisture.

👎 Does not have good aesthetic qualities.

Plywood

A manufactured board formed from layers of veneers bonded by glue to form a flat sheet.

👍 Cross-layered structure gives excellent strength and better impact resistance than the equivalent section of natural wood, no weaknesses.

👎 Poor resistance to moisture as the veneers are porous.

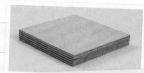

See page 16 for more on plywood

Worked example

Which manufactured board is formed from layers of veneers bonded by glue so it forms a flat sheet? **(1 mark)**

A Plywood ●
B Chipboard ○
C MDF ○
D Pine board ○

Now try this

A table used for school examinations is shown in Figure 1. The top has been made from medium density fibreboard (MDF).

Explain **three** reasons why MDF is a suitable material for making the top of the school table.

(6 marks)

Figure 1

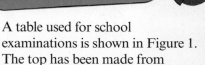

Metals and alloys

Metals are crystalline materials made from elements and compounds. They are typically solid, hard and opaque and good conductors of heat and electricity.

1 Ferrous

Ferrous metals contain iron (ferrite), so most are magnetic and may rust.

Metal	Properties and characteristics	Composition	Melting point	Example uses
Mild steel	Tough, malleable, magnetic, easily joined, poor corrosion resistance	Iron + 0.15 – 0.25% carbon	1400°C	Screws, nails, bolts, girders, car body panels, fridge doors
Cast iron	Hard skin, brittle, soft core, self-lubricating, magnetic	Iron + 2 – 6% carbon	1200°C	Vices, brake discs, manhole covers
High carbon / tool steel	Very hard, difficult to cut, can be hardened and tempered	Iron + 0.8 – 1.5% carbon	1800°C	Chisels, plane blades, saws, drill bits

2 Non-ferrous

Non-ferrous metals do not contain iron, so will not rust. They are not magnetic and tend to be more malleable than ferrous metals.

Metal	Properties and characteristics	Melting point	Example uses
Aluminium	Malleable, ductile, excellent strength to weight ratio, polishes well	660°C	Foil, window frames, engine parts, drinks cans
Copper	Malleable, tough, good hot or cold working, polishes well	1084°C	Electrical wire, gas and water pipes, printed circuits, roofing
Tin	Soft, malleable, high corrosion resistance, low melting point, weak	232°C	Food packaging, solder
Zinc	Brittle, but malleable when heated	419.5°C	Used to galvanise ferrous metals such as steel to prevent corrosion

3 Alloys are a mixture of two or more metals or elements, which has improved properties and characteristics.

Alloy	Properties and characteristics	Composition	Melting point	Example uses
Brass	Easily machined, casts well, polishes well	Alloy: 65% copper 35% zinc	900–940°C	Plumbing / door fittings, musical instruments
Stainless steel	Hard, tough, magnetic	carbon steel + 10.5 to 18% chromium 8% nickel 8% manganese	1400°C	Kitchenware sinks, cutlery, medical equipment
High speed steel	High hardness at temps up to 600°C, resistant to wear, excellent toughness	carbon steel + 18% tungsten 4% chromium 1% vanadium	1400 °C	Drill bits, lathe tools, milling cutters

Worked example

Explain **two** reasons why tin would be a suitable metal for lining the inside of food cans. **(4 marks)**

Tin is corrosion resistant and will not react to the contents of the tin. It is also ductile, so it is easily formed into shape.

Now try this

Explain **three** reasons why stainless steel alloy may be used in the construction of a kettle. **(6 marks)**

Had a look ☐ Nearly there ☐ Nailed it! ☐

Core technical principles
New and emerging technologies
All materials

Polymers

Polymers are developed from oil-based petrochemicals, coal or gas. More recently environmentally-friendly polymers have been developed from plants. Plastics are made from polymers. There are two categories of plastics.

1 Thermoforming polymers

These polymers (plastics) can be recycled and reformed with heat. They are lightweight, low cost and come in a wide range of colours.

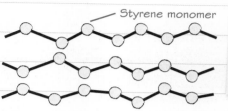
Styrene monomer

A thermoforming polymer comprises millions of connected monomers. For example, styrene monomers become polystyrene.

Features of different thermoforming polymers (plastics)

Acrylic (PMMA polymethyl methacrylate)	Tough, translucent form but easily scratched, used in car lights, shed windows
High impact polystyrene (HIPS)	Tough, impact resistant, food safe, used in refrigerator linings, food containers and children's toys
High density polythene (HDPE)	Tough, high strength to weight ratio, used in shampoo containers and cutlery
Polypropylene (PP)	Tough, durable, hygienic, impact resistant, used in car bumpers
Polyvinyl chloride (PVC)	Tough, strong, durable, flexible, used in drainpipes and rain coats
Polyethylene terephthalate (PET)	Tough, strong, stiff, clear, no porosity, used in drinks bottles

Acrylic is ideal for windows in garden sheds. It is strong and more difficult to break than glass. Although it may scratch, a clear view is not very important.

2 Thermosetting polymers

The cross-linked chains mean that once the polymer has set into shape it **cannot be reformed using heat**. It is hard, rigid but brittle, resistant to electricity, heat and chemicals and cannot be recycled.

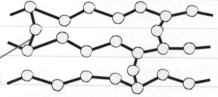
Cross link

A thermosetting polymer has cross links that make the connections more rigid.

Features of different thermosetting polymers (plastics)

Epoxy resin (ER)	Two-part resin and hardener for glue, varnish and paints
Melamine-formaldehyde (MF)	Good fire and heat resistance for kitchen work surfaces
Phenol formaldehyde (PF)	Good fire and heat resistance, for cases for kitchen appliances such as a toasted sandwich maker
Polyester resin (PR)	Starts as a liquid and is set using a catalyst (hardener) in conjunction with glass fibre. Can be combined with strands of glass, carbon or Kevlar to make a very strong composite material. Used in boat hulls and car bodies.
Urea–formaldehyde (UF)	Used for electrical fittings – plugs, sockets and switches, can be coloured or used as glue in materials such as MDF

Worked example

Describe the difference in the structure between thermoforming and thermosetting polymers.
(2 marks)

Thermosetting polymers have cross-linked chains, which means that they do not soften in heat.

Now try this

High impact polystyrene (HIPS) is to be used in the manufacture of children's toys.

Explain **four** reasons why HIPS is a suitable material for this use. **(8 marks)**

Textiles 1

Any flexible fabric that is made from fibres is classified as a textile. It consists of a network of thin thread-like fibres that are combined in a number of ways such as woven, non-woven and knitted.

Natural fibres

These are made from plant or animal sources.

Type	Source	Advantages	Disadvantages	Uses
Wool	Animal hair such as sheep, goats and other animals	Good insulator, breathable, absorbs dyes, lightweight, creases drop out	Prone to shrinking, dries slowly	Pullovers, shirts, trousers
Cotton	Fibrous material encasing seeds of the cotton plant	Soft, breathable, cool, strong, insulating, good abrasion resistance	Shrinkage, wrinkles, attacked by mildew	Shirts, sheets, swimwear, blouses
Silk	Fibres taken from silkworm cocoons	Soft, lustrous, dyes well, very strong, lightweight, comfortable, absorbent	Expensive, needs special care cleaning	Luxury wear, shirts, ties, pyjamas

Synthetic fibres

These are made from coal, oil or petrol-based chemicals.

Type	Advantages	Disadvantages	Uses
Polyester	Strong, durable, quick drying, dyes well, resists shrinkage / chemicals	Low absorbency, static electricity problems	Dresses, curtains, sails
Polyamide (nylon)	Durable, lightweight, chemical / wrinkle resistant, easy to wash	Stains easily, low moisture absorbency	Parachutes, sportswear
Elastane (Lycra)	Lightweight, abrasion / chemical resistant, stretches (elastic), strong	Colours with age, low moisture absorbency	Active sportswear, swimwear

Worked example

Figure 1 shows students in school shirts.

1 Explain why cotton is a suitable fabric for school shirts.   **(2 marks)**

Cotton is a suitable material as it is breathable but will still keep people warm when needed so it is comfortable for the wearer.

2 Explain **one** disadvantage of making school shirts from silk rather than cotton.   **(2 marks)**

A disadvantage of silk is that it is not as durable as cotton and it can tear, discolour or stain easily so it would not be suitable for heavy use.

Figure 1

Now try this

 Evaluate the use of wool fibre as a suitable material in the manufacture of a school pullover.   **(5 marks)**

Had a look ☐   Nearly there ☐   Nailed it! ☐

Core technical principles
New and emerging technologies
All materials

Textiles 2

Fibres can be **combined** in a number of ways. You need to know three methods.

Combining fabrics:

1 Knitted

Knitted fabrics are made by looping warp and weft yarns together making a flexible fabric.

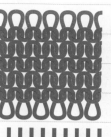

Weft is the yarn that goes across the width of the fabric / loom.
Warp is the yarn going down the length of the fabric / loom.

2 Woven

Plain weave woven fabrics are strong and hardwearing and have fibres interlaced in a criss-cross pattern and the weft and warp aligned at 90° (right angles) to each other.

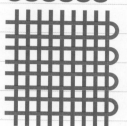

Selvedge is the edge of the fabric where wefts double back forming an edge that does not need to be hemmed to prevent fraying.

3 Non-woven fabrics

Non-woven fabrics are made by tangling fibres together to make sheet materials.

Bonded fabrics use webs of synthetic fibres that are bonded together with heat or chemicals (adhesives). They do not fray and are cheap to produce but are not as strong as woven fabrics. Used for **interlining** in curtains and clothing.

Felted fabrics use wool fibres that are bonded using heat, moisture and pressure. Felted fabric is a good insulator and does not fray, but has little strength or elasticity, is difficult to wash and is susceptible to moths.

As felt is difficult to wash, it is normally used for handicraft projects or hats.

Worked example

1 Explain why felted fabrics made from wool are chosen for making berets, like that shown in Figure 1. **(2 marks)**

Felt would be used as it is a good insulator of heat and will keep the user warm.

2 Explain **one** disadvantage of making the beret from felt. **(2 marks)**

The beret will be difficult to wash, as heat and moisture may make the fibres come apart.

Figure 1

You can blend natural and synthetic fibres to make material with combined properties of the base fibres to improve performance, comfort, strength, insulation or appearance and reduce cost. For example a **cotton / polyester** blended shirt is more durable and resistant to creasing.

Now try this

The jumper and hat shown in Figure 2 are knitted from a wool blend yarn.

Explain **one** reason why knitting is a suitable method of creating a jumper. **(2 marks)**

Figure 2

Materials properties

All materials have specific physical and working properties. Selecting the correct materials for a product is a vital part of the design process.

Physical properties

Physical properties of a material are ones that can be observed or measured **without changing the composition** of a material. These properties include the following:

Absorbency	The ability of a material to soak up a liquid.
Density	The mass per unit volume. This is a measurement of the mass of a material and how much space it takes up. A more dense material will feel heavier for its size.
Fusibility	The ability of a material to melt into a liquid or molten state when heated. Normally associated with metals and polymers.
Electrical conductivity	The ability of materials to conduct electricity. Metals are very good electrical conductors, while polymers are good insulators.
Thermal conductivity	The ability to conduct heat. Metals are very good thermal conductors, while polymers are good insulators.

Working / mechanical properties

The mechanical property of a material is defined as its **ability to resist certain external forces** being applied to it.

Look at page 99 for more about forces.

Strength	The ability to withstand force, e.g. by resisting squashing (compression) or stretching (tension).
Hardness	The ability to resist abrasive wear.
Toughness	The ability to withstand sudden stress or shocks.
Malleability	The ability to permanently deform when worked without breaking, also known as plasticity.
Ductility	The ability to be drawn out or stretched without breaking.
Elasticity	The ability to bend and return to shape without breaking when subjected to a force.

Worked example

Give **three** reasons why polyvinyl chloride (PVC) has been used for the outer covering of the mains electrical cable shown. **(3 marks)**

PVC has been used for the outer covering of the electrical cable because it is easy to strip and easy to handle. It will insulate the electricity running through the power cables. It also has good elasticity, so it will bend without breaking and is very resistant to corrosion, impact, abrasion, weathering, and chemical attack. PVC will burn when exposed to fire, but it is 'self-extinguishing'.

Now try this

Figure 1 shows copper pipes that are part of a domestic plumbing system for heating and running water.

Explain **two** reasons why domestic water pipes are often made from copper. **(4 marks)**

Figure 1

When you need to explain the use of a material, always describe a relevant property and how the property:
- helps the manufacture of the product
- helps the product perform the specific function.

Copper is non-permeable (absorbency) so it will not absorb other substances that it may come into contact with and affect the water supply. and has to be bent into shape (malleability).

Sources and origins

Paper and boards are materials made from fine cellulose fibres and classified by weight or construction.

Raw materials

As much as 85% of the timber used for making paper and boards comes from coniferous trees. Deciduous trees make up the rest with some other materials such as grasses, cotton, straw, bamboo, flax and hemp also used. Trees contain cellulose fibres that are naturally held together by **lignin**, which gives structure to plants. To create paper, a process removes the lignin to allow the cellulose fibres to be separated. The fibres can then be reformed into paper and boards.

> Another important source is recycled paper. This can save energy, water and landfill space and increases sustainability.

Paper making process

1. Trees are specifically grown for paper and harvested.

2. The logs are de-barked (bark is poor quality) and the timber is cut into small 2.5 cm pieces (chipped).

3. The chips are made into **pulp** mechanically or by using chemicals such as sodium hydroxide to break the chips down. The pulp is then washed, refined and cleaned. It may be mixed with other chemicals such as bleach, dyes and **sizing agents**.

> **Pulp** is made by separating the cellulose fibres from wood, fibre crops or waste paper.

4. The pulp slurry is 99% water and only 1% fibres, so it is pumped onto a flat wire screen to allow the water to drain away and leave a mat of damp fibres. These fibres are then put through a roller (calendaring) to remove the rest of the water and press it into a uniform thickness before drying. The more calendaring the higher the gloss.

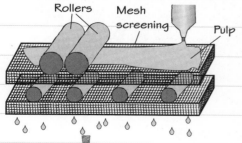

Rollers Mesh screening Pulp

5. The finished paper will be dried and wound into large rolls so that it can be distributed and then sent to factories to be cut into more manageable sizes.

Making board

Board is made in the same way as paper when it is a single sheet. Boards can also be made up of more than one layer such as duplex board, foil-lined board or have a foam core.

Some also have complex structure to provide impact resistance or increase strength, such as corrugated card.

Single-wall (double-faced) corrugated card

> **Sizing agents** are chemicals added to provide water-resistance (to prevent paper from blurring with water or ink) and printability (offset, inkjet, etc.).

Worked example

Describe **two** reasons why corrugated board is the preferred packaging for transporting household electrical goods. **(2 marks)**

Corrugated card boxes are lightweight, so easy to carry but offer protection. They are generally low cost as they are made from a lower grade material.

> You could also say that they can be printed on and recycled.

Now try this

Describe, as a series of stages, the process of producing solid white board that would be suitable for making greetings cards. **(5 marks)**

Stock forms, types and sizes 1

Available formats

Commercially available paper and card is generally available in standard forms.

👍 A set range of available forms is more cost-effective.

👍 Designers can incorporate the standard forms into their designs.

Sheet is the term for a single piece of paper.

Rolls are normally used on an industrial scale as they can be easily fed into machinery for continuous printing runs, such as books and magazines.

Ply is two or more layers of paper combined together using embossing techniques or adhesive to form multi-ply (e.g. two-ply) paper such as napkins, or receipts that self-copy to a second layer (self-carbonating).

A two-ply receipt booklet.

Other types of paper and board

Mounting board (1000–2000 μm) Relatively thick and rigid with colour on one side, used for picture framing.

Newsprint paper (45–55 gsm) Thin paper, low quality, low cost and lightweight. Rough surface, off-white colour.

Tissue paper (10–35 gsm) Lightweight, coloured paper, used for its absorbency properties, and for craft work.

Copier paper (80 gsm) Low cost, very available, smooth surface used for printers, good level of whiteness.

See more types of paper on page 31.

Set standards

These are measured by several criteria:

- **Length** and **width**, normally measured in millimetres (mm).
- **Weight**, measured in grams per square metre (gsm). Most printing paper has a gsm between 60 and 120. Above 160 gsm is card, above 220 gsm is board.
- **Thickness**, measured in microns. One micron (μm) is 1/1000th millimetre. A greetings card would be around 300 microns or 0.3 mm thick.
- **Colour**. White paper is graded on its whiteness. Most copier paper will be graded between 130–170. The higher the number, the whiter the sheet. Coloured paper is also available.

ISO B Series is the range of larger paper sizes used for posters or in industry.
ISO C Series is the range of sizes used for envelopes. A C5 envelope will take an A5 piece of paper, or A4 paper folded in half.

A series

Paper and board is in standard sizes, which have been set by the International Standards Organisation (ISO).

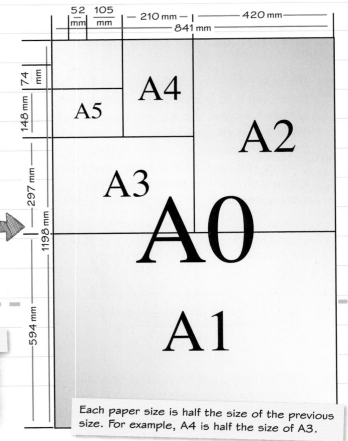

Each paper size is half the size of the previous size. For example, A4 is half the size of A3.

Now try this

1 mm = 1000 microns

A sheet of card is 500 microns thick. Calculate how many sheets there will be in a stack 10 cm tall. **(2 marks)**

Stock forms, types and sizes 2

Fasteners

Fasteners are used to join paper or card temporarily, or more permanently.

Treasury tag
Connects varying numbers of sheets through punched holes.

Paper fastener
Connects lower numbers of sheets through punched holes.

Staple
Popular method to hold sheets together applied with stapling tool.

Binder clip
Holds sheets together using a variety of actions, similar to bulldog clips.

Slide binder
Temporarily holds a number of sheets together.

Paperclip
Simple method to hold a small number of sheets.

Sealing

A paper and board product can be closed securely by **sealing** it in various ways.

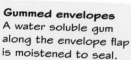

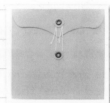

Gummed envelopes
A water soluble gum along the envelope flap is moistened to seal.

Self-adhesive envelope
A covering over the glue is peeled off to be able to seal an envelope. Alternatively, each flap can have a strip of latex which form an instant bond when pressed together.

Wax seal
Wax is melted over the area to seal and it is left to harden to form the bond.

String and button
Uses string wrapped around two buttons to close a package.

Binding

Available binding methods used to combine multiple sheets of paper, using a range of components.

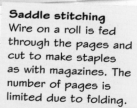

Perfect binding
Pages are gathered in smaller groups with a hard or flexible outer cover and glued at the spine. Used on most book binding.

Comb binding
Combs fit through punched holes and allow pages to lie flat. This is a popular low cost process.

Coil or spiral binding
A spiral of plastic or metal wire is threaded through holes, allowing pages to lie flat.

Saddle stitching
Wire on a roll is fed through the pages and cut to make staples as with magazines. The number of pages is limited due to folding.

Worked example

Staples and paperclips can be used to fasten a number of sheets of paper together. Describe **two** advantages of using a paperclip in preference to a staple. **(2 marks)**

Paperclips would be used in preference to a staple because they do not damage the paper that is being fastened and they are easily removed from the paper and can be reused.

Now try this

Envelopes can be gummed or they can be self-adhesive. Explain **two** reasons why self-adhesive envelopes are likely to be more popular than gummed envelopes. **(4 marks)**

Wastage

Wastage techniques such as cutting, shearing and perforating are used in creating prototypes.

Hand tools for cutting paper, card and boards

Paper shears
Long blade for straight cuts, which uses shear action.

Craft knife / scalpel
Sharp blades used for cutting and scoring.

Rotary cutting / perforating tool
Cuts lines or perforations to allow for tearing or folding.

Steel safety rule
Easy to hold and keeps fingers away from sharp blades.

Cutting mat
Self-healing, non-slip polymer mat that protects surfaces.

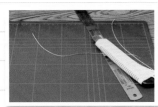

Desktop paper cutter
Used to trim paper and thin card accurately as guides indicate a series of paper sizes.

Die cutting paper and boards (hand process)

Dies are made from sharpened steel strips called 'rules' that are formed to the exact shape of the paper or board and pressed or rolled to make the cut. Examples of products made with die cutters are greetings cards and food packaging.

This method will cut multiple layers – the limit is the thickness of the blade and level of pressure.

Cutters

Corrugated board

A rotary die cutter

The nets of cartons can be die cut and also creased using the die cutter with a rounded edge.

Laser cutting and engraving

This technology is relatively new but used widely in schools. The laser beam cuts through the paper and boards with a focused beam. Care needs to be taken not to burn the edges of the paper or board.

- Work does not need to be held.
- Cuts are extremely precise.
- Used to cut or score.
- Safer than using cutting tools.

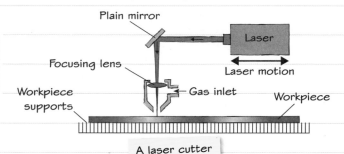

Plain mirror

Focusing lens

Workpiece supports

Laser

Laser motion

Gas inlet

Workpiece

A laser cutter

The advantages of die cutting are that it is a quicker process for large production runs and there is no risk of scorching the cut edges.

Worked example

Describe **three** advantages of laser cutting boards rather than die cutting.   **(3 marks)**

A shaped die will need to be created with the individual design, while laser cutting can have different designs for each piece. Laser cutting can also engrave into the surface of the board. Lasers can also cut more complex shapes than with a die.

Now try this

Describe the steps that must be performed prior to cutting a board that is 1250 microns thick using a laser cutter. The shape to be cut has already been generated on a suitable CAD program.   **(6 marks)**

Addition

Addition processes add to the paper and boards to improve their properties.

1 Laminating

Paper can be laminated with more layers of paper (ply) polymers or foil to improve its properties.

Laminating / encapsulation

A polymer pouch covers the paper or thin board, giving it protection from dirt, water and fading and makes it more rigid and easy to clean. The pouches are bonded by heat in a laminating machine.

When you cover a sheet of paper and create a lip all round, it is **encapsulating**. If you have a layer of plastic with no lip, it is **laminating**.

Commercial laminating

A polythene film covers paper or boards to protect the printed image on items such as books. It can cover one or both surfaces but it does not encapsulate, so edges could be prone to water damage.

The laminate is fed from a roll and can be applied cold or sealed on with heat.

2 Coatings and additives

Paper and board can be treated to prevent them from being absorbent which will improve the quality of printing.

Hot foil blocking

Pre-glued foil is pressed onto card with heat.

Hot foil blocking gives a decorative metallic finish to packaging or greetings cards.

Foil laminated board

Aluminium is laminated onto a card base.

Foil laminate in food packaging forms a barrier between the food and the card.

- Polyethylene (seals in the contents)
- Polyethylene (adhesion layer)
- Aluminium foil (barrier to oxygen, flavour and light)
- Polyethylene (adhesion layer)
- Paperboard (provides strength and stability)
- Polyethylene (protects from the outside elements such as moisture)

Foil laminated card may also have other layers for specific types of packaging such as drinks cartons.

3 Sizing

Sizing is a coating that can be applied to paper to reduce the absorbency. This can be applied at the wet processing stage (internal) or applied to the surface of the paper after it has been made (external).

Sizing materials include clay, chalk or powdered minerals. Wax or acrylic polymer-based coatings can also be used.

Worked example

Explain the purpose of an aluminium and polyethethene layer in a drink carton. **(4 marks)**

The aluminium layer in a drink carton creates a barrier to light and oxygen and helps the drink last longer. The polythene layer creates a water-tight barrier to stop the carton from leaking from inside out and outside in.

Now try this

 1 Explain why an A4 paper poster for an external display board would be encapsulated. **(2 marks)**

 2 Describe the process of encapsulating a sheet of paper that is to be used for an outdoor display board, using a laminating machine. **(3 marks)**

Deforming and reforming

Perforating

Perforating uses a toothed cutter to create a series of cuts that allows the material to be easily torn along the line of the cuts. It is used to separate postage stamps or tear out sections in books.

> Products will often have a combination of **cutting** to create the overall shape of the product, **creasing** to help with folding and **perforating**, which allows a secondary function such as the opening of a package.

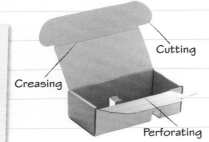

Cutting

Creasing

Perforating

Scoring or creasing

Many paper and board products will need to be **folded** so that they can be used as a product. For example, in boxes or books.

Creasing or scoring are similar processes to cutting but use less pressure. The tools used will be blunt so that the fibres are crushed to make a defined line to fold.

Creasing can be done by hand using a creasing tool, or machinery can be used.

Securing folded paper and board

Tucks and flaps can be carefully designed so that packaging can be folded and securely closed.

Flaps tuck in to close box

Adhesives can also be applied to the flaps that will make a more permanent join or can be designed to be released, as with cereal boxes.

Glue to seal the box closed

Moulded pulp

Pulp is generally made into flat sheets or boards, but it can also be moulded into specific shapes and used for packaging for consumer goods, such as electrical goods or egg boxes. The pulp is pumped into a shaped mould and pressed and dried into shape.

👍 The packaging is environmentally friendly as it is generally made from recycled newspaper and can be recycled again.

👎 It is biodegradable and less expensive than expanded polystyrene.

Moulded pulp is used for egg cartons.

Worked example

1 Give the name of the process that allows the easy separation of two sections of paper along a line. **(1 mark)**

   Perforating

2 Give the name of the process that helps card to be folded along a line. **(1 mark)**

   Creasing or scoring

Now try this

Figure 1 shows a net for a card box that is going to be used to package a bottle of perfume. Glue will be applied to the four flaps. Draw the shape that this net will form when it is folded and glued. **(2 marks)**

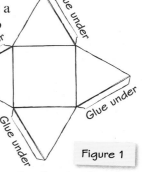

Glue under

Glue under

Glue under

Glue under

Figure 1

Surface treatments and finishes

Surface treatments can enhance functional and aesthetic properties of papers and boards.

1 Printing

All printing processes work on **direct** or **offset (indirect)** transfer.

Process	Advantages	Disadvantages	Uses
Offset lithography Relief printing plate on rollers onto paper. See page 46 for more on this type of printing.	Inexpensive, prints on a variety of papers, high speed, good quality images.	High set up costs, needs to be flat and damp can stretch paper or affect colour.	Books, magazines, packaging or posters.
Flexography Flexible relief printing plate on rollers, papers fed from a roll.	Inexpensive as high volume, inks dry quickly, high speed.	High set up costs, lower quality, print runs in excess of 500,000.	Newspapers, sweet papers low cost magazines.
Screen printing Ink printed through finely woven fabric, non-print area masked.	Prints on a variety of surfaces, good for short runs and volume.	Long drying times, photo screens are accurate, but generally lack detail.	Posters, mugs, T-shirts, point of sale displays.
Gravure Rotary printing using engraved cylinder.	High speed, consistent colour and quality on a variety of papers.	High set up costs, effective for long print runs.	High quality magazines and books, stamps.
Photocopying Drum charged when exposed to original copy, toner fixes to charged areas and transferred to paper and fused by heat.	High speed, good for small batches, can make double sided, low cost and convenient.	Can fade over time, and variable quality as ink is used, expensive for long runs.	Home or business, flyers, documents.

2 Embossing

Embossing is used to create a 3D image on papers and boards.

- A male and female die is made with the relief pattern cut into the surface.
- The plates are then pressed into the paper or boards using heat and pressure.
- It is an extra process after the printing is completed.
- Uses include embossed pattern on packaging to improve aesthetics or raised areas for Braille.

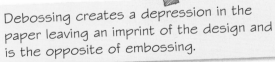

Debossing creates a depression in the paper leaving an imprint of the design and is the opposite of embossing.

3 (Ultraviolet) UV varnishing

Varnishing is a protective finish that can be applied to paper and boards.

- The varnish will be sprayed onto the surface of the paper or boards after printing. This protects the print and gives it a high-gloss finish.
- The varnish can be oil- or water-based but will need to be dried before any further process is carried out, such as folding.
- To speed this up, the sheets will be passed under UV lights, which fixes (dries) the varnish immediately.

Types of UV varnish:
Sparkle – with metal flakes for aesthetic appeal.
Fragrance – which can be activated by scratching.
Silver latex – which can be scratched off, e.g. lottery cards.

Worked example

Identify which printing process is most suited to printing a daily newspaper. **(1 mark)**

A Flexography ⬤
B Gravure ◯
C Photocopying ◯
D Screen printing ◯

Now try this

 Describe the process of UV varnishing onto a sheet of card after it has been printed. **(3 marks)**

Commercial processes

Offset lithography

This process is used for long printing runs, for example, books, magazines, packaging or posters. Offset printing transfers the image to be printed from the plate to a roller or blanket cylinder and then to the paper. The plate does not come in contact with the paper directly.

1 The litho-printing plate cylinder has a relief image (the image stands out from the surface) on it. Plates are made from flexible polymers or aluminium.

2 The litho-printing plate is dampened with water (to repel the ink from non-image areas).

3 Ink is applied to the litho-printing plate as it rotates.

4 The ink is then transferred to the offset blanket cylinder as they rotate against each other.

5 The ink is then transferred to the paper or card as it is pulled through the rollers from the pressure of the blanket cylinder and impression cylinder.

The lithographic printing process

Only one colour can be printed at a time.

Colour models

The **CMYK colour model** uses layers of coloured ink to partially or entirely reduce the light reflected from the lighter background such as white paper.

Colours used are cyan, magenta, yellow and key (meaning black).

The **RGB colour model** adds layers of the three primary colours to produce a broad array of colours. Colours used are red, green and blue.

Die cutting

Once the printing process is completed, the finished sheet needs to be accurately cut to shape using a die cutting machine.

1 The cutters used to create the shapes are called dies. They are made of steel blades called rules. These are made from hardened steel and are expensive to produce but can be used many times.

2 They are fitted to stamping machines to carry out the process of die cutting.

3 The material is cut, then rubber ejectors push the card out.

4 The waste is recycled.

Rollers could also be fitted with cutters to cut continuous runs.

The paper or board can also be creased using rounded rules to allow for folding.

Worked example

Explain why the CMYK colour model is used for printing processes on white paper.   **(2 marks)**

The CMYK colour model uses a combination of individual colours to block out the white paper background at varying levels to create an image that the human eye will see as a full colour image.

Now try this

With the aid of notes and sketches, draw a labelled diagram of an offset lithography printing process for a leaflet printed in black on white paper.   **(6 marks)**

Selecting papers and boards

Properties to consider when selecting materials for a product

Functionality: What the design should do and for whom and the measurable performance factors.	**Availability:** What standard sizes / forms of paper, board and components are available.	**Social factors:** Such as disabilities, religious groups, age or consumer society / obsolescence.
Scale of production: Processing of paper and board, joining methods and manufacturing capability.	**Costs:** Cost of the raw material and conversion into the product. Budget available and what target price is the intended product.	**Ethical factors:** Factors to consider in sourcing raw materials and manufacture, including fair trade organisations.
Environmental factors: Sustainability, waste management, energy demands and recycling.	**Mechanical properties:** Strength, including tension, compression shear.	**Cultural factors:** Fashion, trends, faiths, background or beliefs of the user.
Aesthetics: How it will appear to the customer, use of colours and texture or form.	**Physical properties:** Absorbency, density / weight and fusibility.	**Finishes:** How long it is intended to last and whether it will need further protection against decay.

Worked example

Figure 1 shows a box made from aluminium foil-lined board.

Describe **two** reasons why this box is suitable for food packaging for a takeaway restaurant. **(4 marks)**

Function – The foil lining stops the card from absorbing moisture and keeps the food warm.

Scale of production – Suits high volume production as it can be made in a continuous process.

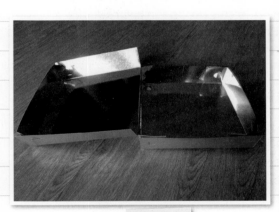

Figure 1

Alternative answers:

Aesthetics – The card is easily printed on with images that promote the company and attract the customer.

Mechanical properties – Strength is suitable for a one-use product, so the card can be at the lower end of thickness.

Costs – Costs are low for card as it is a disposable product.

Make sure your answer relates directly to the needs of a product. In this board-based food packaging, the properties of materials are closely related to the needs for takeaway food.

Improving properties

Papers and boards can also be enhanced by improving their properties for certain uses:

- **Flexibility** is improved by scoring lines so that the material can be bent into boxes or packaging.
- **Rigidity** is improved through folding (stiffening).
- **Surfaces** can be improved through laminating and encapsulation, which also reinforce the material.

Now try this

Explain **two** advantages of using an offset lithography process for printing the leaflets shown in Figure 2 onto plain paper. **(4 marks)**

Figure 2

Sources and origins

Timber has to be converted into workable forms. It goes through two stages: conversion and seasoning.

Conversion

The trunk of the tree is sawn along its length into usable planks.

Slab sawn method
- 👍 Relatively cheap.
- 👎 Poorer quality – prone to faults such as cupping or twisting.

Radial 'quarter' sawn method
- 👍 Better quality timber with short annual rings.
- 👎 More expensive due to more waste.

Faults in timber

Cupping is when the timber is bent across the grain.

Twisting is along the whole length of timber.

Splits occur at the end of planks.

Shakes follow the line of a growth ring.

Knots are where branches were growing, often included in furniture for aesthetic reasons.

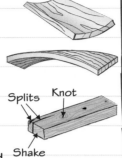

Seasoning

Seasoning is the process that reduces moisture in timber after it has been converted into planks. Well-seasoned timber is around 15% moisture. There are two types of seasoning: natural and kiln.

Natural / air seasoning
- 👍 Cheaper to set up and natural.
- 👎 Takes longer (one year for every 25 mm of timber).
- 👎 Prone to insect attack.
- 👎 Needs large amount of space.

Protection from weather

Piling sticks

Timber bearers

Kiln seasoning
- 👍 More control over moisture levels and consistency, kills insects.
- 👎 More expensive to set up and has greater running costs due to energy requirements.

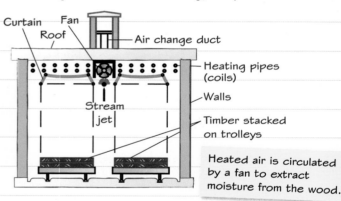

Curtain   Fan
Roof
Air change duct
Heating pipes (coils)
Walls
Stream jet
Timber stacked on trolleys

Heated air is circulated by a fan to extract moisture from the wood.

Manufactured boards

Manufactured boards are man-made to specific dimensions by using cheaper timber or offcuts, chips or fibres. These are combined with adhesive and will have different properties than the original timber. Examples are MDF, plywood and chipboard.

Many manufactured boards have a thin **veneer** or **laminate** to cover the processed surface. A **veneer** is a thin layer of timber that has been taken from a tree.

A **laminate** is also a thin layer of material, but it is not always timber and can be made from other materials such as melamine, which is used for kitchen work surfaces.

Worked example

Give the name of the fault in timber caused by a branch growing out of a trunk. **(1 mark)**

A Shake ◯
B Split ◯
C Twist ◯
D Knot ●

Now try this

Timber is usually seasoned before it is used in the construction of furniture.

Describe the advantages of kiln seasoning over natural seasoning. **(4 marks)**

Stock forms, types and sizes

There are a range of commercially available types and sizes of timbers and manufactured boards. These have the advantage of being more cost-effective and more readily available.

Available stock forms

Commercially available timber is generally available in stock forms.

👍 A set range of available forms is more cost-effective.

👎 It is easier for production if designers incorporate stock forms into their designs.

Standard sizes of timber

When ordering set stock forms of timber, the customer / designer will select from the available sizes and avoid altering width and thickness wherever possible. However, length is easily adjusted.

Ordering stock forms of planks

Planks are long flat pieces of timber with standard width and thickness with two grades of finish.

Standard lengths are normally 1.80 m, 2.10 m, 2.40 m, 2.70 m, 3.0 m and 3.30 m.

Grade of finish

✓ **Rough sawn:** Has not been planed, rough to touch and is more suited to exterior work.

✓ **Planed all round (PAR):** Has been planed and is smooth to touch and dimensions are more precise. Used for interior work.

Standard sizes of manufactured boards

Thickness starts from 3 mm and rises up in steps, e.g. 3 mm, 6 mm, 9 mm, etc. If veneer is applied, thicknesses starts at 4 mm.

Full size will be 2440 mm **long** x 1220 mm **wide**.

Standard mouldings

Mouldings are lengths of timber that have been machined to a defined shape.

Dowels have a circular cross section with a specified diameter.

Rotary cutting a veneer.

A **veneer** is a thin layer of timber that has been taken from a tree and is normally 0.4–1.5 mm thick.

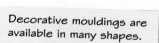

Decorative mouldings are available in many shapes.

Worked example

Explain **two** reasons why a designer may incorporate stock forms of timber into their designs. **(4 marks)**

It is normally cheaper to buy stock forms, which will make the product more cost-effective. It will also be easier to source the timber as stock forms are more readily available.

Now try this

Planks are available in two grades of finish. Explain how these finishes may affect how they are used. **(3 marks)**

You could also say that production will be easier as stock forms are set sizes and so will fit together.

Standard components

Pre-manufactured standard components are used to assemble a product. For timber products, these include woodscrews, nails, pins, knockdown fittings and hinges.

Woodscrews

Woodscrews fix two pieces of timber together.

Traditional woodscrews do not have the thread along the full length of the shank, but **modern screws** do. Both screws need a pilot hole to prevent the timber splitting.

A modern screw

Drive types

Slotted   Pozidrive

Philips

Head types

Flat countersunk   Roundhead   Raised head

Inserting a wood screw

1 Drill pilot hole through both pieces.
2 Drill clearance hole for shank.
3 Drill countersink (if required).
4 Fix screw.

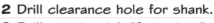
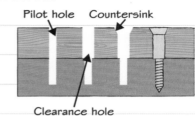

Pilot hole   Countersink

Clearance hole

Nails and pins

These are a popular way of joining timber. They have a sharp point at one end and different shaped heads.

Round wire nail: A general-purpose nail for joining wood.

Oval wire nail: Allows the head to be below the surface.

Panel pin: Smaller diameter pin for fine work.

Knock-down (KD) fittings

These are used for self-assembly furniture, which also allows for dismantling.

Cross dowel

Cam lock

Connecting block

Hinges

Moveable joints called hinges are used on wood such as doors or lids. Generally they are made from metals such as steel or brass.

Butt hinge: Most common hinge for doors, needs to be fitted.

Concealed hinge: Used for kitchen cabinets.

Tee hinge: Used for exterior fittings, sheds, where load is spread.

Piano hinge: Used where long spans are required.

Worked example

Explain **one** reason why it is advisable to drill a pilot hole into timber when preparing it to take a woodscrew. **(2 marks)**

A pilot hole will make the screw easier to fit as it will not be so tight and it will reduce the risk of the timber splitting when the screw is inserted.

Now try this

Describe, using notes and sketches, how to fit a roundhead woodscrew into the two pieces of timber shown in Figure 1.

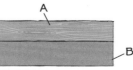

A

B

Figure 1   **(3 marks)**

Wastage 1

Wastage is the process of removing excess timber by cutting the timber to the required shape and size.

Hand tools for sawing timber

Handsaw
Straight cuts on pieces of timber, length is from heel to toe. Types: rip, panel, cross-cut.

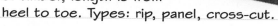

Backsaw
Cutting smaller timber, straight lines, more accurate, depth of cut limited by the back. Types: tenon, dovetail, gent.

Frame saw
For cutting curves, teeth point towards the handle. Types: coping, bow.

Tools for shaping timber

Planes are used to take shavings off the surface of timber. Can be adjusted for depth. Types:

> **Smoothing plane** – for finishing work, a larger version is called a jack plane.
>
> **Shoulder plane** – for cutting into rebates to give a square corner.

Chisels are used to take shavings off the surface of timber and for cutting wood joints.
Types: bevel edge (shown), mortise.

Saw blades

For saws to work effectively, the teeth have to be **set** wider than the **blade** so it does not jam (bind) in the groove made by the cut (**kerf**). Teeth on a saw blade are bent outwards alternately left and right making a saw cut that is actually wider than the width of the blade, stopping it from jamming as it cuts.

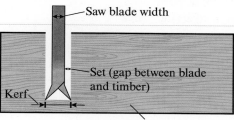

Saw blade width
Set (gap between blade and timber)
Kerf
Timber

> It is important to keep the teeth of a saw sharp. They can be re-sharpened if needed. Saw blade teeth alternate in either direction from the blade to create the set.

Tools for drilling timber

Twist drills can be used for cutting relatively small holes in timber. They are made from high speed steel. The 'wedge' cutting action is used for drilling.

There are some **specialist drills** that are designed for specific tasks:

A **countersink** drill has a 90° angle to create a seating for the screw head so it is flush with the surface.

A **Forstner bit** is used to cut larger flat bottom holes, ranging from 10–50 mm.

Worked example

Name the correct drill that creates space for a screw head to be flush with the surface of timber.

(1 mark)

A Twist ☐
B Countersink ⬤
C Hole saw ☐
D Forstner ☐

A **flat bit** is used to cut larger holes that are deep.

A **hole saw** is used to cut large holes in timber, sizes 19–75 mm.

Now try this

The kerf of a saw is the groove that is created by the saw as it cuts through the timber. Describe **one** reason why the saw kerf should be wider than the thickness of the blade. **(1 mark)**

Wastage 2

Some processes remove smaller amounts of material than cutting and drilling.

Surforms

Surforms are used to shape timber.
- The blades are made from a steel strip that has perforations. The edges of the perforation are sharpened to cut in to the wood.
- Surform blades can be flat, curved or circular.
- Blades can be replaced when they become blunt.
- Generally used for fast removal of wood.

A surform tool

Rasps

Rasps are used to shape timber. They cut smaller amounts of timber than surforms. Each of the teeth will cut into the surface of the timber to remove small pieces of the material. Rasps are a type of file with coarser teeth.

Rasps have coarse teeth and different cross-sectional shapes to create shaped profiles in the wood.

Square Round Half round Flat

Using rasps and surforms

1. Hold the rasp or surform at 45° to the work being abraded.
2. Hold the rasp or surform at both ends.
3. Move along the length of the grain of the timber.

45°

Abrasive paper

Coated abrasive paper, such as glasspaper or sandpaper, is used to smooth timber. The process is called sanding. There are different grades of coarseness. Fine grades have smaller particles (and a higher grit number) and are suitable for giving a smooth or polished surface. Abrasive papers can come in **sheets, rolls, discs and belts**.

Glasspaper has quartz particles (not glass) bonded to a backing paper. It is relatively cheap.

Aluminium oxide paper is used as an alternative and contains aluminium oxide particles instead of quartz and can be used on different materials.

Grit Size	Grade
40-60	Coarse
80-100	Medium
120-150	Medium
180-220	Fine
240 up	Very fine

The bigger the grit number, the finer the grade of paper.

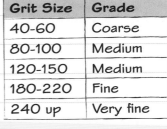

Individual sheets or sections of a roll of glasspaper or aluminium oxide paper are normally used in conjunction with a block, often made from cork, to finish products.

Tailored sheets, discs and belts can be used in conjunction with hand or fixed machine tools.

Worked example

Describe **three** safety precautions when using a handheld sanding machine. **(3 marks)**

When using a handheld sanding machine you must ensure that there is suitable dust extraction. You need to protect your eyes with goggles and you need to ensure that there are no trailing cables.

Now try this

Describe the stages of smoothing and cleaning the curved back of the wooden spoon shown in Figure 1, including the correct tools to be used. The spoon has already been cut to shape. **(4 marks)**

Figure 1

Addition

Timber can be joined in many ways depending on the intended strength and appearance. Three types are carcase, frame and edge joints.

Carcase (box) joints

Carcase (box) joints are used to join planks of wood to make cabinets, drawers or shelves.

Butt	Dowelled	Finger	Dovetail	Housing
Most simple joint, strength is determined by the adhesive used.	The use of dowels can add increased strength to the joint.	The adhesive surface area is increased to make a stronger joint for carcase construction, with improved looks.	The adhesive surface area is increased and dovetails prevent the joint pulling apart. This makes a very strong joint for carcase construction, with improved looks.	Provides larger adhesive area and the shoulder supports the timber in carcase construction.

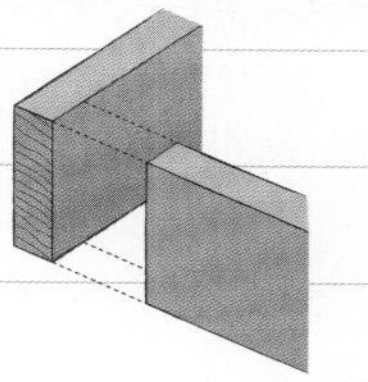

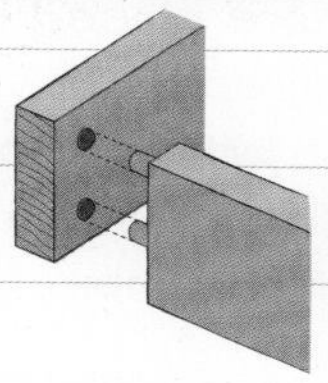

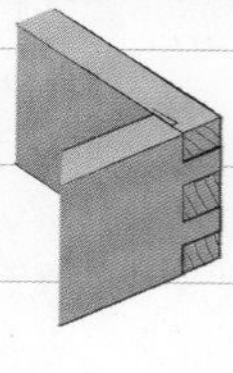

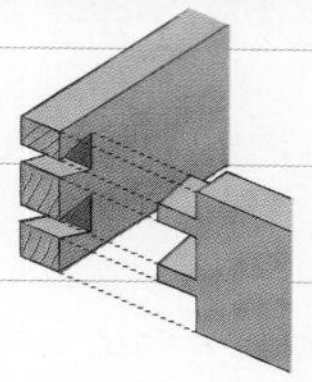

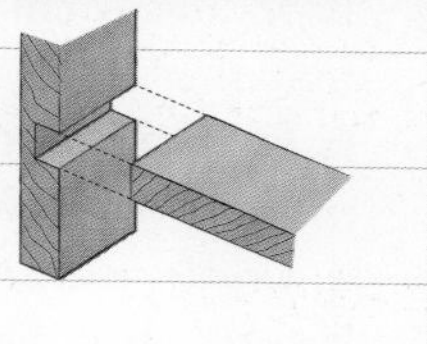

Frame joints

Frame joints are used to create a supporting frame for table or chair construction.

Mortise and tenon	Halving	Mitre
Strong joint for most frame construction, with a large adhesive surface area.	Relatively strong for frame construction. The addition of screws or nails will increase strength.	Attractive joint for corners of frames, but are low strength and may need reinforcing with dowels or nails.

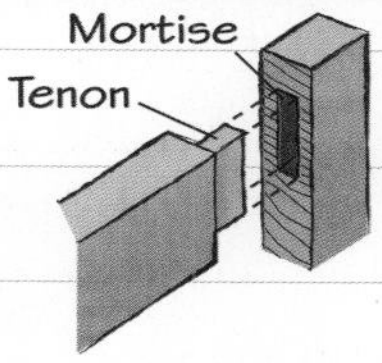

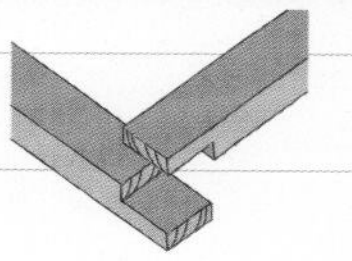

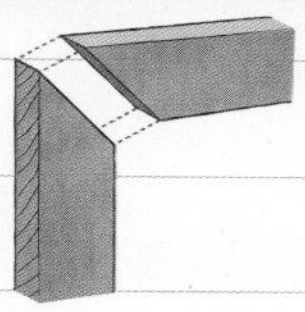

Mortise
Tenon

Worked example

Explain **two** reasons why a biscuit or dowel will increase the strength of a joint made from timber.   **(4 marks)**

Using a dowel or biscuit in a timber joint will increase the adhesive surface area. Modern glues are very strong, so this increases the strength of the joint. Because the dowel or biscuit runs inside the joint, it can only be broken by shearing off, which means that it can withstand greater forces.

Knock-down fittings (see page 50) can also be used in carcase, frame and edge jointing.

Edge joints

Edge jointing is used to join sheets of timber planks along their length.

Biscuit or dowel	Tongue and groove
Increases adhesive surface area and strength.	Increases adhesive surface area and strength.

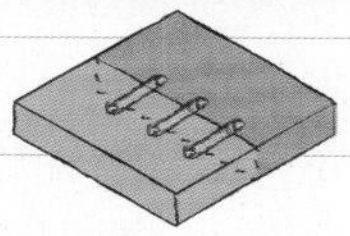

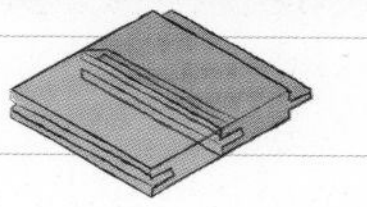

Now try this

Draw a diagram to show how you could strengthen the edge joint shown in Figure 1 with the use of dowels.   **(2 marks)**

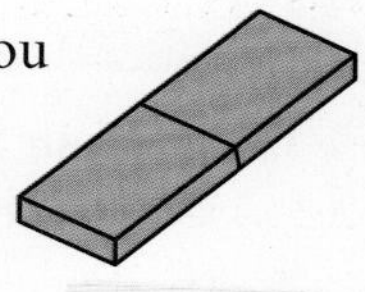

Figure 1

Deforming and reforming

There are two deforming and reforming methods you need to know: laminating and steam bending.

Laminating

Joining two or more layers of timber together is a process called **laminating**.

Any timber can be used for laminating. The thinner the laminates, the tighter the curve.

👍 It forms a thicker and stronger composite material.

👍 It is used in creating plywood or curved shapes that would not be strong if cut from a single piece.

👍 Reduces areas of short grain where the timber will be weaker.

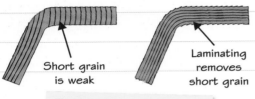

Short grain is weak

Laminating removes short grain

Effects of laminating timber

Process of laminating

1 Adhesive is applied between the layers of laminates.

2 A barrier is placed between a former and the laminates to prevent the two sticking.

3 Laminates are placed in the mould and aligned correctly.

4 Pressure is applied to the former using vacuum bag or clamps.

5 The laminated timber is left to dry.

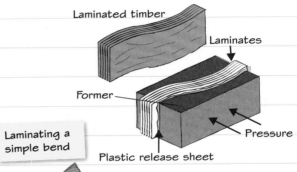

Laminated timber

Laminates

Former

Pressure

Laminating a simple bend

Plastic release sheet

For both laminating and steam bending, a suitable **former** needs to be made that is strong enough to **resist** the forces being applied.

Worked example

A pair of salad servers are to be laminated from strips of beech. Which is the most suitable adhesive for this process?   **(1 mark)**

A Tensol cement ⃝

B Epoxy resin ⃝

C PVA ⬤

D Superglue ⃝

A suitable adhesive for laminating timber is PVA. Contact adhesives can be used if clamping is a problem on thin veneers on curves.

Steam bending

Steam bending is a process of forcing timber into a defined curved shape along its length. **Hardwoods** are more suitable for steam bending such as ash, elm, hickory and oak.

👍 The curved timber will be stronger than if the same shape was cut from a single piece.

👍 Uses include walking stick hooks and curved chair backs.

Process of steam bending

1 Timber is placed in a steam box.

2 The steam increases the moisture content of the timber making it more flexible. This takes around one hour per 25 mm of thickness.

3 The timber is bent around a former and clamped in place.

4 The moisture is then dried from the timber and the shape is kept.

Now try this

1 Give **four** reasons why laminated wood is more suitable than using solid timber for the construction of the curved part of the rocking chair shown in Figure 1.   **(4 marks)**

2 An alternative method of making the rockers is by steam bending. Describe the process of steam bending the rockers of the rocking chair shown in Figure 1.   **(5 marks)**

Figure 1

Surface treatments and finishes

Finishing is used to improve the appearance of timber and protect the surface from damage caused by ultraviolet decay, weather, heat, dirt, liquids, fungus or insects. The type of finish depends on the end use for the timber. Three suitable finishes are paint, varnish or tanalising.

Painting

Painting generally provides a **coloured finish** that can be used inside and outside. Paints can be water-, solvent- or oil-based. Solvent and oil-based paints are being phased out by some manufacturers due to new regulations and environmental issues. **Polyurethane** paints tend to be used where there is a lot of wear or the possibility of scratches, for example on products like children's toys. Before paint can be applied, the timber surface will need to be prepared.

Using paint will conceal the grain of the timber that is being painted.

Preparing timber for painting

1. Timber is cleaned and made smooth using different grades of glasspaper.

2. Knots are treated with knotting solution to prevent any resin seeping out.

3. Timber is sealed with a primer, then this layer is rubbed down lightly with fine glasspaper.

4. An undercoat is painted to provide a smooth surface and even base colour. This layer is rubbed down lightly with fine glasspaper.

5. The final layer is the top coat which will be the final colour and provide a satin, matt or gloss finish.

Varnishing

Varnish provides a **clear finish** that can be used inside and outside.

Varnishes can change the colour of the wood but the grain of the timber will always be seen through the varnish. Varnish is used to protect the timber as it provides a hard, durable and waterproof finish. It also improves the aesthetics.

Timber is prepared for varnish in the same way as for painting and the varnish may be rubbed down between the base coat and the top layer.

Varnish brings out the beauty of the wood.

Tanalising

Tanalising is a preservative process for external timber (generally softwoods) prior to assembly, which prevents water absorption and decay. This results in the timber lasting outdoors for more than 15 years longer.

1. Water is removed from timber with a vacuum.

2. Tank is flooded with a solution of copper sulphate and mineral salts.

3. Pressure is applied to force preservative into timber.

4. Vacuum extracts excess preservative which can be reused.

5. Timber is steam-dried before removing from the tank

Other surface treatments and protection for timber

Preservative	Wax	Oil	Stain
For external use to prevent insect attack and decay.	Applied with wire wool and cloth, can change colour of wood.	Soaks into the grain to give a waterproof barrier.	Used to colour the wood before adding wax or varnish.

Worked example

Give **two** reasons why timber is varnished. **(2 marks)**

Timber is varnished to give it a protective coating and to enhance the colour of the wood as the grain will be seen through the varnish.

Now try this

Describe the process of tanalising a length of pine before it is to be used for constructing a garden fence. **(5 marks)**

Commercial processes

A range of commercial processes is used for shaping and forming wood. You need to know about two of these processes.

Routing

Routers can be used for cutting timber in a controlled way with a large range of shaped cutters.

- A plunging tool is used to cut grooves (A) or recessed shapes.
- A shaped tool can cut along the length of a piece of timber to create a shaped moulding (B).
- Cutters are often guided with a guide wheel for accuracy.

A

B

A commercial CNC router, can be programmed to make many identical items.

A handheld router is used for small-scale production.

A table router is a very good way to add mouldings to wood prior to further manufacturing processes.

'V' Groove   Dovetail   Rebate   Chamfer   Round nose

Other cutters give specific shaped cuts.

Routing and turning machines can be computer numerically controlled (CNC), which means that they are very accurate with repeatable processes, will run 24/7, and are safer and quicker.

Worked example

Explain **two** reasons why a CNC router might be used in preference to a handheld router. **(4 marks)**

A CNC router would be used in preference to a handheld router as it would be safer and more accurate, because there is less chance of human error. It will also be able to repeat the process many times without tiring.

Turning

Woodturning is a process that is used to shape wood, which is spinning on a wood lathe, into a symmetrical shape around an axis. For example, spindle legs or bowls.

- A range of tools will be used to generate the shapes required and they are held firmly by the operator on the tool rest.
- Work can be held on a face plate or between centres (between drive centre and taper centre). On some lathes the drive centre can be replaced with a chuck to hold work.

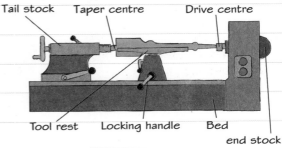

Tail stock   Taper centre   Drive centre

Tool rest   Locking handle   Bed

end stock (covered for safety)

A wood lathe

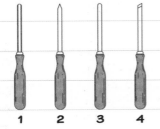

1   2   3   4

1 Roughing gouge to remove most of the material (smaller version called spindle gouge).
2 Parting tool to separate wood
3 Round nose for finer smoother work
4 Skew chisel for planing wood

Now try this

Figure 1 shows a wooden coffee table leg and the block it was shaped from.

Describe the main stages in preparing the square section of timber for mounting onto the wood lathe and turning between centres to make the shape. **(4 marks)**

A

Figure 1

Using and working with timbers

You need to know how and why materials influence the design of a product. See pages 32, 33 and 98 for more on the physical and mechanical properties of materials.

Selecting materials

When deciding on appropriate materials for a product, manufacturers need to examine the following key areas.

Physical properties: Absorbency, density and weight, grain structure, colour, texture, insulator.

Finishes: How long is it intended to last and whether it will need further protection against decay.

Functionality: What the design should do and for whom.

Availability: Availability of the timber and what standard sizes and forms are available and standard components / adhesives to join.

Social factors: Factors such as disabilities, religious groups, age or consumer society / obsolescence.

Aesthetics: How it will appear to the customer, use of colours, texture or form.

Properties and how they influence design

Cultural factors: Factors such as fashion, trends, faiths or beliefs of the user, from a range of backgrounds.

Mechanical properties: Methods to improve properties, such as laminating and steam bending.

Ethical factors: Factors to consider in sourcing raw materials and manufacture, including fair trade organisations.

Environmental factors: Sustainability, deforestation, energy demands, and recycling.

Scale of production: Processing of timber, joining methods and manufacturing capability.

Costs: The cost of the raw material and conversion into the product. Budget available and what target price is the intended product.

Worked example

The children's toy in Figure 1 is constructed out of beech.

Figure 1

Give **two** reasons why beech is suitable for children's toys. **(2 marks)**

Function – Beech is safe because it does not splinter easily and will not harm children.

Aesthetics – Beech has a close grain, which is pleasing to the eye and means it can be painted easily to improve its appearance.

Alternative answers:
Scale of production – Beech is readily available to suit high volume production.
Ethical factors – Beech can be sourced from managed forests so that it is sustainable.
Mechanical properties – Beech is very tough and will resist rough handling.
Environmental – Beech is a sustainable timber and can be regrown over time.

Improving properties

Timbers can be enhanced by reinforcing, bending, or adding treatments or finishes. See pages 54–55 for more on these processes.

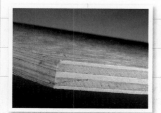

Now try this

Give **two** reasons why medium density fibreboard (MDF) is a suitable material for constructing the flat pack desk shown in Figure 2. **(2 marks)**

Figure 2

It is important to choose reasons that relate to the product's use and target market.

Sources and origins

Metals can be classified as ferrous, or non-ferrous and are elementary substances, which are crystalline when solid. Metals are naturally occurring and found in ores, which are normally contained in solid rock.

Alloys are a mixture of two or more metals or elements, which have improved properties and characteristics.

Metals are **extracted** and **refined** from their ores through two processes, depending on how reactive they are: **carbon reduction** and **electrolysis**.

Sources of common metals

Metal	Ore	Source
Iron ore	Magnetite, haematite	USA, Russia, Sweden
Steel	Manufactured / processed	China
Aluminium	Bauxite	USA, France, Australia
Copper	Chalcopyrite	USA, Chile, Russia
Tin	Extracted from various ores (e.g. cassiterite, stannite, cylindrite)	Indonesia, China

Extraction by carbon reduction

Less reactive metals, such as zinc, iron and tin, are extracted using a blast furnace.
For example:

- Iron ore is fed into the furnace and mixed with coke, limestone and air (oxygen).
- They are heated to 2000°C to chemically reduce and physically convert iron oxides into liquid iron, which falls to the bottom of the furnace and is removed.
- The limestone helps to remove acidic impurities.
- This is called a **reduction reaction**.

Iron ore, coke and limestone

→ Waste gases

← Hot air

→ Molten slag

Molten iron ←

Extraction by electrolysis

More reactive metals, such as aluminium, have to be refined before extraction.

Stage 1 – Refining aluminium from the bauxite

- The bauxite is purified using a hot solution of caustic soda, which dissolves the aluminium oxide (white solid).
- This is washed and dried into a white powder.

Stage 2 – Extracting the aluminium from the aluminium oxide

- The powder is made liquid by dissolving it in molten **cryolite**.
- The liquid is put into an electrolysis tank that contains a negative electrode (cathode) and a positive electrode (anode). These are made from graphite, which is a form of carbon.
- The aluminium is attracted to the negative electrode and sinks to the bottom of the tank, where it can be extracted.

Worked example

Describe the process of electrolysis to extract aluminium from bauxite. **(5 marks)**

To refine aluminium from bauxite, the bauxite is first purified with caustic soda to create a white powder containing the aluminium oxide. The powder is then dissolved in molten cryolite and poured into an electrolysis tank. Cathodes and anodes made from carbon are used to attract the aluminium, which is then collected from the bottom of the tank.

Cryolite is a mineral that consists of aluminium and a fluoride of sodium.

Now try this

Describe the process of carbon reduction to extract iron from iron ore. **(5 marks)**

Stock forms, types and sizes

Stock forms

Commercially available metal comes in standard cross-sectional forms, which saves time in machining and is easier to incorporate into designs.

Metal bar / rod has a solid cross section and is available in a variety of shapes, such as square, round, half round, hexagonal, flat and angle.

Metal tube / pipe has a hollow section and is available in a variety of shapes, such as rectangular, hexagonal, round and square.

Metal sheet comes in a range of flat sheets with a range of thickness from 0.6–3 mm.

Available sizes are measured by **length, width** and:

- **gauge:** the thicknesses of metal; thinner metals have a higher gauge number
- **cross-sectional area:** found by cutting a section through the metal and measuring the solid shape
- **diameter:** the measurement across a round bar
- **wall thickness of tubes:** found by taking the internal diameter from the external diameter.

Typical wire gauge	
Gauge	**Thickness**
10	<3.25 mm
15	<1.83 mm
20	<0.91 mm
25	<0.51 mm

Metal fixings

 Bolts normally have hexagonal head and are used with nuts.

 **Nuts**
Hexagonal head and used with bolts.
Nyloc nuts resist coming loose due to a polymer insert (nylon).
Wingnuts can be tightened by hand, making them easy to assemble.

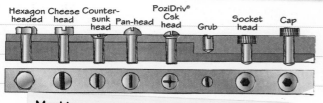

Hexagon Cheese Counter- PoziDriv® Socket
headed head sunk Pan-head Csk Grub head Cap
head head

Machine screws have a parallel thread and a variety of drive systems and head shapes.

 **Washers** spread the load and protect the surface. Spring washers resist coming loose.

 Pop rivets are used for joining metal sheet. A rivet gun is required, but only needs access to one side.

 Snap rivets are used for joining metal sheet. Snap tools are needed and access to both sides.

Worked example

Describe **two** disadvantages of using a nyloc nut.
(2 marks)

Nyloc nuts need tools to attach to a bolt as they are tight, so they may take longer to tighten. They must only be used once as the polymer insert is not as effective if used a second time.

Threads are measured in two ways.
Pitch is the distance a nut would travel if wound one revolution on a screw thread, e.g. 1.5 mm.
Diameter is the outer diameter of the thread, e.g. M12 = 12 mm Ø

 Pitch 1.5mm
'M' 12mm

Now try this

Maths skills

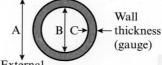 Calculate the cross-sectional area of the tube shaded in Figure 1. Where A = 30 mm, B = 20 mm. Give your answer to three significant figures.
(8 marks)

A — External diameter
B | C — Internal diameter
Wall thickness (gauge)

Figure 1

Wastage 1

There are a range of tools, equipment and processes that are used to shape, fabricate, construct and assemble high quality prototypes. The first of these is wastage.

Sawing metals

Hacksaw Has teeth that point forward and a screw tensions blade.

Junior hacksaw Has fine teeth and a frame tensions blade.

Piercing saw Has very fine blades, tensioned with screws and can cut curves.

Abrafile An abrafile is a thin, round file blade that can be held in a frame saw such as a junior hacksaw and can cut in any direction.

Cutting and shearing metals

Tin snips Uses a shearing action to cut through thin sheet metal in straight lines or curves.

Guillotine
• Has stronger and larger blades that can apply a greater force.
• Allows for thicker sheets of metal to be cut.
• Only cuts in a straight line.

Drilling metal

High speed steel (HSS) twist drills are used to drill metals. The high speed steel is hard, making the twist drills capable of cutting into metals.

A machine countersink drill usually has a 90° angle to create a seating for the screw head so it is flush with the surface.

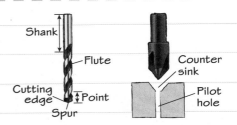

Shank
Flute
Cutting edge
Point
Spur
Counter sink
Pilot hole

Worked example

Name the saw most suited to cutting the 10 mm × 10 mm section mild steel bar shown Figure 1.

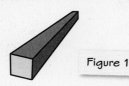

Figure 1

(1 mark)

Hacksaw or junior hacksaw

Now try this

A designer is cutting a number of shapes from 2 mm thick aluminium sheet. Name the saw most suited to cutting out the shapes.

(1 mark)

Wastage 2

Turning metal – metal lathe

A lathe is used to remove metal from a rotating workpiece, using drill bits and a variety of cutting tools made from high speed steel or with tungsten carbide tips.

- The workpiece is held in a chuck and rotated.
- The cutting tool uses a 'wedge' action to remove the material.
- Rotation speeds will depend on the thickness of the bar.
- A lubricant is used to ease the process and wash away swarf.
- Turning can be square to end, parallel or at a taper.
- Centre lathes can be computer numerically controlled (CNC).

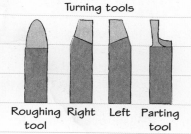

Turning tools

Roughing tool   Right   Left   Parting tool

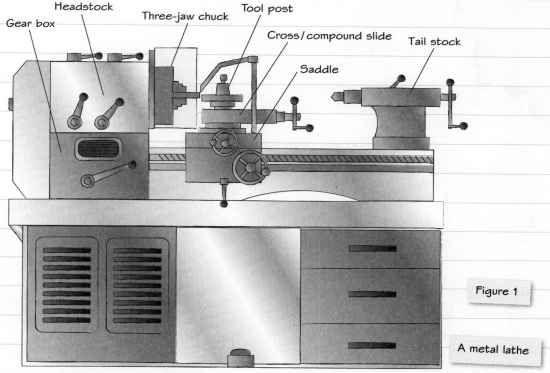

Gear box   Headstock   Three-jaw chuck   Tool post   Cross/compound slide   Tail stock

Saddle

Figure 1

A metal lathe

Wastage is a process that removes unwanted or unusable materials in manufacturing.

Swarf is the fine material removed by machining or cutting.

Worked example

Explain **two** safety features shown on the metal lathe above.   **(4 marks)**

The chuck has a guard around it so that the swarf created from the turning process is not thrown into the operator.

There is a foot switch on the floor which can easily be operated if a person was caught in the machinery.

When describing the process of turning on a metal lathe, it is important that the stages follow a logical order as certain processes cannot be completed until the previous stage is completed.

Now try this

Describe the stages of turning a cylindrical bar (shown in Figure 2) into the shape shown in Figure 3 using a metal turning lathe.   **(8 marks)**

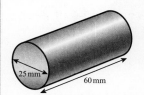

25 mm   60 mm

Figure 2

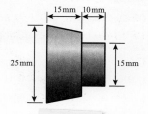

15 mm   10 mm

25 mm   15 mm

Figure 3

Wastage 3

A range of tools, equipment and processes are used to shape, fabricate, construct and assemble high-quality prototypes. In addition to the techniques covered on pages 60–61, the following processes remove smaller amounts of material through cutting or abrading.

Files

A file is a **cutting** tool that is used to remove small amounts of metal. Files are made from high-carbon steel and characterised by their length, shape and cut.

The cut relates to the type of work that is to be carried out and is classified into grades.

1 **Rough cut** is used for coarse work and softer metals.

2 **Second cut** is a general purpose file.

3 **Smooth or dead smooth** are for fine work and finishing.

4 **Dreadnought** has curved teeth for rapid removal of soft metals, such as aluminium and copper.

5 **Needle files** are smaller versions of files that are used for precision work.

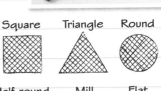

Square   Triangle   Round

Half round   Mill   Flat

Shapes of files

Angle grinder / abrasive wheels

These use an abrasive bonded with resin on a wheel of various sizes. The abrasive material can be made from aluminium oxide or silicon carbide.

Using files

Cross filing (A) removes larger amounts of waste by filing diagonally down the length of the metal.

Draw filing (B) is along the length of the material and is a method of finishing.

Abrasive papers

These have different grades (coarseness) and are used to smooth metal. The grade is measured by particle / grit size. A bigger grit number has smaller particle sizes. A finer grade will give a smoother surface.

Wet and dry paper is a paper backed abrasive and for metals is used wet. It contains silicon carbide abrasive and waterproof glue.

Emery paper is a cloth with an abrasive glued on, such as aluminum oxide or iron oxide abrasives.

Abrasives that can be used wet have the advantages of:
- lubricating the surface of the metal
- washing away the waste material from the surface and not creating dust
- preventing clogging of the abrasive.

Metals must be smoothed when wet. Only card or wood must be dry.

Worked example

Describe **two** advantages of using wet and dry paper on steel when it is wet.   **(2 marks)**

When wet and dry paper is used in its wet state as an abrasive on steel, it will wash away the waste material and it will lubricate the surface to make the process easier.

Now try this

Describe the stages of smoothing and cleaning the end of a mild steel bar that has previously been cut with a hacksaw.   **(6 marks)**

Addition

Addition is joining metals by fusing them together. Three addition processes are:

① Welding

This process joins two pieces of usually the same metal by fusing or melting them together. The joint is as strong as the original metals. Two types of welding are discussed below.

Arc (electrical) welding

- A metal electrode is attached to the work and creates a low voltage but high current of 10–120 amps.
- An arc is produced from the electrode, which melts the metals to be joined and a pool of molten metal is created.

Oxy-fuel (acetylene) welding

- An acetylene torch uses a flame and is lit and adjusted for maximum heat.
- The heat from the flame melts the metal to be joined and a pool of molten metal is created.

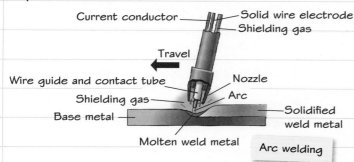
Arc welding

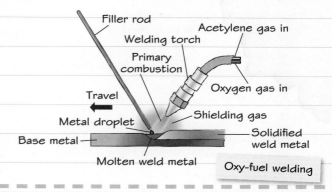
Oxy-fuel welding

② Brazing

This is a permanent method of joining metals such as steel together. It is the strongest method after welding and uses a copper/zinc alloy to form the joint.

Brazing

Stages in the brazing process
1. The area of the steel to be joined is cleaned with abrasive paper to remove oxides.
2. A flux (borax) is spread around the joint to prevent further oxidisation and to allow metal to flow around the joint.
3. The steel is held in place with wire.
4. The joint is heated evenly to reach the correct temperature (875°C).
5. Filler rod (copper / zinc alloy) is melted and allowed to flow into the joint.

③ Hard soldering

Metals with low melting points like copper are joined by hard soldering. The alloys used as soft solders also act as fillers and have a range of melting points, so complex constructions can be assembled in stages.

Worked example

Describe the process of oxy-fuel (acetylene) welding two pieces of steel together. **(5 marks)**

The steel parts must be held securely together. An acetylene torch is adjusted for maximum heat. The heat from the flame melts the steel and creates a pool of molten metal. A filler rod is added to fill any gaps.

Welding joins two pieces of the same metal together by fusing. The filler rod is based on the same material.
Brazing or soldering uses a dissimilar 'filler' metal that melts at a lower temperature to join two metal pieces.

Now try this

Brazing can be used to join two metals together. Describe **five** advantages of brazing in preference to welding when joining two pieces of metal together. **(5 marks)**

Deforming and reforming

Bending and folding

Metals can be changed into a different shape while still in their solid state.

Beaten metal work uses a series of mallets and hammers to beat metal into the required shape. There are several processes:

- **Hollowing** to stretch the copper material into a bowl shape.
- **Planishing** to even out any imperfections. During this process the metals will harden and will need to be annealed to soften the metal.
- **Sinking** will stretch the metal and give a defined edge as the edge of the metal is located against a block and the metal is forced into the desired shape.
- **Raising** can be used to create tall sided shapes. The metal is struck above a stake to force the metal into shape without it thinning but the edge of the metal becomes thickened.

Forging involves heating metal in a hearth, forge or furnace to soften it. The hot metal can then be formed into shape by hammering. Drop forging is a machine process for forging metals using much larger forces with a stationary (die) and a dropping part (hammer).

Methods of bending and folding metals

Sheet metal work is used when the shape is more defined and made from a sheet material. On a small scale the metal can be forced into shape with folding bars or by using a vice. On a larger scale a folding machine could be used for straight lines, or rollers could be used to create curves.

Tube bending uses formers or rollers to bend tubes into curved shapes without the material buckling.

Stamping or press forming is used to cold form a metal sheet into a three-dimensional shape. This is used for car body panels.

Extrusion

Extrusion produces a defined cross-sectional shape by pushing a metal billet (the piece of metal to be formed) through a die. Complex extrusions are used for products such as aluminium window frames. Simple extrusions can be made, such as metal tubes. Extrusion can be done when the metal is hot or cold depending on the relative softness of the metal.

- A die is created with a shaped opening.
- The billet of metal is brought to the die.
- A ram then pushes the billet through the die with great force.
- The extrusion is chopped to the desired length and cooled.

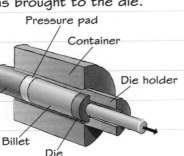

The extrusion process

Labels: Pressure pad, Container, Die holder, Ram, Billet, Die

Worked example

Explain the following two terms in relation to shaping a flat sheet of copper into the bowl shown in Figure 1.

1 Hollowing
2 Planishing   **(4 marks)**

Figure 1

Hollowing stretches the copper material into a bowl shape by using a bossing mallet in the hollow of a sand filled leather bag.

Planishing evens out the imperfections from the hollowing by using a highly polished planishing hammer and a mushroom shaped planishing stake to add smaller and more even indentations.

When describing processes, make sure you note the number of marks that are available. This indicates the number of marking criteria that the examiner is looking for. In this example, 1 mark would be awarded for showing the 'T' section in the die.

Now try this

Figure 2 shows an extruded length of mild steel. Using notes and sketches describe the process of extrusion to produce the section of steel shown in Figure 2.   **(5 marks)**

Figure 2

Modification of properties for specific purposes

Certain properties of metals such as hardness, toughness, ductility and malleability can be modified. You need to know about three modification processes.

① Hardening and tempering

Hardening is a process to make steel harder. However, it increases brittleness.

Carbon steels are heated to their critical temperature (900°C) and cooled quickly (quenched) in water, changing the structure of the carbon.

Tempering reduces hardness and increases toughness in steel.

The process of tempering steel

① Clean the steel with emery cloth so the oxide colours can be seen.

② Heat the steel to a defined temperature, which is indicated by the colour of the steel.

③ When the correct temperature is reached quench the steel in water to give reduced brittleness and increased toughness.

④ Different temperatures are suitable for different purposes.

Main tempering colours for steel

Temperature (°C)	Colour	Examples of tools
316		Spanner
293		Screwdriver
282		Chisel
271		Scissor
260		Plane blade
249		Centre punch
238		Drill
232		Lathe tool

② Annealing

This process softens metal so that it can be shaped or cut more easily.

The process of annealing copper and silver:

① Clean the copper and silver with emery cloth so you can see the colour.

② Heat the copper or silver until it is bright red in colour.

③ Soak it at this temperature to allow the crystal structure to reform.

④ Allow the copper or silver to cool very slowly in air.

Other metals are annealed by heating until they show the following colours.
Mild steel: bright red
Copper: cherry red
Brass: dull red
Aluminium: is covered with a soap solution and is heated until the soap turns black.

③ Case hardening

Case hardening is increasing the carbon content on the outer surface, which will increase the hardness of the surface and improve the steel's wear capabilities. Examples of this use would be bearing, gear or cam surfaces where the wear only occurs on the outer surfaces.

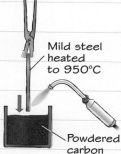
Mild steel heated to 950°C

Powdered carbon

The case hardening process

The process of case hardening steel:

- Heat the steel to 950°C (cherry red).
- Place the steel in a carbon rich environment, like a bath of powdered carbon.
- Repeat until the desired carbon content has been absorbed into the surface.

Worked example

Give **two** reasons why you would need to anneal a sheet of copper if you were forming it into a bowl, using a hammer. **(2 marks)**

You need to anneal the copper sheet because otherwise as you form it into a bowl shape, the copper will harden. This means that it will be more difficult to work and it may cause cracks in the copper. Annealing softens the metal to prevent this.

Now try this

Describe the process of hardening and tempering a length of high carbon steel that is to be used as the blade of a screwdriver shown in Figure 1. **(5 marks)**

Figure 1

Surface treatments and finishes

There is a range of surface treatments and finishes to enhance functional and aesthetic properties of metals. Finishing is used to improve the appearance of metal and protect the surface from decay caused by weather, dirt and liquids. The type of finish depends on the end use for the metal.

Dip coating

A thick polymer such as PVC is applied to protect the metal from wear and also provides a barrier to air and moisture to prevent corrosion.

Dip coating can be used for products such as tool handles and fridge shelves.

The dip coating process

1 The metal part is heated to above the melting temperature of the polymer (230°C). The polymer is a fine powder. Clean air is pumped into the tank which causes the powder to rise and move around (fluidise) to ensure an even coating.

2 The metal part is lowered into the liquidised polymer. The polymer sticks to the metal and solidifies as it cools.

3 The metal part is removed and allowed to cool.

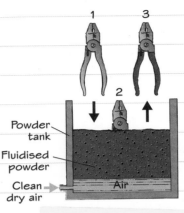

Powder tank
Fluidised powder
Clean dry air
Air

The dip coating process

When mild steel that is coated in zinc is scratched, the zinc layer becomes a sacrificial layer.
This means that the zinc oxidises more quickly than the mild steel and reforms the protective layer over the mild steel.

Galvanising

A very thin layer of zinc is applied onto mild steel by dipping it into molten zinc. This protects the metal from oxidising and therefore prevents rusting and can last for 50–100 years. It can be used for products such as garden fencing, girders, ducting and car bodies.

Powder coating

This finishing method applies a layer of paint to protect a metal and gives a smooth, high gloss finish that is much harder and tougher than could be achieved with painting. It can be used for products such as bicycle frames.

1 The metal needs to be prepared and is normally sandblasted.

2 The metal to be coated is statically charged (negatively) and is sprayed with a powder paint that is positively charged.

3 The powder paint is attracted to the metal to give an even coat.

4 The metal is then baked in an oven to melt the powder to give a smooth, high gloss finish as it cools.

Other finishes for metal

Metal lacquer	A clear finish finished or painted onto metal.
Metal paint and primers	A coloured protective finish sprayed or painted onto metals.
Electroplating and anodising	Uses electrolysis to apply a very thin metal coating to another metal.
Shot / sandblasting	Cleans the metal and gives a uniform satin finish.
Hot blacking	Uses chemicals to add a very thin and dark black iron oxide finish.
Polishing and brushing	Provides a natural polished or a uniform brushed satin finish.

Worked example

Give **two** reasons why a finish is applied to mild steel. **(2 marks)**

The finish protects the mild steel from wear and corrosion.

Now try this

The handles of the scissors shown in Figure 1 have been dip coated.

Describe the process involved in dip coating the scissor handles. **(7 marks)**

Figure 1

Commercial processes

There are a range of commercial processes that are used for shaping and forming metal. You need to know about two of these processes.

① Milling

A milling machine uses multi-toothed rotating cutters to shape metal. The work is firmly fixed to the machine table that moves on three axes. The milling cutter rotates and the workpiece is moved left and right (long travel) and in and out (cross-travel) to ensure metal is removed in the desired area. The depth of cut is increased by raising the machine table by rotating the vertical travel handle.

Milling machines can be computer numerically controlled (CNC), which means that they are very accurate with repeatable processes, will run 24/7, and are safer and quicker than manually operated conventional milling machines.

② Casting

Casting is a shaping process where the metal is heated to a molten state and then poured into a shaped mould. You need to know about two casting processes.

Die casting is generally used for smaller products as the process is repeatable in large quantities and gives a high quality finish.

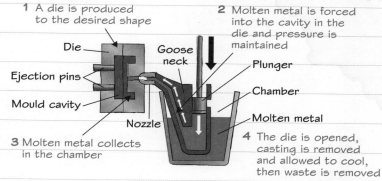

1 A die is produced to the desired shape

2 Molten metal is forced into the cavity in the die and pressure is maintained

Die

Goose neck

Plunger

Ejection pins

Chamber

Mould cavity

Molten metal

Nozzle

3 Molten metal collects in the chamber

4 The die is opened, casting is removed and allowed to cool, then waste is removed

Sand casting is used for larger objects such as vices or G clamps that have a lower quality finish. They are made in smaller quantities as the mould has to be re-made each time.

①
Strickling off
Sand — Drag

A split pattern is created and half is placed in the moulding box (drag), dusted with parting powder and sand is packed around the pattern and smoothed off.

②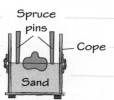
Spruce pins
Cope
Sand

The drag is turned over and the cope, the spruce pins and the second half of the pattern are added and again dusted with parting powder.

③ Strickling off
Sand — Drag

Sand is packed around the pattern and smoothed off.

④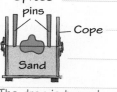
Vents
Mould
Sand

The pattern, runners and riser are removed and the channels and vents are put in to allow the metal to flow.

⑤ Vents
Mould
Sand

The metal is poured into the runner until it appears in the riser, then left to cool before being trimmed.

Worked example

Explain **two** reasons why the use of a computer numerically controlled (CNC) milling machine can improve the amount of products made, in comparison to a manually operated conventional milling machine. **(4 marks)**

There will be fewer errors and wasted parts as the CNC machine will have repeatable accuracy. The machine will not need to have breaks so it can work 24/7.

Now try this

Figure 1 shows a model car that has been die cast in aluminium. Describe **three** reasons why the model car has been made using the die casting process, in preference to sand casting. **(3 marks)**

Figure 1

Using and working with metals

When deciding on materials for a product, a manufacturer will examine all aspects of the material to ensure that it meets all the needs. The properties of metals can be altered through alloying, hardening and tempering.

Physical properties: density and weight, fusibility, electrical and thermal conductivity.

Finishes: How long the product is intended to last and whether it will need further protection against corrosion.

Functionality: What the design should do and for whom and measurable performance factors.

Availability: Availability of the metals and what standard sizes / forms are available and standard components and fixings.

Social factors: Factors such as disabilities, religious groups, age or consumer society / obsolescence.

Aesthetics: How it will appear to the customer, use of colours and texture or form.

Costs: The cost of raw material and conversion into the product. Budget available and what target price is the intended market.

Cultural factors: Factors such as fashion, trends, faiths or beliefs of the user, from a range of backgrounds.

Mechanical properties: Strength (tension) (compression), hardness, toughness, malleability, ductility, elasticity, plasticity.

Ethical factors: Factors affecting sourcing raw materials and manufacture, including fair trade organisations.

Environmental factors: Sustainability, waste management, energy demands, and recycling.

Scale of production: Processing of metal, joining methods and manufacturing capability.

> **Properties and how they influence design**

Enhancing metals

Metals can also be enhanced by bending or folding to create a more rigid structure.

The metal in the legs of this aluminium chair is thin, but the tube structure makes it strong.

Metal sheet is not very rigid. Folding or bending the sheet makes it much more rigid.

Worked example

Stainless steel is used for making utensils that are used in the kitchen for cooking.

Describe **two** reasons why the kitchen utensils shown in Figure 1 are made from stainless steel.

(2 marks)

Figure 1

1 **Function** – The stainless steel is easy to clean, making it hygienic for cooking.

2 **Aesthetics** – Stainless steel has a shiny surface that looks good and will not scratch easily.

Alternative answers:
Scale of production – The steel can be easily pressed and formed to shape.
Finishes – The stainless steel does not require a specific finish as it is self-finishing. It is also corrosion resistant.
Mechanical properties – Stainless steel has high strength allowing it to be used in the kitchen without breaking.
Costs – Costs are relatively high, but stainless steel is long lasting.

Now try this

Describe **two** reasons why cast iron is a suitable material for the construction of the body of the engineer's vice shown in Figure 2.

(2 marks)

Figure 2

Sources and origins

You need to know how polymers are processed from crude oil.

See page 35 for more on classification of polymers.

Crude oil

Crude oil is a naturally occurring material that comes from the Earth's crust. It is made from organic materials that have been heated and compressed over millions of years. It is normally extracted from the ground by drilling and pumping it to the surface. It consists of many different chemicals but mostly **hydrocarbons**.

Fractional distillation of crude oil

Crude oil needs to be separated or refined into **fractions** (its component parts) by processing in an oil refinery to make more useable products.

1 The oil is heated until it boils (around 400°C) and then evaporated.

2 The gases enter the fractioning tower, where they will condense back into liquid as they cool.

3 The smaller hydrocarbons condense at lower temperatures and so rise further up the tower as gases. Larger ones remain lower and condense at higher temperatures.

4 The fractions are then extracted at the different temperatures. Each fraction has different uses.

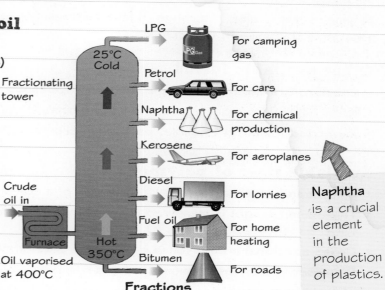

Naphtha is a crucial element in the production of plastics.

Hydrocarbons

Hydrocarbons are chains of molecules of varying lengths that are made up of hydrogen and carbon atoms.

- **Alkenes** are a type of hydrocarbon, which form **monomers**.
- Identical monomers can be joined end-to-end by the process of **polymerisation**.
- Polymerisation forms **polymers**.
- Polymers can be converted into different plastics.

Propene can be polymerised to form poly(propene) or **polypropylene** which is used to make many injection-moulded products, such as garden chairs.
Ethylene or **ethene** can be polymerised to form **poly(ethylene)** or **poly(ethene)**, which is used for carrier bags.

Cracking

The large hydrocarbon molecules produced from distillation are broken down into smaller hydrocarbons. After distillation, they are subjected to heat and pressure, which breaks the bonds in the long molecules making a smaller, more useful version. This process is known as **cracking**. The smaller hydrocarbons called **alkenes** are then used in the production of polymers such as polypropylene and polyethene.

Fractional distillation and cracking can have some potential risks. There needs to be rigorous safety measures in place to reduce the risk of explosion.
Care must also be taken to reduce any environmental impact and the release of any harmful chemicals.

Worked example

1 Explain the term 'polymer'.   **(2 marks)**

A polymer is a string of identical monomers joined end-to-end.

2 Name **three** polymers formed in this way.   **(3 marks)**

Polystyrene, polypropylene, polythene

Now try this

Describe the process of fractional distillation of crude oil to produce alkenes used in the production of polymers.

(5 marks)

Polymers

Stock forms, types and sizes

Available sections of polymers

Polymer rod has a solid cross section and is available in a variety of shapes in 2–100 mm sections.

Polymer tube has a hollow section and is available in a variety of wall thickness and shapes in 5–1000 mm sections.

Polymer sheet comes in a range of flat sheets with a range of thickness from 1–20 mm.

Other available forms

- **Powder / granules:** For example, polymer processes such as dip coating and injection moulding.
- **Rolls / films:** For example, cling film and laminated sheets.
- **Expanded foam:** For example, packaging, cups and insulation.

Available sizes of polymer

- **Length and width** are generally variations of a standard size 2440 mm x 1220 mm large sheet.
- **Thickness (gauge)** is measured in millimetres or microns. 100 gauge = 25 microns (0.025 mm), 1000 gauge = 250 microns (0.25 mm).
- **Cross-sectional area** is found by cutting a section of the polymer and measuring the solid shape.
- **Diameter** is the measurement across a round bar.
- **Wall thickness** of tubes is found by taking the internal diameter from the external diameter.

Standard components

Fixings should be appropriate to how brittle the polymer is. Components include the following:

Nuts and bolts: Bolts normally have a hexagonal head, are used with nuts to create a strong fixing.

Washers: Spread load and protect surfaces. Spring washers resist coming loose.

Nyloc nuts: Has polymer (nylon) insert to stop loosening, need tools to tighten.

Wingnuts: Tightened by hand so easy to assemble, but can work loose.

Hinges: Used to join two polymers that need to move.

Metal hinges are bolted on. Some are just for use with polymer sheets.

   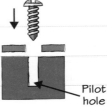

Flexible polymer can be used as an integrated hinge.

Polymore hinges are bolted or glued on.

Self-tapping screws: Form own thread in pilot hole when inserted into polymer.

Pilot hole

Worked example

Describe **one** advantage and **one** disadvantage of using a nyloc nut. **(2 marks)**

An advantage is that the nylon insert prevents the nut from coming loose. A disadvantage is that they need tools to attach to a bolt as they are tight.

Now try this

Calculate the wall thickness of the polymer tube shown in Figure 1. Where A = 25 mm, B = 20 mm.

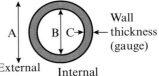

A — External diameter
B | C — Internal diameter
Wall thickness (gauge)

Figure 1 **(2 marks)**

Wastage 1

There are a range of tools, equipment and processes that are used to shape, fabricate, construct and assemble high quality prototypes. The first of these is wastage.

Hand tools for sawing polymers

Junior hacksaw
Has fine teeth and a frame tensions blade.

Hacksaw
Has teeth that point forward and a screw tensions blade.

Laminate cutter

Sheet polymers can be scored, allowing them to be snapped along the line of the cut.

Machine tool for cutting polymers

A **scroll saw** uses a fine blade that has a reciprocating action to cut through the polymers.

Abrafile
An abrafile is a thin round file blade that can be held in a frame saw, such as a coping saw, and can cut in any direction.

Coping saw
Used for cutting curves, has teeth pointing towards the handle.

For larger work, a band saw can be used, but care must be taken as the machine saw generates heat that could melt the plastics as it cuts.

Laser cutting polymers

This technology is relatively new but used widely in schools. The laser beam cuts through the polymers with a focused beam.

- Work does not need to be held.
- Cuts are extremely accurate.
- Used to cut or engrave.
- Increased safety when cutting.

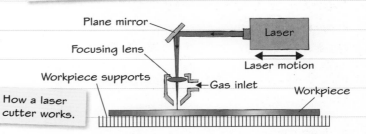

Plane mirror

Laser

Focusing lens

Laser motion

Workpiece supports

Gas inlet

Workpiece

How a laser cutter works.

Tools for drilling polymers

A **hole saw** is used to cut larger holes in timber, sizes 19–75 mm.

A **machine countersink** drill bit has a 90° angle to create a seating for a countersunk screw head so it is flush with the surface.

Twist drills are the most commonly used drills for polymers. They are made from high speed steel and use the 'wedge' cutting action.

Describe **two** hazards and **two** control measures when drilling acrylic sheet on a pillar drill. **(4 marks)**

Acrylic is a brittle material and is likely to snap, catch or wind up the drill. To avoid this you need to use the correct speed for the drill and make sure the work is clamped to the drill table or platform. The drilling operation will also produce swarf, so the user needs to protect their eyes with goggles.

Describe the stages for cutting a shaped piece of acrylic using a laser cutter.

The image to be cut has already been generated on a suitable computer aided drawing program.

(6 marks)

Wastage 2

In addition to the techniques covered on page 71, there are processes that remove smaller amounts of material through cutting or abrading.

Filing

Files are made from high-carbon steel and are used to remove small amounts of polymer. Files are characterised by their length, shape and cut. The cut relates to the type of work that is to be carried out and are classified into grades.

1. **Rough cut** is used for coarse work.
2. **Second cut** is a general purpose file.
3. **Smooth or dead smooth** are for fine work and finishing.
4. **Needle files** are smaller versions of files that are used for precision work.

Examples of files

Square   Triangle   Round

Half round   Mill   Flat

CNC router

Computer numerical controlled (CNC) routers can be used for cutting outline shapes on polymer sheets or to create relief shapes.

- The processes are quick as they are automated.
- They are very precise with a high degree of accuracy.
- They are safe to use as the process can be carried out behind screens or guards.

Using files

A **Cross filing** removes larger amounts of waste by filing away from you diagonally down the length of the metal.

B **Draw filing** is along the length of the material. This is a method of finishing.

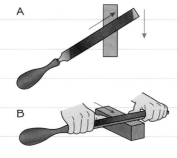

Hot wire cutter
This contains a thin wire made from stainless steel or nickel chrome stretched from the base to a cantilever arm. The wire is electrically heated (at low voltage) to 200°C. The polymer is passed through the wire and it is melted.

When cutting expanded polystyrene, **fume extraction** must be used.

Handheld hot wire cutter
This works in the same way as the hot wire cutter, but it is more flexible allowing the user to cut more intricate shapes. Some handheld hot wire cutters allow the wire to be shaped to give a precise cut.

Worked example

Give **two** advantages of using a CNC router for cutting a shape from a solid polymer, over using a handheld router. **(2 marks)**

The CNC router will run to a program so the operation can be easily repeated. There is less risk of human error as a virtual test could be run first.

Now try this

Describe the stages using files to smooth and clean the edge of a 5 mm acrylic sheet that has previously been cut with a band saw.

(4 marks)

Addition and deforming 1

You need to know about the different ways of working with polymers.

Line bending

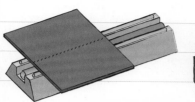 

Strip heaters are used to apply heat to make thermoplastic sheets bendable.

A **jig** is used to make bends at a desired angle.

Press forming (plug and yoke)

① Thermoplastic is heated and placed between a male plug and female yoke.

② The layers are clamped into place.

③ Once cooled, the former is removed.

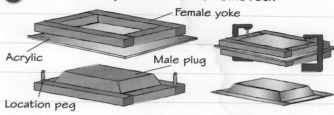

Female yoke

Acrylic

Male plug

Location peg

Vacuum forming

In this process the plastic sheet is softened by heat. Air pressure forces the polymer around the former. High impact polystyrene (HIPS) is a suitable polymer for this process.

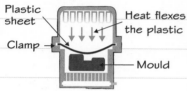 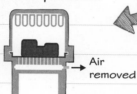

Plastic sheet

Heat flexes the plastic

Clamp

Mould

Air removed

Polymer softened with heat

Air blown in and former is raised

Vacuum pulls polymer around former and cools

Design of formers must include:
- draft angle, radiused (rounded) corners, vent holes and a smooth finish.

Avoid:
- undercuts
- large height that overstretches the polymer.

Laminating polymers

Thin layers of materials are combined to make a stronger composite material.

For example, to prevent glass in car windows from shattering a layer of polyvinyl butyral (PVB) or ethylene-vinyl acetate (EVA) is laminated between two layers of glass. Melamine formaldehyde is a laminated polymer used for worktops.

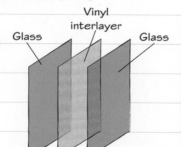

Glass

Vinyl interlayer

Glass

Worked example

Describe the process of line bending a sheet of acrylic 200 mm × 300 mm in half along its length.
(4 marks)

1 Mark the line to be bent on the acrylic using a steel rule and chinagraph pencil.

2 Place the acrylic on a strip heater with the line over the heat.

3 Allow heat to soften the acrylic and turn if needed for even heat.

4 When flexible, use a jig to bend the acrylic and hold it until it cools and is rigid again.

Advantages of laminated polymers / glass
- It can block up to 99% of harmful ultraviolet light.
- The polymer layer creates shatterproof glass.
- It insulates from heat, cold and sound.
- It can also be used to contain a heating element for front windscreens on cars.

Now try this

Describe the process of vacuum forming the cutlery tray.

A mould with the correct draft angles and vent holes has already been made.

(6 marks)

Polymers

Addition and deforming 2

You need to know about the different ways of working with polymers.

3D printing

3D printing converts a CAD model into a physical model that is built up layer by layer. The 3D printers available include the following.

Fused deposit modelling (FDM): The most common 3D printing method in schools. It uses thermoplastics such as ABS and polystyrene. It can be used to print prosthetics and even spare parts on board a space station!

- The CAD program controls a liquefier head, which moves in all planes to extrude (print) the molten polymer into a defined path.

- A support material is used to hold up overhangs and will be dissolved after printing.

- Printing large objects can take a relatively long time, but it is generally quicker than making by hand.

Stereolithography: A process where a liquid resin polymer is selectively cured (hardened) by a laser to build up a 3D shape.

Laser sintering: A process where a powdered polymer is selectively melted by heat from the laser and then solidifies to build up a 3D shape.

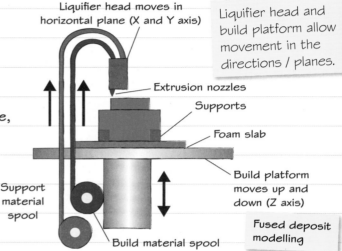

Liquifier head moves in horizontal plane (X and Y axis)

Liquifier head and build platform allow movement in the directions / planes.

Extrusion nozzles

Supports

Foam slab

Build platform moves up and down (Z axis)

Support material spool

Build material spool

Fused deposit modelling

Welding

Welding is a process used to fuse together thermoplastic polymers.

Chemical welding uses a solvent to melt the polymers and blend them together to create a permanent join. Specific solvents are used for different polymers.

- **Dichloromethane methyl methacrylate** is a liquid solvent that is drawn along a joint and fuses the polymers where they touch, but does not fill gaps. It is quick curing.

- **Tensol 12** cement is a thicker solvent and can fill small gaps but takes longer to cure.

Heat welding of polymers such as HDPE, LDPE, ABS, PP or rigid PVC uses a heat gun to soften the parts to be joined and a filler rod of a similar polymer to fuse the parts together.

Resin casting

Resin casting is a process where a liquid thermosetting polymer such as polyester resin is mixed with a catalyst (hardener) and poured into a mould to take on the shape of the mould as it cures.

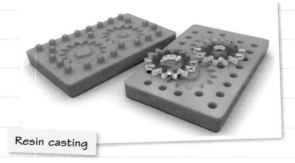

Resin casting

Worked example

Describe **two** hazards, and their **two** control measures, to consider when using Tensol 12 cement to join two pieces of acrylic.

(4 marks)

The fumes given off by the polymer present a hazard, which can be controlled with good ventilation. The liquid resin could also be harmful to the skin, so protective gloves need to be worn.

Now try this

Figure 1 shows a 3D printed chess playing piece.

Explain **two** reasons why a support material may be required when printing this piece.   **(4 marks)**

Figure 1

Modification of properties

Polymers often have other ingredients to enhance or change their properties. These are called additives. You also need to understand about biodegradable polymers.

Additives

① Stabilisers

Help to slow down or prevent degradation in polymers. Three of these are:

- **ultraviolet light stabiliser**, which prevents the polymers discolouring or turning brittle when exposed to sunlight
- **bio-stabilisers**, which are added to reduce the effects of microbiological attack
- **heat stabilisers** which are used to prevent plastics decomposing when exposed to high temperature during manufacture.

② Fibres

Glass fibres reinforce a polymer resin to make rigid structures, for example in car bodies.

③ Filler and foamants

Bulk is added to polymers at lower cost, for example expanded foam products.

④ Plasticisers

Plasticisers improve the flow of polymers during moulding and make polymers less brittle.

⑤ Pigments

Pigments change the colours from the base colour for aesthetics.

⑥ Fragrances

Fragrances added in the moulding process mask smells, such as in bin bags.

Reasons for using additives:

- To make it easier to process the polymer.
- To improve aesthetics (colours).
- To make the polymer cheaper.
- To improve mechanical properties, making products strong, durable and less brittle.
- To extend the life of the polymer.
- To be more environmentally friendly.

Foamants and fibres are used in surfboard construction. The polymer foamant gives buoyancy, while the glass fibres mixed with resin create the hard outer shell.

Biodegradable polymers

Polymers made from crude oil do not biodegrade very easily so new polymers have been developed from vegetable starches and are fully biodegradable by bacteria when exposed to moisture and warmth.

These polymers are non-toxic but cannot be recycled unlike some oil-based polymers. Examples of starch based biopolymers are:

- **Polyactic acid (PLA)**: Easily moulded and used on reels in 3D printers, disposable cutlery and compost bags.

- **Polycaprolactone (PCL)**: Polymorph 62° or Coolmorph 42° can be easily moulded and remoulded at a low temperature by hand and easily coloured.

- **Polyhydroxybutyrate (PHB)**: Also known as Biopol™, it is easily coloured, but has a low chemical resistance. It is useful for short-term use, such as food packaging and shampoo bottles.

Worked example

Give **three** reasons why you need to add stabilisers to PVC that is to be used for guttering and drainpipes on the outside of a building. **(3 marks)**

The PVC would need an ultraviolet light stabiliser adding to prevent it from fading and becoming brittle in the sun. It would also need to have a bio-stabiliser to reduce the effects of microbiological attack from the microorganisms in the liquids put through the pipe. A heat stabiliser will also need to be added to prevent the PVC decomposing when exposed to high temperatures during the manufacturing processes.

Now try this

The surfboard shown above has a core made from expanded polymer. Explain **three** reasons for using expanded foam in the core of the surfboard. **(3 marks)**

Had a look ☐   Nearly there ☐   Nailed it! ☐

Surface treatments and finishes

Finishing improves the appearance of polymers or adds patterns. The type of finish depends on the end use for the polymer. Three suitable finishes are polishing, printing and the addition of vinyl decals.

Polishing

Polymers can be scratched very easily, which affects the aesthetics. Polymers are polished to remove the scratches with smaller scratches until they are reduced, creating a polished surface. There are three stages.

Wet and dry paper is made from silicon carbide grit bonded to paper. Common grades include coarse 60–120 grit, medium 200–320 grit and fine 400–600 grit.

1 Use a coarse abrasive to remove the marks from saw cuts or filing.

2 Use fine wet and dry paper to remove marks left by abrasive paper.

3 Polish with appropriate abrasive polish, for example Perspex No 1 or 2.

Printing

Colour or patterns may be printed onto the polymer. You need to know about two methods of printing on polymers:

1 Hydrographic printing (water transfer) is used to print a design onto a 3D surface.

- The design is printed on a water soluble film. When placed in water an activator dissolves the film and the ink floats on the water.

- The polymer object is dipped into the water and the ink transfers to the object. The activator softens the outer layer of the polymer to help the ink bond to the surface before it dries.

- A lacquer is used to protect the ink.

2 Heat transfer printing is an easy, cost-effective process that produces high quality photo-realistic prints.

- The image is printed on a backing paper.

- The paper is placed on the polymer and heat is applied in a press.

- The print transfers to the polymer.

Vinyl decals

Vinyl decals can be used to add colours or patterns to the surface of different materials. Decals are often used for shop signs where they are known as 'peel-and-stick'.

A decal is a term used for a vinyl sticker that is bonded onto paper and then transferred to the polymer surface (a separate transfer tape is sometimes used).

- The vinyl will be graded for internal and external use to withstand UV degradation.

- The decals are cut with a computer numerically controlled (CNC) vinyl cutter.

Vinyl decals are a quick way to decorate or add information

Worked example

Give **two** reasons why you would wet the 'wet and dry' paper when polishing the surface of acrylic.

(2 marks)

It prevents the paper clogging and washes away the fine waste material to help give a uniform surface.

Now try this

Describe the process of hydrographic printing used to add the pattern onto the polymer cycle helmet.

(5 marks)

Commercial processes

The properties of thermoforming polymers mean that they can be softened with heat and reformed into a different shape. These include injection moulding and extrusion. Polymers suitable for these processes include polystyrene, nylon, polypropylene and polythene.

Injection moulding

This process is used to turn polymer granules into specified shapes. It is used for a large scale of production with repeatable accuracy.

Stages of injection moulding

1 Plastification

Polymer granules are put in the hopper and they fall into the barrel with the Archimedes screw, which moves the granules along past the heaters where they will melt.

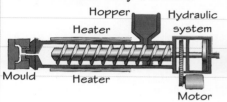

2 Injection / cooling

The Archimedes screw plunges forward to inject the polymer into the die under pressure. Polymer fills the cavity and pressure is maintained to ensure all cavities are filled.

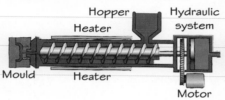

3 Cooling / ejection

When the die has been filled, water channels cool the polymer. The die opens and ejector pins push out the moulding ready for the next cycle.

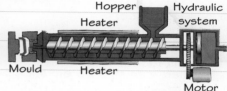

Extrusion

This is very similar to injection moulding but the polymer is formed through a die into a shaped cross section profile.

The shape is then cooled as it leaves the die.

A mandrel needs to be used for hollow sections.

A mandrel is a core that the polymer is formed around to make a tube.

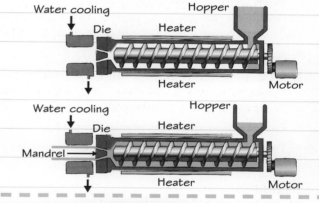

Pipes are commonly formed by extrusion, but many different cross sections can be achieved.

Worked example

Describe how to produce a hollow section of extruded tube. **(3 marks)**

To create hollow tube the melted polymer will be pushed through a die that has a mandrel incorporated into it. The mandrel is a solid core that is used to force the polymer around it so that it forms a hollow pipe.

With questions that ask for notes and/or sketches, it is advised to provide both as the marks for the answer can be awarded from the notes or the sketches and it ensures you have fully answered the question.

Now try this

With notes and/or sketches, describe the process of injection moulding. **(6 marks)**

Using and working with polymers

You need to know how and why materials influence the design of a product.

See pages 38 and 98 for more on the physical and mechanical properties of materials.

Selecting materials

Manufacturers need to examine the following when deciding on appropriate materials for a product:

- **Functionality:** What the design should do and for whom, including measurable performance factors.
- **Availability:** Availability of the polymer and what standard sizes / forms and standard components to join are available.
- **Scale of production:** Processing of polymers, joining methods and manufacturing capability.
- **Costs:** Cost of raw material and conversion into the product. Budget available and target price.

- **Ethical factors:** Sourcing raw materials and manufacture, fair trade organisations.
- **Environmental factors:** Sustainability, waste management, energy demands and recycling.
- **Mechanical properties:** Strength (tension) (compression), hardness, toughness, malleability, ductility, elasticity, plasticity.
- **Aesthetics:** How it will appear to the customer, use of colours, texture or form.
- **Physical properties:** Absorbency, density / weight, fusibility, electrical and thermal conductivity, fluidity, additives.

Enhancing materials

Polymers can also be **enhanced** by **reinforcing** or **stiffening** to improve their properties.

Laminating (reinforcing)

Glass fibres reinforce a polymer resin to make rigid structures, such as car bodies and canoes.

- A shaped mould is produced.
- A release agent is used and the polymer is mixed with a catalyst (hardener) and painted or sprayed onto the mould.
- The strands of glass are laid into the resin.
- The process is repeated and the moulding is left to cure.

Stiffening

Plastics mouldings can be made more rigid by using ribs and gussets of polymer to increase strength.

Gusset

Rib

Worked example

The outdoor chair in Figure 1 is made from high density polyethylene (HDPE). Give **two** reasons why HDPE is suitable for outdoor seating. **(2 marks)**

Figure 1

1 **Mechanical properties** – The strength of HDPE makes it suitable for a chair as it can take the weight of the user.

2 **Physical properties** – The HDPE softens in heat, which means that it can be easily injection moulded.

In your answer relate the properties to the needs of the product. Alternative answers include:

Environment – HDPE can be easily recycled.
Costs – The cost of HDPE is relatively low to suit use and weathering in the garden.
Availability – Availability is good as the polymer is derived from oil.
Aesthetics – HDPE is available in a range of colours to suit the garden environment.

Now try this

There will be many reasons why a material is used for a product. It is important to ensure that the reasons you give relate to the use of the product; in this case the prime reason will be safety.

State **two** reasons why urea formaldehyde (UF) is a suitable material for the construction of the electrical socket in Figure 2.
(2 marks)

Figure 2

Sources and origins

Fibres used in textiles can be **natural** or **synthetic** and come from a variety of primary sources.

To remind yourself about what textiles are, go to pages 36 and 37.

Animal-based fibres

Wool is valued for its warmth and availability.

Wool/hair	**Wool** is produced from the coats of sheep and other animals. It is naturally coated with a wax substance called lanolin and is used for warm clothing. Other wools include: **cashmere** – soft wool from cashmere goats **angora** – soft wool from rabbits **camel hair** – may be blended with other wool to produce softer yarn.
Silk	Silk is the fibre taken from the cocoon of the silkworm. It is produced by the silk moth caterpillar.

Vegetable sources

Cotton	Cotton is the white and fluffy fibre found on the seed pods of the cotton plant. It is versatile, strong and has a good colour retention.
Linen	Linen is found in the long stems of the flax plant, found in cool parts of the world. It is durable, strong, absorbs moisture and does not stretch. It is expensive.

Chemical sources

Chemical sources are oil-based and have been designed to have specific properties. In addition to **polyester, polyamide (nylon)** and **elastane (Lycra)** there are other synthetic fibres:

Polypropylene	Used in carpets
Acrylic	Used as a yarn in clothing
PVC	Stretchy waterproof fabric
Kevlar	Used in motorbike jackets

Processing

All the fibres above need to be **processed** before they can be used.

- **Wool / hair** is removed from the animal, then sorted and cleaned before it is **carded** and then spun.
- **Silk** fibres are collected from the cocoons, steamed and then unwound before spinning.
- **Cotton** is died and cleaned. Seeds and lint are separated from raw cotton in a process called '**ginning**'. The cotton is then carded before spinning.
- **Linen** fibres are obtained by thrashing the flax stalks after drying.
- **Synthetic fibres** are produced from a polymer solution. The fibres are then extruded, cooled and solidified.

Spinning

Spinning converts fibres into a thread or yarn, making them strong enough to be used in fabrics.

Spinning traditionally uses a spinning wheel to twist the fibres together. This gives the thread a uniform thickness.

Modern industrial methods use similar techniques. Carding separates the fibres into one direction and produces strands called 'silvers', which are then fed through rollers and twisted together.

Wool fibres are twisted together to form a yarn.

Carding is a mechanical process to disentangle and straighten fibres.

Worked example

Explain how chemical-based yarns are made from oil-based polymers.   **(2 marks)**

The oil is refined to the particular polymer that is required, such as polyester. The strands of polyester or nylon are then extruded into fine strands before they are spun together to form a yarn.

Now try this

1   Explain the process of obtaining cotton fibres from the cotton plant prior to the spinning process.   **(2 marks)**

2   Explain the process of obtaining silk fibres from the silkworm cocoon prior to the spinning process.   **(2 marks)**

Stock forms, types and sizes

There is a range of commercially available types and sizes of materials and components that can be used with textiles.

Available forms

Commercially available textiles are generally available in standard forms, which make them more cost-effective as waste can be minimised when planning designs.

Rolls of fabric are usually available in standard widths, such as 0.9 and 1.5 metres (many other widths will be available depending on the manufacturer). Designers need to know the width of fabric they are working with when planning their designs. The lengths are dependent on the production runs but will also conform to standard sizes.

Cotton

Width 0.9 – 1.5m

| 25 cm x width (long quarter) | 50 cm x half width (fat quarter) | 50 cm x width (half metre) | 100 cm x width (full metre) |

50 cm x half width (fat quarter)

Standard sections of fabric cut from a roll

Threads are long fibres used to sew garments or products such as cotton, nylon, silk, polyester, rayon, or wool.

Yarns are interlinked by spinning threads into a twisting pattern, making it stronger than a thread in the same material. Yarns are available in hanks, skeins, balls and reels and used to weave or knit into a textile fabric.

Hank   Skein   Ball   Reel

Yarns are available in 1 or 2 ply – this is the number of threads twisted together.

Available sizes

Fabrics are measured by width, linear metre and:

- **Weight** – The weight of the yarn refers to the thickness of the yarn which ranges from super fine to bulky. Specific weights of yarn will produce a specific number of stitches, weave or knit. This will also indicate how strong, thick or warm a fabric is.
- **Pattern repeat** – This is the number of centimetres before the pattern starts again. Large distances between repeats make it difficult to match patterns.
- **Thread count** – This is the number of threads in a given area or how tightly woven the fabric is.

Standard components

Zips have interlocking parts on a flexible strip and open and close with a sliding fastener. They come in many sizes and colours and work in different situations, such as fixed at one end (trousers), concealed (cushions), open-ended (jackets) and two-way (bags).

Buttons are small fasteners sewn onto material that fit through a button hole.

Toggles are similar to buttons but are pushed through a loop on the side to be connected.

Press studs or poppers are interlocking discs. One has a projection that snaps into a hole in the other disc. They are made from metal or plastic.

VELCRO® is made from two strips of materials that have tiny hooks and loops that can be easily fastened and unfastened.

Other standard components:

- Hook and eye
- Buckle
- Eyelet
- Drawstring
- Ribbons / braids
- Elastic
- Beads / sequins

Worked example

Give **two** advantages of using a zip for a trouser fastening, compared to buttons. **(2 marks)**

Zips are easier to operate with one hand, and a zip has one long fixing method, whereas buttons may need to have multiple fastenings

Now try this

VELCRO® is a popular type of fastener on children's clothing. Give **three** reasons why VELCRO® is a suitable fastening on a school coat for a child. **(3 marks)**

Wastage

A range of tools, equipment and processes is used to cut high quality prototypes.

Hand tools for cutting and shearing textiles

Paper scissors
Used for cutting paper patterns.

Craft knives
Used for cutting paper patterns and stencils.

Dressmaking scissors
Has a long blade for long straight cuts.

Seam ripper
Quickly unpicks seams with minimal damage to fabric.

Embroidery
Short sharp blades for fine work and cutting threads.

Cutting wheels
Cuts accurate lines and curves in fabrics of multiple layers. Different shaped blades can cut other lines such as zig-zags.

Pinking shears
Cut a zig-zag edge in fabric to prevent fraying and as decoration.

In commercial settings, electrical versions will speed up the cutting process.

Machine tools for cutting and shearing textiles

Band knife
A band knife has a continuous knife blade that cuts through the fabric. It will cut multiple layers of fabric and is suited to soft fabrics such as felt. It is used commercially and can be computer controlled.

Laser cutting
This is used to cut intricate shapes and patterns in paper, card and some fabrics, such as cotton, silk, polyester and felt.

Die cutting
Dies are made from sharpened steel strips that are formed to the exact shape of the pattern. They are then pressed into the textile to cut the same shape. This method will cut multiple layers of fabric, but there is a limit on the thickness of the blade. Often used in the fashion industry.

1 Place the fabric on the mat and the cutter on top.

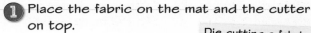

Die cutting a fabric.

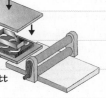

Pressure
Cutting matt
Steel cutter
Layers of fabric
Cutting matt

2 Cutters forced through fabric (rollers or press).

3 Waste fabric is removed.

Worked example

Give **three** precautions you need to take when using a laser to cut fabric or patterns to shape.
(3 marks)

Suitable extraction is needed to remove any fumes. Materials must be appropriate to laser cutting and not burn. The material needs to be kept flat, to allow accurate shape cutting.

Now try this

1 Give the name of the tool that is most suited to unpicking stiches made in a piece of cloth. **(1 mark)**

2 Explain how the use of pinking shears helps reduce the amount of fraying in a cut fabric. **(2 marks)**

Addition 1

A range of tools, equipment and processes are used to join textiles.

Sewing

Sewing joins fabrics together with stitches, by hand or by machine. The chosen needle should suit the weight of the thread.

Sewing by hand

1 Select the appropriate size needle.
2 Unravel the length of thread.
3 Weave the thread though the loop at the end of the needle.
4 Tie a knot in the end of the thread.
5 Sew using the chosen stitch.
6 Tie final knot and cut away excess.

Sewing by machine

Sewing machines have the following advantages:

- They are faster.
- They give a much more professional look because all stitches will be uniform.
- They make more stitches per length, so garments tend to be stronger.

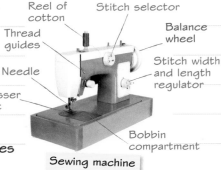

Reel of cotton — Stitch selector — Balance wheel — Stitch width and length regulator — Thread guides — Needle — Presser foot — Bobbin compartment

Sewing machine

Types of stitch

Stitch		Description
Running stitch (basting for tacking)	Running stitch 4 3 2 1	Simple stitch for general work. Stitches vary in length depending on use.
Back stitch	Back stitch 3 1 2	Loops back on itself and prevents any movement in the fabric.
Blanket stitch	Blanket stitch	Reinforces edges of thick materials, to prevent them from fraying, or for decorative purposes.
Zig-zag stitch	Zig-zag stitch	Reinforces edges, stretchable fabrics or used for joining fabrics edge to edge.
Chain stitch	Chain stitch	A decorative stitch made from a series of loops in a chain-like pattern.
Overlock stitch	3 thread overlock 4 thread overlock	Multiple threads can be used for finishing edges of a fabric and stopping them from fraying.

Embroidery

Embroidery is the application of stitches sewn by hand or machine directly onto fabric for decoration. For example, company logos on clothing.

CNC machines can be programmed and have repeatable accuracy. They can produce an embroidered image in a fraction of the time that it would take to hand embroider.

Worked example

 1 Give **one** reason for using a blanket stitch.
(1 mark)

A blanket stitch strengthens an edge of material and prevents it from fraying.

 2 Give the name of the process that uses a needle and thread to decorate a fabric.
(1 mark)

Embroidery

To **tack** or **baste** is to make a quick, temporary stitch to hold fabric together but the tack can be removed later.

Point — Needle — Eye

Needles vary in size from 1 to 12. A higher number indicates a finer needle. Needles should be small enough to fit through fabric without stretching it. The eye needs to be large enough to fit the thread.

Now try this

A running or basting stitch is the simplest form of stitch.

Give **two** situations working with fabrics when you would use a basting stitch.   (2 marks)

Addition 2

There is a range of tools, equipment and processes that add features and textures to fabrics.

Laminated or layered textiles

Laminating or layering textiles improves the properties of the final garment and creates a composite material.

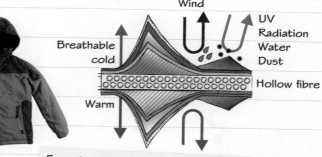

- 👍 This uses the specific properties of a number of different fabric layers (ply) to create the desired effect.
- 👍 Different layers could be used for comfort, water resistance, heat resistance and breathability.
- 👍 The layers can be sewn or bonded together with an adhesive or heat.

Examples of laminated or layered textiles include clothing for sports, firefighters and PVC-backed fibres for jackets and sports bags.

Piping

Piping is used along the edges or seams of a fabric to strengthen, protect, neaten or highlight them.

It is used on cushions, furniture and clothing, often in a contrasting colour. Cord can be used to give a strong definition.

Cord sewn into cushions for protection.

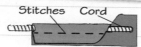

Stitches   Cord

Appliqué

Appliqué is when fabric shapes are sewn onto another fabric. It creates colour, pattern and adds texture to fabrics.

Often used with felts as they do not fray. Otherwise, the whole edge of the applied fabric will need edging with stitching, such as zig-zag stitching.

Felted fabrics sewn onto material for decoration.

Batik

This is a traditional fabric colouring technique from Java (Indonesia) that masks areas with wax in fine lines or a block before adding dye.

1   Draw the pattern on the fabric.
2   Apply the first layer of wax.
3   Apply the first layer of dye.
4   Repeat until all colours have been built up.
5   Remove wax by ironing or boiling.

Batik in progress

Worked example

Explain **two** ways that laminating fabrics to make race suits can give protection to a Formula 1 racing driver.   **(4 marks)**

The race suits worn by Formula 1 drivers could be made from different layers of material with different properties. The layer closest to the skin would give the driver comfort and would also be breathable so the driver is protected from overheating. Another layer would be fire or heat resistant to protect the driver if there was a fire.

Now try this

1   Explain **two** reasons why PVC is a suitable material to laminate with a fabric for the sports bag shown in Figure 1.   **(4 marks)**

Figure 1

2   Explain **two** reasons why piping is often used around the edges of the sports bag shown in Figure 1.   **(4 marks)**

Deforming and reforming

There are a range of tools, equipment and processes that are used to shape textiles. You need to know about a number of ways to shape fabrics.

Draping

Draping is a way of manipulating fabric into a desired shape.

The first method of draping is used to shape fabric into three dimensions by forming it over a mannequin (tailor's dummy). It makes it easy for the tailor or dressmaker to see how the garment will look as it develops.

Shaping using a mannequin

The second method of draping is used to shape felt. The felt is soaked in hot water and then a former is used to stretch the felt into shape. When the felt is dried, it remains in the formed shape. This method is often used for making hats.

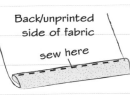
Shaping felt

Seams

A seam is a strong and secure method of joining two fabrics together by stitching. As the main purpose is functional they should be as flat as possible so that they are not seen.

A flat seam is the most basic type and leaves a neat, almost invisible line on the right side of the fabric.

Fronts of fabrics facing each other — Seam allowance — Machine stitching

Hems

A hem is used to give a neat edge to a fabric by folding over and sewing along it. This also prevents the fabric from unravelling or fraying.

Back/unprinted side of fabric — sew here

Quilting

This is achieved by using layers of fabric. Padding (wadding) is added in between the two outer layers to raise the surface of the material.

Pleats and tucks

These are folds in fabric that allow it to fan out in places and still be fitted in others. It is often used to give skirts their shape.

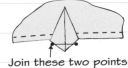
Pleat

Gathering

This is used to pull a few rows of stitching in the material together to reduce the fullness. Used for the top of curtains or for waist bands.

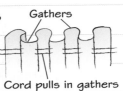
Gathers — Cord pulls in gathers

Darts

These are used to fit fabric closer to the body as they remove some of the excess material in triangular folds at the waist or on the bust of shirts.

Join these two points

Worked example

Describe **two** reasons why the material at the bottom of the trouser legs in Figure 1 will be hemmed. **(2 marks)**

The material will be hemmed so that there is a neat and straight finish across the material. The hem will also provide strength and stop the material from fraying.

Figure 1

Now try this

 1 Give the name of the sewing technique that allows the skirt shown in Figure 2 to fan out at the bottom. **(1 mark)**

 2 Give the name of the sewing technique that prevents the bottom of the skirt shown in Figure 2 from unravelling or fraying. **(1 mark)**

 3 Give the name of the sewing technique that gives fullness to a garment evenly. **(1 mark)**

Figure 2

Surface treatments and finishes

Surface treatments and finishes enhance the functional and aesthetic properties of textiles. Finishing techniques can help to protect against heat, dirt, liquids and wear.

Dyeing

Dyeing is a manual or industrial process that uses coloured pigments to change the colour of the yarn, fibre or completed fabric. There are two major types of dyes:

- **Natural** dye is made from natural sources such as plants, roots, berries and flowers. It is environmentally friendly.
- **Chemical** dyes are made from petroleum by-products and minerals, which may be harmful to people and the environment. They give bright, exact colours, and are cheaper and easier to process.

Types of dyeing

Apart from fully immersing the fabric or yarn into a dye, there are other types of dyeing.

- Some dyes need to be 'fixed' with a **mordant** such as salt, which prevents it coming out through washing or wearing.
- Natural fibres absorb colour more easily than synthetic fibres. The final colour is dependent on the original colour of the fibre, which may need to be bleached to create a stronger colour.

Dip – Only parts of the fabric are dipped into the dye and change colour.	**Direct** – Colour is transferred to the fabric by a printing block made of materials such as wood and foam.
Resist – Part of the fabric is treated to resist the dye to create a pattern.	**Mordant** – A fixing agent that is applied to fabric before dyeing. The mordant combines with the dye and fabric to fix the colour.
Batik – Similar to resist, but this uses wax to mask areas that should not be dyed. 	**Tie** – The fabric is tied or folded so the dye does not have uniform coverage and interesting patterns can be created.

Fabric protection

Fabric protection can prolong a fabric's life and keep it looking good. It can provide protection against fire, dirt, liquids and from creasing. The protection can be applied to the yarn or applied to the finished fabric, in the form of a chemical.

There are four types of fabric protection you need to know:

- **Flame retardant** – A halogenated or phosphorus chemical is applied to reduce the risk of igniting or burning.

- **Stain protection** – A chemical is applied that prevents the absorption of dirt into the fibres.

- **Crease resistance** – A resinous chemical is applied that prevents creases when material is worn or used.

- **Water proofing** – Materials such as PVC or polyurethane are applied to a fabric to repel water.

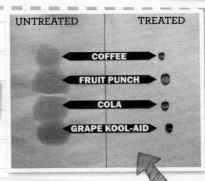

Stain protection on fabric

The same fabric will prevent liquids soaking in when treated with a stain or water proofing. This will make the product easier to clean, and should extend its useful life.

Now try this

Explain **two** suitable forms of fabric protection that could be used on the fabric used to make a soft toy for a baby.   **(4 marks)**

Commercial processes

Weaving

Weaving is done by interlacing two yarns that run in different directions. **Weft** yarns run from left to right and **warp** yarns run up and down.

Plain weave
The weft yarns pass over and under warp yarns. Used for cotton-based fabrics such as shirts.

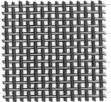

👍 Cheap to produce, strong and hard wearing. Good for printing on.

Satin weave
The weft yarns pass over four or more warp yarns and under one. Used for blouses.

👍 Makes shiny fabrics that are delicate but easy to snag.

Twill weave
The weft yarns pass over two warp yarns and under one. Used for trousers and curtains.

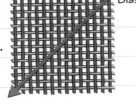
Bias

👍 Creates a diagonal pattern (bias), which improves elasticity and movement. Strong weave for softer yarns such as denim.

Dyeing
Dyes can be added at different stages in the process. The dye can be applied to the fibres before they are made into yarn (stock dyeing), to the yarn (yarn dyeing), to a length of cloth (piece dyeing), or to a whole garment.

Printing

Printing uses ink, dyes or paint to apply patterns or markings to the surface of a fabric. Fabrics that have a tight weave will give a better finish.

Block printing		Dye is applied to a block with a pattern engraved on and then pressed onto the fabric. Blocks can be made from wood, rubber, metal or even a sponge.
Screen printing		A fine mesh is held in a frame with a stencil blocking off areas of the screen, which forms a pattern when the ink is applied, one colour at a time.
Engraved or screen roller printing		A roller or series of rollers are engraved with the pattern, or screens are wrapped around the rollers. The ink is applied as the rollers rotate. The print run can be continuous, making it suitable for large print runs.
Transfer printing or sublimation		The image is digitally printed onto a backing paper. Heat and pressure is used to turn the inks into gas to transfer the image onto the fabric.
Stencilling		The pattern required is cut from acetate or card and a brush, spray or sponge can be used to apply the dye. Stencils can be computer designed and used many times.

Worked example

Describe the meaning of the term weft and warp when working with yarns or fabrics. **(2 marks)**

A weft is a yarn that runs across the width of a fabric from left to right. A warp is a yarn that runs the length of a fabric going up and down.

Now try this

Evaluate the use of chemical dyes over natural dyes when colouring fabrics. **(4 marks)**

Using and working with textiles

Materials are selected for certain physical and mechanical properties, as defined on pages 38 and 98. You need to understand how they have influenced the design of a product.

Selecting materials

When deciding on appropriate materials, a manufacturer will examine all aspects of the material including methods to improve properties:

- **Functionality:** What the design should do including factors such as strength.
- **Availability:** Availability of textiles and the standard sizes, forms and components.
- **Social factors:** Disabilities, religious groups, age or consumer society / obsolescence.
- **Scale of production:** Processing of textiles, joining methods, dyeing and manufacturing capability.
- **Cultural factors:** Fashion, trends, faiths or beliefs of the user, from a range of backgrounds and ethnicities.

- **Costs:** Raw material and conversion into product costs. Budget available and target price.
- **Ethical factors:** Sourcing raw materials and manufacture, fair trade organisations, child labour or exploitation of adult labour.
- **Environmental factors:** Sustainability, waste management, energy demands and recycling.
- **Mechanical properties:** Strength (tension), elasticity and flexibility.
- **Aesthetics:** Use of colours, texture, lustre or sheen.
- **Physical properties:** Absorbency, density / weight, fusibility, thermal conductivity and ability to colour or be printed on.
- **Finishes:** How long it needs to last and if it will need a protective finish.

Worked example

The cycling clothing in Figure 1 contains elastane™. Give **two** reasons why elastane is suitable for cycling clothing. **(2 marks)**

Figure 1

Function – Elastane™ is lightweight and covers the cyclist for warmth and protection and provides greater aerodynamics.

Finishes – Elastane™ is polymer-based and will be machine washable, making it easily washed by the user.

Make sure you relate the properties of the material to the needs of the user. Other answers could include:

Physical properties – Elastane™ is durable, to withstand the rigours of the cycling.

Mechanical properties – It is an elastic material and stretches to fit the user.

Functionality – It is lightweight so it does not add to the work of the cyclist and it is quick drying so it does not interfere with the drying qualities of the clothing.

There will be many reasons why a material is used for a product. It is important to ensure that the reasons relate to the use the product; in this case, aesthetics, comfort and safety are very important.

Reinforcing

Textiles can be enhanced by reinforcing and stiffening to improve their properties.

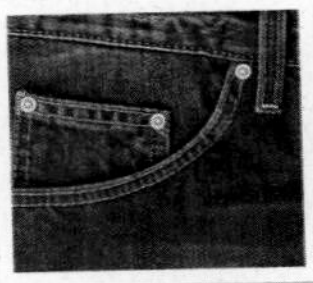

- **Rivets** strengthen areas under stress, such as the corner of jean pockets.

- **Webbing** is a very strong woven fabric made from synthetic fibres such as nylon and polypropylene. They have high breaking strengths and are used when tensile strength is important, such as seatbelts, straps or upholstery.

- **Stiffening (fabric interfacing)** is often hidden when constructing fabrics, for example in shirt collars or baseball cap peaks. Interfacing can be sewn in or ironed on.

Now try this

Describe **two** reasons why wool is a suitable material for the construction of the stair carpet shown in Figure 2. **(2 marks)**

Figure 2

Stock forms – circuit boards

Electronic systems are made up of many different components that are connected together on **printed circuit boards** (PCBs).

Electronic system

An electronic system is the physical connection of components. It uses a signal in the form of electrical energy from an input, which is processed to operate an output device.

Printed circuit boards (PCBs)

The connections on a PCB are usually made from copper foil bonded onto a substrate made from glass reinforced plastic (GRP) or paper reinforced phenolic resin, which is less expensive and often used in household appliances.

The fine lines in this PCB are copper tracks connecting the components (resistors). The tracks appear green as the PCB has been coated with a protective lacquer.

Copper clad board

Copper clad board has a thin layer of copper on either side of a GRP sheet. The tracks are created by cutting or etching away the excess copper using one of these methods:

1 CNC router / miller
The copper to be removed is programmed into the CNC machine and small cutters will cut around the tracks and drill the holes.

2 Photo-resist PCB
The track layout is drawn onto the copper with an ultraviolet (UV) mask. The rest of the copper is exposed to UV light, which will soften it. It is then removed with a chemical such as ferric chloride.

3 Etch resist masking
The track layout is drawn onto the copper with an etch resist mask (tape or ink). The board is then immersed in a chemical such as ferric chloride to remove the copper that has not been masked.

Voltage and current

Electrical components have a voltage or current rating at which they can work.

Voltage (V) is the energy required to move a small electric charge along a path. The voltage in domestic homes is 240V.

Current is the amount of electrical charge that flows through a circuit. It is measured in amperes (amps or A).

An electric kettle plug will be rated as 13A, but tracks and components on a circuit board may operate in milliamps (mA). 1A = 1000 mA.

Batteries come in a range of voltages.
- AA or AAA battery for remote controls 1.5V
- Mobile phone lithium batteries 3.7–4.2V
- Car battery 12.6V

Stripboard

Stripboard has copper tracks already laid out in parallel lines on the GRP.

Circuits need to be carefully planned so that they can be assembled across the tracks. Links, components or breaks in the tracks ensure the circuit functions.

Worked example

Explain the process of making a printed circuit board using etch resist pens. **(4 marks)**

1 Design the track layout.
2 Draw the track onto the copper board with the etch resist pen.
3 Place the copper board into the ferric chloride solution.
4 Rinse the excess solution.

Now try this

Draw a labelled diagram to show the construction of a copper clad board that is suitable for a circuit board. **(3 marks)**

Stock forms – resistors

Current, voltage and resistance

Voltage (V) is the strength of an electrical supply. The higher the voltage, the stronger the supply.

Current (I) is the flow of electricity around an electrical circuit – how fast it is flowing.

Resistance (R) is how hard it is for the current to flow. Resistance is measured in ohms (Ω).

Ohm's law is the relationship between voltage, current and resistance: $V = I \times R$

Resistors

Resistors can be used in a circuit to regulate current flow or to provide a specific voltage for a device, such as a light-emitting diode (LED).

Circuit symbols

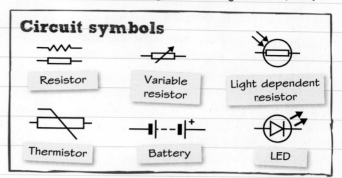

Resistor   Variable resistor   Light dependent resistor

Thermistor   Battery   LED

Variable resistors

Variable resistors can be used to change the resistance in an electrical device.

Light, temperature and pressure sensors can be used in a circuit with varying degrees of resistance.

Variable resistors can be found in electrical products in the form of knobs or sliders.

Resistor codes

A resistor uses a series of coloured bands to indicate its value.

Resistor colour code

Band colour	Value
Black	0
Brown	1
Red	2
Orange	3
Yellow	4
Green	5
Blue	6
Violet	7
Grey	8
White	9
Gold	0.1
Silver	0.01

Tolerance colour code

Band colour	±%
Gold	5
Silver	10
None	20

Band 1 First figure value

Band 2 Second figure value

Band 3 Number of zeros/multiplier

Band 4 Tolerance (±%) See below

Brown	Green	Orange	Gold
1	5	000	5%

Resistor is 15000Ω or 1.5K ±5%

Yellow	Violet	Silver	Red
4	7	x00	10%

Resistor is 4700 or 0.47K Ohms ±10%

To be practical, the options are reduced to a standard range of **preferred values**. The E12 range has 12 values and has a 10% tolerence.

Worked example

Figure 1 shows a simple LED circuit. The battery is 9 volts (V) and the current in the circuit is 13 milliamps (mA). The LED is protected by a resistor.

Calculate the value of the resistor, if the LED is rated at 3.1V. **(6 marks)**

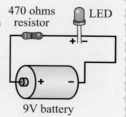

470 ohms resistor   LED

9V battery

Current = 13mA = $\frac{13}{1000}$ amps

Voltage drop = 9V – 3.1V = 5.9V

Using Ohm's law R = $\frac{V}{I}$

Resistance = $5.9 / \left(\frac{13}{1000}\right)$ = 454 Ω

The closest resistor on the E12 scale will be 470 Ω

Now try this

Electrical circuits are normally represented as a circuit diagram. Draw the circuit diagram for the LED circuit shown in Figure 1. **(4 marks)**

Had a look ☐   Nearly there ☐   Nailed it! ☐

Stock forms – dual in-line packages and microcontrollers

On page 20 you looked at single chip micro-computer components. You need to know about the stock forms and how they are fitted onto circuit boards.

Integrated circuits

Integrated circuits contain all the components needed to perform a particular function. Minute resistors, diodes and transistors are etched onto a silicon chip, which means that products can be much smaller and also cheaper.

An integrated circuit

DIL Socket

Soldering DIL packages directly onto circuit boards can easily overheat and damage the chips. It is advisable to solder a socket directly onto a printed circuit board where the DIL package can be fitted without soldering. This also means the DIL package can be easily replaced.

14-pin DIL chip with socket

Microcontrollers (PICs)

Programmable interface controllers are more complex than standard integrated circuits as they have processors, memory, more inputs and outputs and can be programmable.
PICs can perform the function of many integrated circuits, have flash memory, take up less space and allow products to be smaller, but they can be very expensive.
They form the central processing unit for many household electrical items such as PCs, washing machines and radios.

Dual in-line packages (DILs)

Silicon chips are too small to be used alone so they are housed in dual in-line packages. These are rectangular plastic or ceramic casings with two parallel rows of metal pins.

The integrated circuit is connected to the pins by fine wires and the pins connect to other devices on a circuit board. Pins are 2.54 mm apart.

The pins on a DIL are in pairs, and the number varies between 6 to 40 pins.

In-line package

DIL chip numbering

Chips must be inserted into the board or socket the correct way around for them to work. Most pins have a specific function but they may not all be connected inside the package. This is because it is cheaper to make the chips and sockets standard sizes, but connections within the chip may be designed differently.

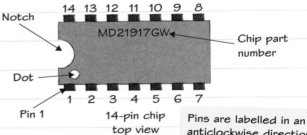

Notch

MD21917GW — Chip part number

Dot

Pin 1   14-pin chip top view

14 13 12 11 10 9 8

1 2 3 4 5 6 7

Pins are labelled in an anticlockwise direction from the notch or dot.

Flash memory retains data when there is a power loss.

Ribbon cable is a flat strip of many wires that can be used to connect the multiple pins on a DIL or microcontrollers to other components.

Worked example

Explain **two** advantages of a manufacturer of digital alarm clocks using a microcontroller in the circuit of the alarm clock. **(4 marks)**

The advantage of using a microcontroller is that it combines many functions of individual circuits and will take up less space, allowing the alarm clock to be more compact. It can also be programmed, adding extra functions to the alarm clock, like multiple alarms or a sleep function.

Now try this

Explain **one** advantage of having flash memory in the microcontroller of a digital radio alarm clock. **(2 marks)**

Stock forms – mechanical

Having standard forms and components is cost-effective as it saves time in machining. Levers, linkages, gears, pulleys, belts, cams and followers were explained on pages 29–30. There are also other components that interconnect mechanically to control movement and force.

Chain and sprocket

On pages 25 and 30 you saw that a pulley and gears can transmit rotary motion. A chain and sprocket can also do this. It is used on bicycles or motorbikes and is stronger than a pulley system and does not slip.

The direction of rotation of the output would also be in the same direction as the input. Lubrication is required.

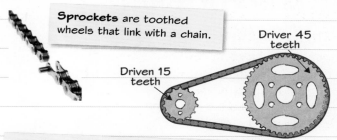

Sprockets are toothed wheels that link with a chain.

Driver 45 teeth

Driven 15 teeth

See page 26 for more on velocity ratio.

The **chain** is a series of links and rings / rollers to make a flexible coupling.
The **velocity ratio** for a chain and sprocket is found from the relationship between the number of teeth.

Pulleys as lifting systems

As well as transmitting rotary motion, pulleys can also gain mechanical advantage (MA) in a lifting system with a cable and grooved pulley. A simple single pulley system can be used to raise a weight, but there is no advantage apart from being able to lift the load.

Increasing the number of pulleys and supporting ropes will increase the mechanical advantage.

Mechanical advantage (MA)

The mechanical advantage (MA) is found by counting the number of supporting ropes, belts or cables in the system.

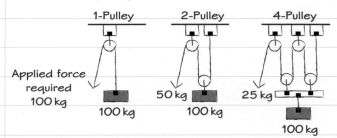

1-Pulley   2-Pulley   4-Pulley

Applied force required 100 kg

50 kg   25 kg

100 kg   100 kg   100 kg

Standard components

Nuts and bolts: Normally hexagonal and used together.

Nyloc nuts resist coming loose due to polymer insert.

Wingnuts can be tightened by hand.

Washers: Spread the load and protect surfaces.

Plain or bush bearings: Give a bearing surface, reduce wear and come in a range of materials.

Springs: Used to apply force flexibly or can store energy. This is due to the helical design. They can be used in tension or compression.

Ball bearing and roller bearing races are used on axles that run at high speeds, such as cars or bicycles.

Worked example

1 Describe **two** disadvantages of using a nyloc nut.   **(2 marks)**

Nyloc nuts need tools to attach them tightly. Once used, the polymer insert is not as effective and may come loose if reused.

2 Figure 1 shows two arrangements of pulleys and cable in a lifting system. Calculate the mechanical advantage of each pulley system.   **(2 marks)**

A – 4:1
B – 4:1

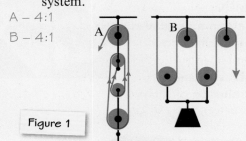

A   B

Figure 1

Question 2 is simple – you just need to count the number of supporting ropes in each case.

Now try this

Explain **two** reasons why the first arrangement of pulleys in Figure 1 (A) would be preferred over the second arrangement (B).   **(4 marks)**

Wastage

There are a range of tools, equipment and processes that are used to shape, fabricate, construct and assemble high quality prototypes. The first of these is wastage.

Hand tools for systems

Side cutters
Used for cutting wires close to the circuit board for neatness.

Wire strippers
Used to remove the outer layer of plastic on an insulated wire.

Desoldering pump or desolder braid
Used to remove excess solder.

Tools for cutting PCBs

Guillotine
A guillotine is an accurate way to cut printed circuit board (PCB). Other methods could include cutting with a hacksaw or scoring with a craft knife in order to snap along the line.

Tools for drilling circuit boards

Stripboard cutter
A stripboard cutter is a simple tool for breaking the copper tracks on stripboard with a drilling action.

PCB drill
Small twist drills are used for drilling circuit boards, with sizes ranging from 0.2–1.5 mm to suit the components.

The size makes them difficult to hold in a standard chuck, so they tend to have enlarged shanks. This also gives them more strength.

Drills are held in a specialist PCB drilling machine to enable them to drill perfectly straight and reduce the chance of snapping.

Laser cutting materials for systems

This technology is relatively new but is used widely to make accurate mechanical parts. For example, gears and cams can be made in a range of materials, such as polymers, wood and some metals. PCBs can also be cut and track layout etched.
The laser cuts materials with a focused beam.

👍 Work does not need to be held.
👍 Cuts are extremely precise.
👍 Used to cut or engrave.
👍 Increased safety.

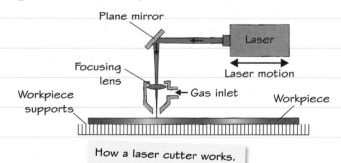

How a laser cutter works.

Worked example

Describe **two** hazards and their necessary control measures when drilling a series of 1 mm holes in a PCB prior to component assembly. **(4 marks)**

The drill is very fine so it is likely to break. It must be held vertically in a drill press and the PCB moved under the drill to avoid any chance of breaking the drill. The drilling operation will also produce swarf or the drill may snap, so the user needs to protect their eyes with goggles.

Now try this

Describe the stages for cutting a PCB using a laser cutter. The image to be cut has already been generated on a suitable computer-aided drawing program. **(6 marks)**

Addition

Tools required for soldering components onto a circuit board.

Soldering iron, stand and sponge: Has a heated tip to melt solder and a damp sponge for cleaning the tip between tasks.

Helping hands tool: Holds work steady to solder. Has a light and magnifying glass for close work.

Fume extractor: Has pads that absorb solder fumes. This is vital for safe working.

Solder: Made from 60% tin and 40% lead, giving it a low melting point. Lead free versions are used in school.

Soldering is precise – if solder crosses a track, it will create a short circuit. A desolder pump is used to suck up excess molten solder.

PCB track cleaner: An abrasive that removes oxides that may prevent solder from adhering.

Setting up for soldering by hand

1. Heat soldering iron, switch on extraction.
2. Clean tracks to ensure a clean join.
3. Steady circuit board in the helping hand tool.
4. Insert components to be soldered.

Worked example

Explain **two** reasons why solder contains a flux.

(4 marks)

Flux contains a cleaning agent that stops the metal surfaces from oxidising and forming a bad joint. It also improves the flow of the solder across the surface as it assists the heat transfer of the soldering iron to the surface.

Soldering the components onto a printed circuit board

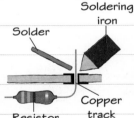
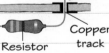
Solder — Soldering iron — Copper track — Resistor

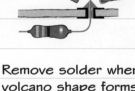

Steady the work, make sure soldering iron is hot. Hold iron with one hand and solder with the other.

Preheat track and component for a few seconds to raise the temperature.

Introduce solder to touch the heated track The solder will then melt.

Solder should flow around the joint filling the gap to make a good joint and not a **dry joint**.

Remove solder when a volcano shape forms. Remove the soldering iron and the solder will solidify. Trim excess wire with side cutters.

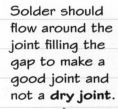

A dry joint is when the solder is not connecting the component and track.

Now try this

Explain how excess solder can be removed from a circuit board.   **(2 marks)**

Modification of properties

Metals prone to significant wear, such as gears and bearings, can be strengthened by **hardening**.

Hardening and tempering

Hardening moves the carbon in carbon steels into a new structure, which is harder but more brittle. The carbon steel is heated to its critical temperature (900°C) and then cooled quickly (quenched) in water.

Tempering reduces the brittleness and increases toughness and impact resistance.

1. The steel must be cleaned with emery cloth so the oxide colours can be seen.
2. Heat it to a defined temperature (e.g. 293°C), indicated by the colour of the steel.
3. Quench the steel in water.

Case hardening

Gears and cams undergo a lot of surface wear. Case hardening increases the carbon content on the outer surface of steels to improve wear but leave a tough core.

1. Heat steel to around 950°C (cherry red).
2. Place it in carbon rich bath of case hardening compound.

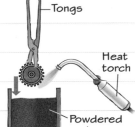
Tongs
Heat torch
Powdered carbon

The process is repeated until the desired carbon content is absorbed into the outer surface.

Anodising aluminium

Aluminium is a good material for electronic goods as it does not rust. However, it does oxidise, which gives a hard dull finish. Anodising provides aluminium with a decorative, durable, corrosion-resistant, oxide finish.

'Hardcoat' anodising process

1. The aluminium part is cleaned.
2. The aluminium part (anode) is immersed in an acid electrolyte bath with a cathode of lead or aluminium.
3. A current is passed through it, which flows from the anode to the cathode.
4. Oxygen atoms are released from the acid electrolyte. These react with the surface of the aluminium part to create a thick oxide layer.
5. Dye is added and it is sealed to prevent fading.

Sulphuric acid electrolyte
Aluminium torch body
Anode
Cathode (lead or aluminium)

Anodising aluminium

Making photo-resist printed circuit boards (PCBs)

The Printed Circuit Board (PCB) layout can be designed on a computer and printed. This can be used to create a photo-resist mask to help produce the PCB.

Photo-resist board
Peel back
Plastic film
Sensitive side of board

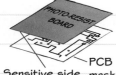
PHOTO-RESIST BOARD
Sensitive side of board
PCB mask

UV Light Box

DEVELOPER TANK

ETCHANT TANK

1. Cut PCB photo-resist board to size and peel off protective layer.
2. Place photo-resist mask on the sensitive side of PCB board.
3. Expose board to UV light for a set length of time.
4. Develop with dilute sodium carbonate for 15–30 seconds and rinse.
5. Etch with ferric chloride for 15–45 minutes and rinse.

Now try this

Describe the process of case hardening the outer layer of the gear wheels that is to be used in an electric hand drill, shown in Figure 1.   **(5 marks)**

Figure 1

Surface treatments and finishes

There are a range of surface treatments and finishes to improve or maintain performance and help protect against heat, dirt, liquids and wear.

PCB lacquering or conformal coatings

A PCB (printed circuit board) is covered with a protective layer made from polymers and called a lacquer. It prevents failure of the circuit board and protects against fine strands of solder that could cause a short circuit.

👍 PCB lacquering reduces the need for an expensive enclosure, as it protects against liquid and chemical corrosion and degradation.

👍 It is virtually weightless, so adds no weight to the product.

👎 It is highly flammable, harmful if inhaled or swallowed.

👎 It is irritating to eyes and skin.

👎 The vapours may cause drowsiness and dizziness.

PCB lacquer is sprayed on once the assembly processes have been completed.

Lubrication

Lubrication is used in **mechanical systems**. A lubricant aids the movement of mechanical parts to prevent them seizing or overheating due to friction or abrasion.

* Lubricants can be solid, semi-solid, liquid or gas.
* Three common lubricants are oils, greases or dry lubricants.

Viscosity is a measure of a liquid's resistance to flow. Water has low viscosity and grease has high viscosity. Viscosity changes with temperature and pressure.

	• Oils are generally polymer-based with added ingredients that give a specific performance, such as reducing corrosion or preventing deposits forming using detergents. • Oil is graded by **viscosity** (such as 20W or 10W). Thinner oils have a lower number.	Uses: tool maintenance, engine parts, hinges
	• Grease is made from oils with thickeners mixed in to give different grades, such as white lithium, marine or silicone grease. • Greases act as a barrier to corrosion and the high viscosity means that they stay where they are placed.	Uses: bearings, gears
	• Lubricants are made from particles of silicone or graphite, which allows two surfaces to slide against each other. • They are suspended in a solvent, which dissolves when sprayed onto the component surface leaving the lubricating film.	Uses: locks, hinges, linkages

Methods of applying lubricants

1 Oil drip feed applies oil onto the surface at regular intervals.

2 Oil splash feed uses moving parts to splatter the oil from a sump.

3 Oil force feed uses a pump to continually apply the oil to a moving component.

4 Grease is forced into place usually through a nozzle and it stays in place.

Lubricants need to stick to bearing surfaces. When choosing a lubricant you need to consider: load to be carried, space between surfaces, running temperature or speeds, porosity of surface, flow rate and viscosity.

Worked example

Give **two** safety precautions necessary when using a PCB lacquer or a dry lubricant. **(2 marks)**

When using PCB lacquer you need to ensure there is suitable ventilation so that you do not breathe the fine droplets which could be harmful. You must wear personal protective equipment to ensure that the PCB lacquer or dry lubricants do not come into contact with skin.

Now try this

Explain why grease is used in bearings in preference to oil. **(2 marks)**

Commercial processes

There are a range of commercial processes that are used for shaping and forming electrical and mechanical systems. You need to know about two of these processes.

Pick and place (PNP) assembly

Pick and place assembly machines work with extreme accuracy at high speed.

This is a process that is used for placing components such as resistors, capacitors and integrated circuits onto a circuit board in a production line, also known as populating.

- A programmable robotic device is used to pick the components at high speed and accurately place them in position and is suitable for surface mount and through-hole components.
- **Surface mount technology (SMT)** is a robotic system that uses a vacuum to quickly pick the component from the dispenser and place it on the paste or pads.
- **Through-hole technology** is more conventional and the leads of the components are placed through holes drilled in the PCB.

Commercial soldering

Soldering components onto a circuit board is a time consuming process and there are two commercial methods for carrying this out on a large scale. They are both quick processes with reliable joints that are strong and have good conductivity.

Flow or re-flow soldering is most popular for surface mount components but can also be used for through-hole components. Components can be easily fitted on both sides of the circuit board.

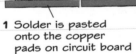

2 PNP places the components onto the paste

4 Solder cools and solidifies. Heat sensitive chips can be placed

1 Solder is pasted onto the copper pads on circuit board

3 The board and components go into re-flow oven. Heat melts paste to attach components

Flow soldering

The solder paste is precisely added to the circuit board with the use of stencils.

Wave flow soldering is when a circuit board to be soldered is passed over a wave of molten solder in a bath. The process is suitable for surface mount and through-hole components.

1. Components are placed using PNP. The circuit is then placed on the conveyer and fluxing is used to help the flow of solder and prevent oxidising.
2. Preheaters reduce sudden change in temperature.
3. A pump produces a solder wave that solders the components to the board.
4. Circuit board cools.

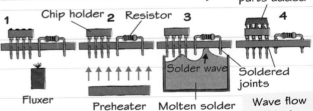

Circuit board moves along a conveyor

Heat sensitive parts added

Chip holder   Resistor

Fluxer   Preheater   Molten solder   Soldered joints

Wave flow soldering

Both soldering processes will need a flux applied. In re-flow, the flux is mixed into the paste, while in wave flow, the flux is added separately.

Explain **three** advantages of using pick and place (PNP) to assemble a circuit board on a production line, over manual methods of assembly. **(6 marks)**

The use of PNP machines means that there is no human error as the components will be accurately placed every time. The PNP machine can also run without taking breaks, resulting in higher productivity. The PNP machine can work at a much faster rate than a human.

Now try this

Give **two** advantages of re-flow soldering over the wave soldering process for assembling and soldering a printed circuit board. **(2 marks)**

Using and working with electronic and mechanical systems

Mechanical and electronic systems

Systems are organised or connected to perform a particular function. Systems can be electronic or mechanical. Mechanical and electronic systems may be connected to each other.

Mechanical systems use mechanical components that connect to manage a mechanical power source and change it into force and movement using levers, linkages, pulleys, gears or cam bearings.

Electronic systems use electronic components that connect to manage electrical power sources and process them into a desired output.

Selecting materials

The following key areas will be used to analyse when deciding on materials for a product.

Functionality: What the design should do and for whom, including measurable performance factors.	**Availability:** Availability of the component parts and standard sizes and forms and the availability of standard components.	**Social factors:** Factors such as disabilities, religious groups, age or consumer society / obsolescence.
Aesthetics: How it will appear to the customer, use of colours and the finished system.	**Costs:** Cost of the components and conversion into the product. Budget available and the target price for the intended market.	**Ethical factors:** Factors in sourcing raw materials and manufacture, including fair trade organisations.
Environmental factors: Sustainability, waste management, energy demands and recycling.	**Mechanical properties:** Strength tension / compression, hardness, toughness, malleability, ductility, elasticity and plasticity.	**Cultural factors:** Factors such as fashion, trends, faiths or beliefs of the user, from a range of backgrounds.
Scale of production: Connecting all the different parts, manufacturing capability, mass, batch or continuous.	**Physical properties:** Absorbency, density / weight, fusibility, electrical and thermal conductivity, size, miniaturisation and battery life.	**Finishes:** How long is it intended to last and whether it will need further protection against corrosion depending on intended environment.

Worked example

Figure 1 shows gears used as a drive system in the gearbox of a vehicle.

Give **two** reasons why gears are suitable in this application. **(2 marks)**

Figure 1

Mechanical properties – Have high strength and toughness as the gears will be transmitting a lot of force.

Availability – The gears can provide large speed increase or reduction in a small space, as they are directly connected rather than alternative rotary systems such as pulleys.

Alternative answers:
Finishes – The gears will be heat treated so that they are hard and resistant to wear and can operate at high speeds.

Now try this

Give **two** reasons why the manufacturers of the microwave oven shown in Figure 2 have chosen to use an electrical system to control its functions. **(2 marks)**

Figure 2

There will be many reasons why a material is used for a product. The reasons must relate to the product use, such as range of functions, miniaturisation, cost of manufacture or product life span.

Function – Gears can have different numbers of teeth, allowing different speeds to be created.
Scale of production – The gears used can be mass produced to satisfy high demand.

Selection of materials or components

In addition to the specific working properties of a particular material, designers will need to take many factors into consideration when choosing a material for a product. Here are the key factors.

Functionality		What the material is intended to do and how it performs for the user.
Aesthetics		How attractive or pleasing the material needs to be in a product in terms of form, colour and texture.
Environmental factors		The energy consumption, pollution and sustainability from the material's initial sourcing and extraction, manufacture, use and disposal.
Availability		Materials need to be readily available in their raw form or as components. Materials that are specialist, scarce or difficult to source will have a higher cost. The use of stock materials will benefit designers and customers.
Cost		The cost of the raw material and processing, through to the manufacture of the product. This is heavily influenced by the scale of production.
Social factors		Companies must consider social factors when selecting materials. The needs of the people have high priority. Examples are the specific needs of children, disabled or elderly where safety may be a critical factor. Factors in a consumer society, such as trends and fashions, may drive the quality of materials used.
Cultural factors		Different faiths and beliefs may impact the development of products. This does not just impact design; the origin of materials may also be important, for example materials that have been derived from animals need to be carefully considered.
Ethical factors		Materials can be purchased from ethical sources, such as wood that has been responsibly managed and accredited by the Forest Stewardship Council (FSC) or products endorsed by the Fairtrade Foundation.

Many materials used in design and manufacturing are generally available in standard / stock forms. This makes the material more cost-effective as it gives designers ready-made materials that can be incorporated into their designs.

Worked example

Explain **three** factors that might influence a designer when selecting materials for a product that is being sold at a craft fair. **(6 marks)**

The choice of materials by the designer will be influenced by the availability of the materials. The use of standard / stock materials will help the design process as there will be set measurements that can be used for the materials or components. How and where the materials are sourced is important as customers may want to know whether the product is ethically made or has been endorsed by a company such as Fairtrade, which means that the workers have not been exploited. Finally, the designer will want to use materials that are environmentally friendly so that it is not impacting on limited material resources or the processes used in manufacturing do not produce harmful emissions.

When considering the choice of materials for a product you could look at other products on the market and evaluate the materials used. These will have been selected for good reasons based on the original brief and specification from the company.

Now try this

Apart from availability, cultural and ethical factors, explain **three** further factors that will influence a designer when designing a child's toy that is being sold in a toy shop. **(6 marks)**

Forces and stresses

All materials need to be able to withstand a variety of forces and stresses to be successful. There are five different ways force and stress can be experienced.

A **force** is a load that has been applied. It is measured in newtons and it is represented by the symbol N.

As a load is applied to a material it produces a **stress** and may cause the material to deform.

Loads and stresses can be applied in a number of ways.

① Tension

This is a pulling force that can be exerted on a material.

The rope is resisting the pull from the people and is experiencing tension.

② Compression

This is the force pressing on a material.

The legs of the chair are resisting load from the elephant and are experiencing compression.

③ Bending

Bending forces create tension and compression. When a beam is supported at both ends and a load is applied, the upper part of the beam is being compressed while the lower part is experiencing tension. The point between these two forces is known as the **neutral axis**.

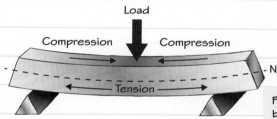

Forces in different parts of a beam supported at both ends.

Loads can be either static or dynamic.

A **static load** is a load that does not move and is constant, such as books sitting on a shelf.

A **dynamic load** is unstable or may be moving, which tends to increase the force applied to the material, such as a person walking over a footbridge.

④ Torsion

This is a twisting force. Often along the length of a material.

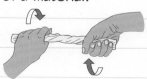

The material is being twisted from opposing ends and is experiencing torsion.

⑤ Shear

This is when two parallel forces that are out of alignment are acting against each other.

The blades of the scissors are acting against each other to shear the material.

Worked example

Name the main force acting in the following examples. **(4 marks)**

1 The leg of a stool, when a person is sitting on it.
Compression

2 A rope used to tow one car behind another.
Tension

3 The blades of a tin snips used to cut thin metal.
Shear

4 The handle of a screwdriver, when putting in a screw.
Torsion

Now try this

1 Explain how a single beam shown in Figure 1 can be experiencing tension and compression when carrying a load.

(4 marks)

2 Name the dotted line shown in Figure 1.

(1 mark)

Figure 1

Ecological issues 1

Ecological concerns

There are ecological issues associated with product design:

- Loss of wildlife and soil erosion through **deforestation**.
- Changes to the landscape, loss of habitat, noise and vibration through **mining**.
- **Farming** requires good soil, so farmers expand into new areas, destroying habitats. Pesticides cause pollution and rivers are diverted, impacting on ecosystems.
- Vehicles **transporting** products use a lot of fuel, which causes pollution.
- The production of carbon during the manufacture of products.
- The use of **finite raw materials**.
- The use of landfill, which can cause dangerous chemicals to leak into the ground, poisoning wildlife and possibly humans.

Sustainability

Companies must consider the **sustainability** of the manufacture, use and disposal of their products. Sustainable products reduce demand on non-renewable raw materials and energy sources, produce less waste and reduce pollution.

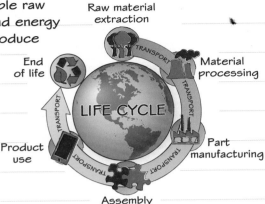

When a company analyses its environmental impact at each stage of the product's life, it is called a **Life Cycle Assessment (LCA)**.

Carbon footprint

A carbon footprint is the amount of CO_2 emissions that is directly or indirectly attributed to an individual or company. It includes:

- extraction, transportation, processing and manufacture of products
- power consumption, such as electrical power
- recycling and end-of-life disposal of products
- travel, such as commuting, holidays, etc.

Companies and individuals should continuously look for ways to reduce their carbon footprint.

Reducing your carbon footprint

- **Energy:** Use efficient house insulation, low energy lighting, alternative energies and turn down heating.
- **Water:** Reduce water use and turn off taps.
- **Travel:** Use low carbon vehicles, car sharing, and minimise number of journeys.
- **Recycling:** Recycle used glass, plastics and paper.
- **Offsetting:** Offset carbon emissions by a tree planting programme.

Worked example

Give **four** ways that an individual could reduce their carbon footprint at home. **(4 marks)**

An individual could insulate their home, turn down temperature levels for water and heating, use energy efficient lighting, and take showers instead of baths.

Now try this

1 Examine the two tables and identify the greatest environmental impact for each and give a reason for this. **(4 marks)**

2 Describe **two** ways that the environmental impact for each product can be reduced. **(4 marks)**

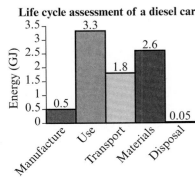

Life cycle assessment of a diesel car

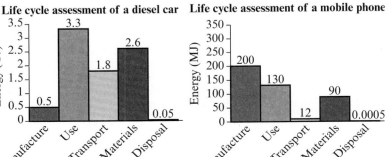

Life cycle assessment of a mobile phone

Ecological issues 2

There are a number of areas where significant improvements in sustainability are being made.

Transportation

The materials, parts and the product need to be transported, which could result in a large number of 'product miles'. These can be minimised by:

- reducing the **number of journeys** by fitting more onto transport vehicles by making products smaller, lighter and with less packaging
- reducing the **length of journeys** by using distribution hubs and moving processing plants closer to the source of raw materials
- changing the **energy source** of vehicles from fossil fuels to renewable energy sources.

Leaner design

Ecological impact should be considered right at the beginning of the life of a product, at the design stage. The designer could:

- use less materials or parts and include renewable materials or standardised parts
- design the product with parts that are easily separated for recycling
- simplify or use energy efficient or repeatable manufacturing processes
- reduce the amount or type of packaging
- make products more sustainable, such as recharging, and easy maintenance.

Recycling or reuse

Recycling or reuse of products or materials is ecologically responsible, it improves sustainability and benefits the environment.

Goods can sometimes be made cheaper by not using new materials. For example, newly extracted aluminium costs twice as much as using recycled aluminium; 90% more energy is needed to extract aluminium from its raw form.

Modern multi-layered packaging, e.g. drinks containers, makes material separation difficult, so that it is easier to use new raw materials than to recycle. This is a big issue.

See pages 100 and 103 for more on sustainability and recycling

Ways to reduce ecological issues relating to materials

Paper and boards	• Farm trees effectively to renew supply and reduce deforestation, habitat loss and soil erosion. • Recycle to reduce demand on raw material. • Use fewer toxic chemicals in processing.	Metals	• Recycle to reduce demand on raw materials. • Reduce environmental impact of mining, such as deforestation. • More efficient processing methods.
Timber	• Forest Stewardship Council (FSC) to manage timber use and supply. • Farm trees effectively to sustain supply.	Textiles	• Recycle to reduce demand on raw materials. • Use natural rather than synthetic fibres. • Invest in reuse schemes for clothing and fabrics, such as charitable donations. • Use fewer toxic chemicals in processing.
Systems	• Create rechargeable, energy efficient products to conserve energy. • Recycle batteries to reuse chemicals. • Use efficient processing methods. • Make printed circuit board parts easier to recycle.	Polymers	• Minimise the environmental impact of drilling, fracking and processing oil. • Encourage development of biodegradable polymers. • Recycle to reduce demand on raw material.

Now try this

In your chosen material discipline, carry out the following tasks:

1 Identify a home consumer product that has been constructed from the material. **(1 mark)**

2 Explain how the product could be made so that it is more sustainable. **(2 marks)**

Social issues

A large organised group of people living together, such as a town, country or continent, is called a society. You need to understand the social issues related to making products.

Safe working conditions

In Britain, companies have to ensure, so far as is reasonably practicable, the health, safety and welfare at work of all their employees.

- There is strict legislation about health and safety at work (Health and Safety at Work Act 1974) and it is monitored and enforced by the Health and Safety Executive (HSE).

- Since April 1999, workers' pay is also protected with the introduction of the minimum wage.

ALL PERSONS MUST COMPLY WITH THE HEALTH AND SAFETY AT WORK ACT 1974

The Health and Safety at Work Act 1974 covers health and safety, welfare facilities, ventilation, cleanliness, space, lighting, temperature, working (flexible) hours, shift patterns and training.

Fair trade

In other countries, workers may not have the same protection as workers in the UK. The **Fairtrade** organisation looks at the interests of farmers and workers to ensure they have good working conditions, are not discriminated against and are paid a fair price.

Impact on others

Companies have a responsibility to ensure that their products have a positive impact on people. Examples include the following:

- Companies that source local produce are helping the local economy and support other jobs in the wider community.

- Products must be designed so that they do not offend, such as offensive logos or branding on products.

- Companies could donate to local, national and world charities, or help at local volunteer events.

Reducing pollution

Pollution has harmful effects on people's lives. For example, air pollution can cause respiratory diseases and chemical pollution of soil or water is thought to contribute to a variety of illnesses.

Atmospheric pollution is due to substances, such as CO_2 emissions, toxic fumes, and particles from factories being released into the atmosphere. CO_2 emissions contribute to **global warming**. Some countries committed to reducing this, in the Paris Agreement (2014), which has been signed by 175 countries to date. This aims to keep the rise in global temperature below 2°C during this century.

Oceanic pollution is due to harmful substances such as household waste, chemicals, particles or plastics released into the ocean. **80% of oceanic pollution is from outside the water**, such as dumping of waste, sewerage or chemical spills. Legislation is being introduced to reduce oceanic pollution, such as the ban on microbeads in cosmetics.

Worked example

1 Explain the term 'global warming'. **(2 marks)**

Global warming is the gradual increase of the temperature of the Earth's atmosphere due to human activity (including manufacturing processes) creating carbon dioxide, which traps heat from the sun, causing the earth to heat up.

2 Describe **three** causes of oceanic pollution **(3 marks)**

Oceanic pollution can be caused by waste being towed out and dumped at sea. It is caused by oil leaks from tankers or oil rigs. It can also be caused by untreated sewage, factory waste or pesticides and fertilisers from agriculture that are left to drain into the oceans.

Now try this

The Health and Safety Executive is there to monitor the health and welfare of all workers. Describe **four** ways that companies look after the health and welfare of workers. **(4 marks)**

The six Rs and the environment

Product designers need to minimise the impact of their products on the environment. It is important that finite natural resources are not exhausted and that sustainable alternatives are found and used. The six Rs are a checklist of points that should be considered in the development of a product.

1 Reduce

Consider if it is possible to reduce the amount of:

- **material** in the manufacture of a product
- **consumables** that are needed in the product, for example, changing a vacuum cleaner to be bagless
- **energy usage** by using more energy efficient processes.

3 Recycle

Polymers, metals, textiles, timbers, paper and boards can all be recycled. Consider if it is possible to:

- **reprocess** the waste in a product in the same system or to make something else
- collect waste for **commercial recycling**
- **use recycled materials** in a product
- **substitute** unrecyclable materials for ones that are easier to recycle
- design products that are easy to **dismantle** to make it easier to recycle parts.

5 Rethink

This strategy examines what is actually needed and considers if there is a more environmentally friendly solution. It considers:

- how many should be made?
- do we actually need the product?
- how do we minimise the processes and use of resources?

2 Reuse

Consider if it is possible to reuse:

- the product again for the **same purpose** by refilling it, such as ink cartridges or carrier bags or getting the maximum use of the product before it wears out or has to be discarded
- the product or parts of the product for a **different purpose**, such as drinks bottles, textile insulation or bags for life.

4 Repair

Try to ensure:

- the product can be easily repaired to extend its life and reduce the need for a replacement and to reduce manufacturing
- spare parts are readily available – this is true, for example, of home appliances or vehicles.

6 Refuse

Question the need for products and materials and, where possible, do **not**:

- buy a product if you do not need it
- use materials that are bad for the environment
- add unnecessary packaging or use carrier bags if not needed.

Worked example

 1 Describe **three** advantages to the customer of designing products that can be easily repaired. **(3 marks)**

The product will last longer and could save the customer money, as well as meaning that fewer materials are sent to landfill.

 2 Describe **one** disadvantage to the manufacturer of designing products that can be easily repaired. **(1 mark)**

The manufacturer will sell fewer products and may have money tied up in stock for repairs.

Now try this

 A department store has decided to change its carrier bags from polyethylene to the textile one shown in Figure 1. Explain **two** reasons how a designer has used the principles of the six Rs to design the new carrier bag. **(4 marks)**

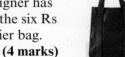

Figure 1

 Since the government introduced the tax on plastic bags, bags for life have become trendy and people like to display their 'green' credentials. Bags for life are being designed to meet this demand.

Scales of production

It is important to know the scale of production as this will influence the selection of materials used for a product. There are four scales of production you need to know about.

❶ Prototype

'One-off' designs are single unique products that are individually designed, such as furniture or wedding dresses.

A prototype is an example of one-off production as it is a unique concept experimental model. It is the first example of a design that can be a product in its own right or a full-scale working model used in the development process.

👍 High quality to exact specifications.

👍 Made by skilled workers and are unique.

👎 Expensive as cost of materials is higher.

👎 Labour intensive and production times are longer.

❷ Batch

A set number of products (a batch) are made either in limited quantities or for a limited time.

👍 Can allow customers a wider choice of designs.

👍 Quick response to demand.

👍 Economies of scale due to high unit output, so materials can be bought in bulk.

👎 Batches must be stored.

👎 Re-tooling the machines for different processes may be costly.

👎 Some processes will be repetitive as larger numbers made.

Examples include textbooks, designer clothes.

Batch produced products can respond to seasonal demand.

❸ Mass

Mass production efficiently and consistently produces many products at a low cost per unit. This system is often automated with parts added in sequence in a production line.

👍 Materials can be cheaper in high quantities.

👍 High level of quality control.

👍 Low unit cost.

👍 Cheaper labour.

👎 Initial set-up costs can be high.

👎 If a production line breaks, manufacture is halted.

👎 Repetitive.

👎 Less flexibility to respond to the market.

Examples include household appliances, children's toys and clothing, where design changes are limited.

Production lines for mass production date back to the early 1900s

❹ Continuous

This involves manufacturing thousands of identical high-demand product components or materials 24 hours a day.

👍 Removes the cost of stopping and starting the production process.

👍 Materials can be cheaper in high quantities.

👎 Automation can lead to staff redundancy.

👎 Little flexibility to change production without large costs.

Examples include standard single components such as buttons, nuts, bolts, rivets, LEGO® blocks, drinks cans and sheet materials such as glass and steel.

It is important that designers consider the scale of production when designing products, including the availability and cost of materials, technology involved, quantities required, speed of manufacturing processes and selling price.

Worked example

Give the name of the scale of production that would be most suited to the production of the water bottle shown in Figure 1.

A Mass ◯

B Continuous ⬤

C Prototype ◯

D Batch ◯

Figure 1

Now try this

Justify **three** reasons why mass production methods would be used to produce the computer mouse shown in Figure 2.

(6 marks)

Figure 2

The use of production aids

Manufacturing can be very labour intensive so manufacturers will use a variety of different aids to help speed up processes. You need to know about different production aids.

1 Reference points / datums

It is important to have a constant point to make measurements from on any work.

It is identified before any marking out process.

If needed, the reference point will be machined first so it is accurate and all measurements taken from the datum.

For most work, the reference point will be a square edge or corner.

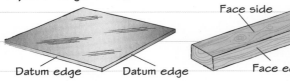

Datum edge for a metal or plastics workpiece

Face side and face edge for a wooden workpiece

2 Patterns

Patterns are replicas of the product that is to be made.

The accuracy of the pattern is directly related to the quality of the product to be made.

Patterns can be made from cheaper material, such as paper or wood, which is easier to work and can be used many times or re-made as the design changes.

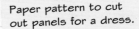

Paper pattern to cut out panels for a dress.

3 Templates

Templates are used if you need to mark out the same points, or shape, onto material a number of times.

The template is made to the exact size of the shape to be cut or the location of holes. The template can be fixed to the material and marks can be transferred easily, or it may be **sacrificial** and used once and another copy created when required.

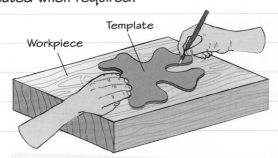

Template used to mark a shape onto timber.

4 Jigs

A jig is a device for holding work in place, which helps when carrying out repetitive manufacturing methods. The jig holds the work in the same position and then the cutting tool is guided to the correct place. For example, a jig for drilling accurate holes in wood.

A jig used to guide a router to cut finger joints accurately.

Advantages of patterns, templates and jigs:

- Greater productivity and quicker production.
- Simplifies more complex processes.
- Reduced costs.
- Increased accuracy, quality and **tolerance**.

Tolerance is the level of accuracy that a product will be constructed to. It will be set by the manufacturer at the start of the process. More expensive products tend to have closer / tighter tolerance.

See page 106 for more on quality control and tolerance.

Worked example

Explain **two** advantages of using a jig in a manufacturing process. **(4 marks)**

The advantage of using a jig is that it can increase the speed of carrying out a manufacturing process as points do not need to be marked out. It will also reduce the possibility of human error as it will produce the same results every time.

Now try this

Describe **two** advantages of using a pattern in a manufacturing process. **(2 marks)**

All materials

Quality control during manufacture

All manufacturers want their products or prototypes to be as accurate as possible. However, it is impractical to expect all materials, components and products to be 100% accurate.

Tolerance

Manufacturers set 'an allowable margin of error' to ensure that a part will still function as long as the part is within the tolerance range.

Tolerances are set with an upper and lower limit, which is plus or minus (±) a set figure. They can be set for all materials and can relate to size, weight, colour, strength and quantity.

Parts manufactured within tolerance will always fit. It can be dangerous if parts do not fit properly, e.g. a nut and bolt being loose in an aircraft engine.

Quality control (QC)

A quality control system is set up throughout the manufacturing process to check that parts and assembled products have been made to the correct standard, and **within tolerance**.

QC equipment is expensive to set up so most companies use **random sampling**, which is more cost-effective than checking every product individually.

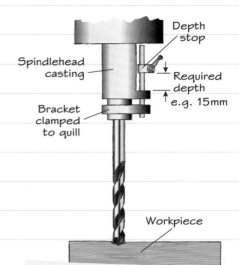

In a pillar drill, the depth stop can be set so that the drill will only move down the required depth.

There are many **specific quality control tests** that manufacturers can use.

Paper and boards	Registration marks or colour charts	Registration marks are used for multiple printing processes. They show that each process has been accurately lined up.	
Timber	Go / no go fixture tool / gauges	This tool is used to check the upper and lower limits of tolerance. The material is in tolerance if it fits within the larger opening (go) and does not fit in the smaller opening (no go). This tool can be used very quickly as there is no measuring involved.	No GO +9 GO −4
Textiles	Inspection of printed material	Printed fabric often has a mismatch in the pattern. This is particularly important when fabric is joined. The fabric is visually inspected in manufacture and when sewn together as a garment.	
Electrical and mechanical systems	Timers for exposure 'soak' times	It is important to time how long a PCB should be exposed to the UV light, developer or etchant. Overexposure can lead to breaks in tracks.	
Metals	Depth stops and guides	Depth stops are normally fitted to machinery to ensure work is cut to the correct length or depth.	
Polymers	CNC laser settings	It is important that laser cutters have correct information about kerf allowance, material and thickness so that they will cut accurately.	

Worked example

A steel leg for a chair must be 720 mm long (±) 5 mm. Which of the following dimensions would be within tolerance? **(1 mark)**

A 726 mm ○
B 770 mm ○
C 716 mm ●
D 670 mm ○

Now try this

Explain **three** quality control checks that may be carried out by a manufacturer when producing the radio shown in Figure 1. **(6 marks)**

Figure 1

Investigation using primary and secondary data

To identify design opportunities and to develop a design brief and manufacturing specification, you need to understand the needs of a client or user and ways to gather information.

Clients and users

All design starts from the **needs** of a person or group of people. These people are called the client or user. Basic human needs include warmth, water, food and shelter. People may also identify specific needs that improve their lives, whether related to leisure, work, age, gender or disability.

Market research

Market research is a method of gathering, analysing and interpreting primary data about a potential product.

It can target past, existing or potential customers and gathers information about them, such as spending habits, likes and dislikes. Information can be collected through questionnaires, surveys, interviews or focus groups.

User or client needs

Before starting any design process, a designer needs to analyse the client or user's needs and formulate an action plan to gather information to help them develop a **design brief** and **design specification**.

A **design brief** is a clear statement of intent and should include:

- the identity of the client or user
- the needs of the client or user
- details of any constraints such as cost, time or space.

A **design specification** sets out the specific criteria found in the research that the product must achieve and will be used in the evaluation. Specification points should be measurable where possible. A good specification should detail function, appearance, ergonomics, time, materials, environment and cost.

Sources of research data

Primary data is collected directly from people or user groups using questionnaires, surveys, interviews, focus groups or individual research, such as material testing or site visits.

Secondary data is information that has already been collated by other people and presented in any of the following ways:

- books (libraries), magazines or the internet
- government data or reference books
- trade organisations
- analysing the work of other designers.

Designing questionnaires

To gain relevant and accurate feedback, the design of the interview or questionnaire is important. Questions should be:

- short and to the point
- focused on solving the problem (will it help develop a specification?)
- objective (ask questions that give a measurable answer, avoid subjective questions)
- relevant to the individual answering. For example, if a device is for the elderly, the questions should be relevant for the elderly.

Worked example

Explain **two** advantages of gathering secondary data for research in a design problem.   **(4 marks)**

The advantages of gathering secondary data are that it is economical as the gathering process has already been completed, saving time. It will provide a wider range of detailed data that could not have been concluded from a small number of people, especially when investigating human dimensions.

Quantitative data can be counted and is usually factual. Qualitative data is more about opinions.

Now try this

Explain **two** advantages or gathering primary data for research in a design problem.

(4 marks)

107

Investigating using secondary data

An important aspect of secondary information is how the product interacts with the client or user.

Ergonomics

Ergonomics is the relationship between people and the products they use – how they can be made more comfortable and efficient.
Examples include the following:

- **Signs:** First aid signs are green to be instantly recognisable.
- **Layout:** Keyboard layouts and fonts on keys are standardised for ease of use.
- **Strength:** Operating strengths are within user range to reduce potential accidents.

Anthropometrics

Anthropometrics is the study of human sizes in relation to the products that they use and can be applied to the design of products. For example, sizes for furniture, clothing and bicycles.

Anthropometrics uses statistical data that has been gathered by measuring all human dimensions. This includes height, hand size and reach. The data are broken down by different genders, ages and ethnic groups, etc., as these groups will have a different range of measurements.

Targeting more customers

Some designs cannot be made to be an exact fit for all users so designers use strategies to maximise the use of their products.

1. Make one design suitable for as many as possible. For example, cinema seats are designed to fit the maximum range of body sizes.
2. Design products in different sizes to hit certain points on the distribution curve, such as clothing.
3. Design adjustable products, such as rucksack straps or car seats.
4. Design accessories for an original design, such as foam inserts for a cycle helmet.

Normal distribution

Normally distributed results produce a bell shaped graph with the most common dimension being the 50th percentile or mean. The graph below shows the normal distribution for adult seat height in the UK. Designers and companies tend to focus on the middle 90% of the target user group (shown in green). The top and bottom 5% are seen as extremes and it would be costly to design to the full range of dimensions.

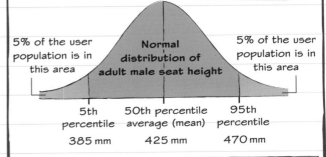

The seat height normal distribution curve for male adults used for anthropometrics

5% of the user population is in this area

Normal distribution of adult male seat height

5% of the user population is in this area

5th percentile 385 mm   50th percentile average (mean) 425 mm   95th percentile 470 mm

	Percentile		
	5th	50th	95th
Adults			
Males	385 mm	425 mm	470 mm
Females	355 mm	395 mm	440 mm

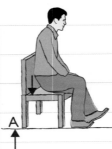

The seat height (A) of a fixed height chair for an adult male will be close to 425 mm (50th percentile), while an adjustable seat may fit the full range from 355 mm (5th) to 470 mm (95th), which is the extremes of both men and women.

Sometimes a designer needs to know the 100th percentile in a data set, such as the maximum weight of a user.

Describe **three** ways in which anthropometrics has influenced the design of the hair dryer shown in Figure 1.   **(3 marks)**

Figure 1

The controls on the handle are within reach of the user without them having to remove their hand. The size of the handle will fit into the palm of the hand of the user. The length of the handle fits the user and is balanced.

Explain **four** ergonomic features of the office chair shown in Figure 2.   **(8 marks)**

Figure 2

108

Investigation using secondary data

When designing new products, it is important to analyse similar existing products to help you to identify good or bad points. This can give you ideas for improvements to your design solution.

Analysing an existing design

Function and purpose: What should the design do and who for and are there any measurable performance factors?	**Ergonomics and anthropometrics:** What human factors have been incorporated into the design, such as physical dimensions, colour, temperature?	**Client social factors:** What society is being targeted and how, such as disabilities, religious groups or age?
Safety: How has safety been incorporated into the design of the product in production, use or end of life?	**Costs:** What are the costs of the raw materials and conversion into the product? What is the intended market and pricing?	**Ethical factors:** What factors are relevant when sourcing raw materials for manufacture?
Environmental factors: How does the product fulfil sustainability concerns?	**Materials:** What mechanical and physical properties are needed and how available are they?	**Cultural factors:** What fashion, trends, faiths or beliefs are being targeted?
Aesthetics: Does it need to be good looking? Consider shape, form, colour, decoration and texture.	**Construction methods:** What construction or assembly methods have been used? What is the scale of production and processing?	**Finishes:** What finishes have been used? What level of protection do they give?

Worked example

Evaluate the stool shown in Figure 1 in terms of its:

1 suitability for the user   **(4 marks)**

The materials can be easily cleaned. The stool is strong enough to take the weight of the student. The stool has been priced to be affordable for a school budget. Beech is very strong and can be easily varnished to extend the life of the stool. Overall it is a cheap solution, as it is strong, cheap and can be placed easily under the benches.

2 ergonomics.   **(4 marks)**

The stool is a suitable height for students to sit on and fit under laboratory benches and the slot in the top makes it easy to pick up. The design is pleasing to the eye with rounded corners and is comfortable to hold. The stool is made from solid timber so it will be heavy to move. Overall the stool is the correct dimensions to fit the user and is easy to move around due to the handle on top.

A traditionally designed stool for use in a school science laboratory.

- Each stool costs £45.00.
- Made from beech with a MDF top.
- Finished with varnish.

600 mm

Figure 1

Now try this

Figure 2 shows a polyester sports bag used by an athlete attending a gym.

Specification:
- Lightweight, with dimensions 900 × 400 × 400 mm
- Waterproof textile material
- Two straps and separate compartments
- Low cost (£28.00) sold in high street store

Evaluate the bag shown in Figure 2 in terms of its:

Figure 2

1 suitability for the user   **(4 marks)**

2 aesthetics.   **(4 marks)**

Product analysis could help you:
- make a product better or cheaper than those available on the market
- save time by using good elements of an existing solution, such as design features, mechanisms or standard components.

The work of other designers 1

It is important to understand the work of present and past designers to inform your research and designing. You should investigate, analyse and evaluate the work of a minimum of **two** of the 16 designers on pages 110–111.

Designer	Known for	Key information	Example
William Morris (1834–1896)	Hand-crafted products, textile furnishings and wallpapers	Prominent role in the Arts and Craft movement. His designs had simple forms, were hand crafted and well made. His designs often reflected forms from nature and have been used in a range of domestic furnishings, furniture and wallpapers.	
Louis Comfort Tiffany (1848–1933)	Decorative arts designer	Known for artistic work in many materials, such as metals, pottery and stained glass. He produced innovative jewellery and interior decoration in the Art Nouveau style. Inspired by nature and colour. His designs are still popular today.	
Charles Rennie Mackintosh (1868–1928)	Architect, furniture, textile and interior designer	Produced innovative, simple, stylish and functional designs. Influenced by Arts and Crafts, Art Nouveau and Japanese styles as he moved to Modernism. Used geometric and natural materials. He did not design for mass production.	
Coco Chanel (1883–1971)	Fashion designer	Challenged post-war traditional corseted wear and introduced practical designs with clean lines. This included cropped skirts that were more feminine, comfortable, natural, sporty and chic. The brand is still popular and includes fragrances and jewellery.	
Gerrit Rietveld (1888–1964)	Architect and furniture designer	Member of the De Stijl (Dutch) modernist group. Advocated the use of simple shapes, primary colours, geometric shapes and horizontal and vertical lines in both product design and in the design of buildings.	
Raymond Templier (1891–1968)	Jewellery designer	Innovative jewellery designer. Important figure in Art Deco movement. Interested in Cubism and how it translated into jewellery designs, which included semi-circles, triangles, geometric lines, a variety of precious stones and rare metals.	
Marcel Breuer (1902–1981)	Architect and furniture designer	A student and head of carpentry at the Bauhaus (Germany). Experimented with new materials, such as tubular steel in furniture designs (Wassily Chair) and concrete in buildings. Developed the idea of modular construction.	
Harry Beck (1902–1974)	Technical draughtsman	Changed the rules on drawing maps by producing a simplified colour-coded map of the London Underground in the 1930s. He linked the relative locations of stations rather than exact geographical locations to make a schematic diagram that reduced the detail to what was essential to the user.	

When you investigate, analyse and evaluate the work of other designers, give specific and relevant pieces of information that need to be researched, for example:

- what area of design they were famous for
- chronology of their work / life
- notable examples of their work
- philosophy or style
- what design movements they were involved in.

Now try this

Modernist designers rejected the styles from the past and were able to develop more innovative designs. Explain **two** reasons why they were able to do this.

(4 marks)

The work of other designers 2

You'll need to understand the work of present and past designers to inform your research and designing.

Designer	Known for	Key information	Example
Sir Alec Issigonis (1906–1988)	Car designer	Designed the iconic Mini in the 1950s, which had the largest possible interior from such a small footprint as well as a transverse engine, making it very economical. Also designed the Morris Minor, which was the first million-selling British car.	
Ettore Sottsass (1917–2007)	Product designer and architect	Influential designer and part of the Memphis design movement, which he called the 'New International Style'. Challenged the black humourless design of products and introduced colours, textures and patterns to reinvigorate everyday designs, such as the Carlton room divider.	
Aldo Rossi (1931–1997)	Architect and product designer	Influential in the Post-Modern movement. He wanted to design buildings or products that would stand the test of time and he had a desire to produce buildings that tied their form into the way of life for the people using them.	
Mary Quant (1934–present)	Fashion designer	Made famous for her youth-oriented fashions, such as her mini-skirt and hot-pants designs in the 1960s. She wanted to make clothes that were 'fun to wear' and that she would wear herself. Her Chelsea look or 'Mod style' became very popular.	
Norman Foster (1935–present)	Architect	Designed many high profile projects, including Wembley and the Gherkin in London. His designs include a lot of glass and steel with clear structure and coherent forms. His designs are also constructed to be sustainable and environmentally friendly.	
Vivienne Westwood (1941–present)	Fashion designer	Combined traditional elements of British design, such as tartan and Harris Tweed, with historical influences, such as corsets and crinoline, to produce very modern designs. Heavily involved in the 'Punk' style of the 1970s.	
Philippe Starck (1949–present)	Product designer and architect	Wanted to create products that had durability and longevity and were uniquely 'in fashion'. He wanted designers to be honest and objective and his products were influenced by fashion and novelty, were often stylized, streamlined and organic but often over-designed.	
Alexander McQueen (1969–2010)	Fashion designer	Experimental and innovative designer who pushed fashion limits to the extreme. Known for dramatic designs that were often shocking and unconventional. He displayed his theatrical designs with powerful runway shows.	

The **iterative** design process is where designers use a cycle of prototyping, testing, analysing and refining products to make changes and refinements to a design.

Now try this

Designing is an iterative process where many scale models and prototypes will be created before the final design is produced.
Explain **three** reasons why a designer will produce scale models or prototypes of a design. **(6 marks)**

The work of other companies

It is important to understand the work of product design companies to inform your research and designing. You should have an understanding of the work of a minimum of **two** of the following design companies.

Designer	Known for	Key information	Example
Alessi (Founded 1921)	Italian design company producing household items	Mass-produced products constructed from stainless steel and bright colours that are fun, functional and visually appealing. Alessi has employed a range of famous designers, including Philippe Stark, Ettore Sottsass and Aldo Rossi.	
Apple (Founded 1976)	American consumer electronics company	Known for cutting-edge technology and software, in sleek and simple products, such as the iPhone and iPad. Key concept was to make computers more intuitive, accessible and user-friendly. Founded by **Steve Jobs**, **Steve Wozniak** and **Ronald Wayne**.	
Braun (Founded 1921)	German electrical consumer appliance company	Works to the principle that 'less is better' to produce functional electrical appliances that are simple, innovative, aesthetic, easy to use, long lasting and environmentally friendly with no unnecessary detail.	
Dyson (Founded 1991)	British electrical consumer appliance company	Founded by James Dyson who was the designer of the first bagless vacuum cleaner. Other Dyson products, such as fans, hair / hand dryers, have subsequently been designed following the same principle of innovation and efficiency.	
Gap (Founded 1969)	American clothing company	Focus on casual, everyday clothing. It was founded on the **principle** of doing **business** responsibly, honestly, ethically and with integrity. Founded by Doris and Don Fisher to make it easier to find a pair of jeans.	
Primark (Founded 1969)	Irish clothing company	Brings current trends in fashion to a wide market with reasonable quality. Popular for customers that want the latest look on a budget. The original store, opened by Arthur Ryan in Dublin, is called Penneys.	
Under Armour (Founded 1996)	American sportswear company	Known for innovative designs such as synthetic fabric with moisture wicking to remove sweat. Launched by former American football captain, Kevin Plank. It now sells a wide range of sport-enhancing clothing and equipment.	
Zara (Founded 1974)	Spanish clothing company	One of the world's most successful retail brands, which has the customer at the heart of their business model. Introduced the idea of 'fast fashion' by reducing lead times and reacting to new trends quickly through new technologies in manufacturing and distribution.	

When researching the work of companies, you need to know about when they were established, their underlying design principles, what products they are noted for and any significant people within the organisation.

Now try this

Give the name of **two** product design companies from the ones listed above and give **two** key principles that each company works towards.   **(4 marks)**

Design strategies

Designing is a complex process and you need to use a range of strategies to generate imaginative, innovative and creative designs. You need to know about four different strategies.

① Collaboration

Collaboration allows you to draw on the experience and specialist knowledge of others.

- This could be from your client or user or from an expert or professional in your chosen material, such as a welder or a carpenter.
- The input could come at any stage in the design process, such as initial research, reviewing design ideas and prototypes, manufacturing or evaluating the final design.
- In industry, designers will work in teams as this will give a wider range of contributions and people may be inspired by others.

② User-centred design

This design strategy focuses on an explicit understanding of the needs of the client or user and involves them throughout the design and development process.

- The input is also collaborative and could come at any stage in the design process, such as initial research, reviewing design ideas and prototypes, manufacturing or evaluating the final design.
- In industry, feedback will continue to be sought after the product has been launched.

③ A systems approach

The design process is broken into distinct stages that can be worked through in a logical, sequential order, from the development of the design brief and specification, through to the design stages and the final evaluation at the end.

Feedback loops will be used in stages, such as designing so that testing or user feedback can be analysed.

④ Iterative design

This process takes a cyclic approach to design where there is a continuous process of designing, prototyping, testing and evaluating at all stages of the design process. This will include using client feedback on sketches, material testing, modelling, field trials and evaluation.

Each iteration of the design moves the solution forward to resolve problems until a finished design is produced.

Worked example

Explain **two** advantages of using a collaborative approach in solving a design problem. **(4 marks)**

A collaborative approach gives you a wide range of views and feedback, which should reduce the number of mistakes or design fixation. It also means that expert information, such as manufacturing techniques or materials that are not fully understood by the designer, can be incorporated and this may save time and money.

The iterative process comes at all stages in the design process. The key to success is that feedback is given and the design is refined and evolves. The process includes:

sketching in design and development to record changes

modelling to visualise or test aspects of the design before moving on

testing aspects of the design to ensure they function correctly

evaluation of each design, the developed idea and final construction.

Avoiding design fixation

Designing is an imaginative, innovative and creative process but it does not always run smoothly. You may find that your prototype does not work exactly as you had anticipated. It is important that you are flexible in your approach and do not become fixated on your original design. Try to:

- use a collaborative approach and seek advice from others
- start modelling rather than drawing as it may highlight issues by looking at the problem in a different way
- go back to the problem and take a fresh approach that may be more experimental, with different shapes or materials.

Now try this

Iterative design is a cyclic approach to the design process. Explain **four** ways that you could use iterative design in the development of a design solution. **(8 marks)**

113

Communication of design ideas 1

There is a range of communication techniques that you will need to understand, in order to understand drawings and to use them to explain ideas to others.

Freehand sketching

Sketching is a convenient way of recording ideas and communicating them to other people.

- Sketching should be done carefully using a suitable pencil (HB).
- Decide on 2D or 3D and use light lines.
- Use crating to create a framework.
- Go back over the detail on the object and 'line in' once you are happy with the drawing.

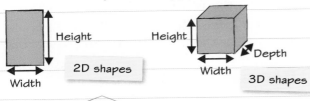

2D shapes — Height, Width
3D shapes — Height, Width, Depth

Crating provides a framework for detailed drawings to be **lined in**.

Isometric projection

This is a way of representing 3D shapes. All dimensions are actual size and vertical lines remain vertical. Horizontal lines are drawn at 30° to the horizontal.

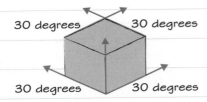

30 degrees   30 degrees
30 degrees   30 degrees

One point perspective represents a 3D shape by drawing the front shape and then extending the lines to a notional vanishing point (VP). The position of the VP is normally the horizon line to represent your eye level when looking at the object.

Two point perspective more realistically represents a 3D shape by drawing the sides of the object extending to two notional vanishing points (VP).

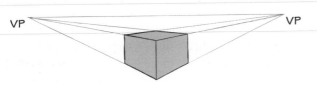

VP   VP

Working or orthographic drawings

Orthographic drawings are in 2D. One form of orthographic projection is called **third angle projection** and it lays out the different views of a shape in a precise order.

You will need to convert drawings from 3D to third angle projection and also in reverse. A second end view can be added to the left if needed.

Plan
End — A —
Front

Plan
A
Front   End

A **third angle projection** should have this symbol shown.

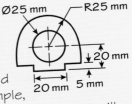
Ø25 mm   R25 mm
20 mm
20 mm   5 mm

All drawings in 2D or 3D benefit from **dimensions** so that the product can be visualised or constructed from the drawing. You should scale the drawing. For example, a scale of 4:1 means that each line drawn will be four times larger when full scale.

Many objects have internal features that cannot be seen, such as holes. How are these represented on a 2D or 3D drawing?   **(1 mark)**

A Shading ◯
B Dashed line ●
C Zig-zag line ◯
D Continuous line ◯

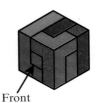

The puzzle cube shown to the right has been drawn in isometric projection. Draw the puzzle in third angle projection showing the pattern on all three views. The front view is indicated.   **(6 marks)**

Front

114

Communication of design ideas 2

It is important to understand drawings and to be able to communicate ideas graphically to others.

Annotated drawings

Annotated drawings give detail, such as the labelling and justification of materials, parts or components within a design. They can also be used to show manufacturing processes, dimensions or design features.

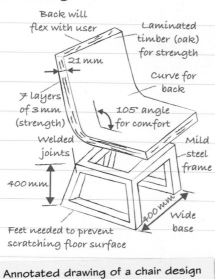

Back will flex with user

Laminated timber (oak) for strength

21 mm

Curve for back

7 layers of 3 mm (strength)

105° angle for comfort

Welded joints

Mild steel frame

400 mm

400 mm

Wide base

Feet needed to prevent scratching floor surface

Annotated drawing of a chair design

System diagrams

System diagrams use input, process and output boxes with feedback loops to represent how a system would work. These are often used in electronic systems to break down the system into smaller stages, such as a heating system.

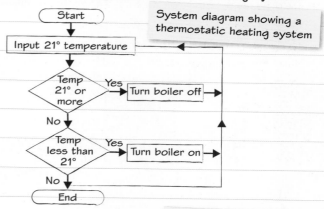

System diagram showing a thermostatic heating system

Start

Input 21° temperature

Temp 21° or more → Yes → Turn boiler off

No

Temp less than 21° → Yes → Turn boiler on

No

End

Schematic diagrams

Schematic diagrams represent the elements of a system using graphic symbols rather than pictures of the individual items. Schematic diagrams are often used to represent circuits.

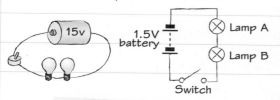

15v

1.5V battery

Lamp A

Lamp B

Switch

An electrical circuit and its schematic diagram

Exploded drawings

Exploded drawings show constructional detail or assembly. The diagram of the train clearly shows all the individual parts. The use of annotation would give information about joints, adhesives or materials.

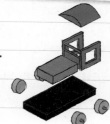

Exploded drawing of a train

Other methods

Audio / visual recordings of interviews for research or to show clients work in progress.
Computer aided design (CAD) packages to draw designs.
3D modelling to make scale versions of designs to test different aspects.

CAD can help with the communication of ideas in a number of ways:
• Reduces human error.
• Drawings can be more accurate as you can zoom in to parts.
• Easier to save and edit ideas.
• Much quicker than drawing by hand.

Worked example

Draw the system diagram for a simple alarm that has a snooze function to wake a student.

(3 marks)

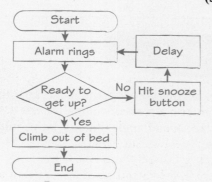

Start

Alarm rings ← Delay

Ready to get up? → No → Hit snooze button

Yes

Climb out of bed

End

Now try this

A design student has made a simple alarm system using two metal plates as a switch. It is powered by a 9V battery to sound a buzzer when a connection is made. Draw an annotated schematic diagram of the simple alarm system.

(4 marks)

Marking out

All materials used in design and technology need to be accurately marked out before they are cut.

Marking tools

These tools leave an imprint on the material to show where to cut, drill or join.

Scriber: Scratches lines into metal or polymers, made from tool steel.		**Engineer's blue:** Makes it easier to see marks on metal.	**Tailor's chalk:** For marking onto fabrics, easily removable.
Pencil: Easily erased, used on most material surfaces.		**Odd leg calliper:** Mark lines parallel to the edge of materials.	**Marking knife:** Marks fine accurate lines on timber, often across grain.
Marker pens: Permanent and non-permanent on paper, board and fabric.		**Compass:** Marking out curves or circles on timber, paper and boards.	**Marking gauge:** Marking lines parallel to edge of timber, can also have a cutter.
Centre punch: Marks centres for holes to be drilled in metal.		**Dividers:** Marks out curves or circles on metal.	**Mortise gauge:** Marks two lines parallel to edge of timber in mortise and tenon joints.

Measuring tools

These tools will have dimensions that can be read.

Steel rule: Measuring and drawing straight lines.		**Micrometer:** Measuring thicknesses and diameters very accurately to within 0.01 mm.	
Tape measure: Measuring straight and curved lines.		**Vernier calipers:** Measure length, thicknesses and depth accurately to within 0.01 mm.	

Guide tools

Guide tools are used for marking and measuring tools (see page 105 for more on patterns and templates).

Try square: Marking lines at 90° to the edge of wood, or to check for square edges.		**Engineer's square:** Marking lines at 90° to the edge of metal, or to check for square edges.	**Sliding bevel:** Marking angles that are not 90° to the edge of wood.
Mitre square: Marking lines at 45° to the edge of wood.		**Outside callipers:** Help to measure outside diameter or dimensions, with a steel rule.	**Inside callipers:** Help measure inside diameter or dimensions, with steel rule.

Worked example

1 Give the name of a tool that will mark a line parallel to the edge of a piece of timber. **(1 mark)**

   Marking gauge

2 Give the name for a tool that will mark a line parallel to the edge of a piece of metal. **(1 mark)**

   Odd leg callipers

Now try this

Mitre squares are excellent at checking that a mitre cut on a piece of timber is exactly 45°. Give the second angle that is set on a mitre square. **(1 mark)**

Material management

It is important to plan the cutting of materials efficiently to minimise waste and use appropriate marking out methods and datum points.

The cost of waste

All material that is not used in manufacturing is classed as waste. For a manufacturer, waste means loss of money and reduces profits. Manufacturers need to look at ways to minimise waste in the marking out and cutting of materials. Strategies include planning, tessellating, using standard forms and pattern matching.

Always allow for some waste when cutting material to size. Waste between pieces that need to be cut should be kept to a minimum, such as the width of saw, laser cut or overlap needed.

Standard forms

As discussed in the materials section, all materials will come in standard forms. It is important for designers to know the standard sizes available so they can use this information to plan their designs.

For example, if materials come in 1 m lengths, try and incorporate this size or use multiples, i.e. four 250 mm pieces.

Planning

When cutting materials, it is important to plan where the material will be cut. Try to:
- minimise areas of waste
- align to edges or corners
- group parts close together.

For example, a manufacturer wants to cut out a large number of circles. Here, in:
a) the circles are in a square formation
b) the circles are in a triangular formation, which is the closest that they can be packed.
When the scrap for each is worked out:
a) produces 21.4% waste
b) produces only 9.3% waste.

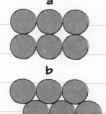

Tessellation

Tessellation or tiling is a method of maximising the use of the material by fitting shapes together so that there are no overlaps or gaps. This is particularly good for laser cutting where there is little waste between each part.

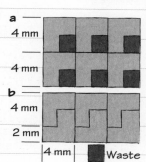

In the first example, the sheet size is 96 cm². The waste in **a** is 2 cm x 2 cm x 6 = 24 cm² which is 25% of the sheet.
However, in **b** there is virtually no waste.

Pattern and grain matching

By limiting the repeat on a pattern, you can generate less waste. For example, the pattern shown here has a pattern repeat of 10 cm.

You could lose up to 10 cm of material each time you match the material.

A closer pattern will produce less waste. This is also important when matching grain on timber.

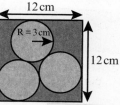
Pattern and grain matching

Now try this

Three circles with the radius of 3 cm are to be cut from a square piece of material that is 12 cm square, shown in Figure 1. Calculate the amount of waste generated. Give your answer to one decimal place. **(6 marks)**

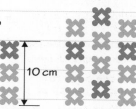
Figure 1

Working safely

Risk assessment

A **risk assessment** is a systematic process to identify any risks in a process or workshop activity. It also identifies suitable precautions or control measures that will reduce or eliminate the risk.

The main forms of hazard include:

- hot items or liquids
- electrical risk
- bright flashes
- sharp items
- flying debris
- entrapment in moving parts
- loud noises
- tripping or slipping
- work at heights
- operating strength of the worker / operator
- toxic substances (fumes, spillages and splashes)
- vibrations.

Safe working

In order to work safely, you must:

- 👍 Keep your work area clean and tidy, know where the emergency stops are and do not work alone.
- 👍 Walk and never run, carry tools and equipment in a safe manner.
- 👍 **Behave safely** and **do not distract** others.
- 👍 Make sure **tools** are all in **good working condition**.
- 👍 Only use machines or tools you have been taught to use and for the intended purpose and **follow all instructions**.
- 👍 Ensure all machines have the **appropriate guards** in place and **never leave machines unattended** or switched on, always switch off when changing tooling.
- 👍 **Report all accidents** and breakages.
- 👍 Always **clamp work** when required.
- 👍 Ensure there is **extraction** for dust and fumes.
- 👍 **Tie back** any loose clothing or hair.

Worked example

Figure 1 shows a resistor being soldered to a circuit board. Identify **five** potential hazards when soldering resistors onto the circuit board.   **(5 marks)**

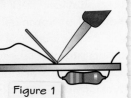
Figure 1

1 Breathing in the fumes.
2 Burns from the soldering iron or solder.
3 Electrical risk from accidentally burning the cable.
4 Cutting yourself on the sharp exposed wires.
5 Damaging posture if not at correct working height.

Personal protective equipment (PPE)

Types of PPE include the following:

Eyes	Safety glasses, goggles, masks
Respiration	Face mask, breathing gear
Ears	Plugs, defenders
Head	Hat, tie hair back
Hands / arms	Gloves, gauntlets
Body	Overalls, apron
Feet / legs	Stout shoes, gaiters

Safety signs

Know your signs as they will help identify hazards and provide safety information.

Prohibition signs indicate and prohibit behaviour likely to cause a risk to health or safety.	**Mandatory signs** show the correct action to be carried out or followed.	**Warning signs** indicate that there is a potential danger.
Direction signs indicate areas of safety or medical assistance. They often include directions.	**Fire equipment signs** show the location of any firefighting equipment.	**Chemical hazard warning signs** about hazardous substances used with COSHH.

The law requiring employers to prevent or reduce workers' exposure to hazardous substances is the **Care of Substances Hazardous to Health (COSHH)**. It requires employers to find out what the health hazards are and decide how to prevent harm to health by using risk assessments.

Now try this

 Computer Aided Manufacture (CAM) is increasingly used in manufacturing. Explain **four** ways that using CAM has improved the safety of manufacturing.   **(8 marks)**

Maths skills 1

In all materials sections you should be able to apply the following mathematical skills.

Area

The **area** of a shape is the 2-dimensional space that is covered. It is measured in square units, such as square metres (m²) and square centimetres (cm²).

Typical area calculations are:

Square / rectangle / parallelogram
= base × height
Triangle = ½ base × height
Circle = πr^2 (where π = 3.142 and r = radius of circle)
Trapezium = ½ (a + b) × h

Volume

The **volume** of a shape is the 3-dimensional space occupied by an object. It is measured in cubed units, such as cubic metres (m³) and cubic centimetres (cm³). Typical volumes include:

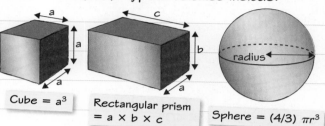

Cube = a^3

Rectangular prism = a × b × c

Sphere = (4/3) πr^3

Surface area

The **surface area of a 3-dimensional** shape is the sum of areas of all faces. For example, this cube has six identical faces, so the total surface area is $a^2 \times 6$.

The surface area of curved surfaces can be found in the same way, but you need to break the shape down into component parts.

An extruded part with a uniform cross-section will be the cross-sectional area × length (or height).

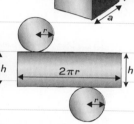

To find the surface area of a cylinder:

1 Find the area of the circles at the ends of the cylinder.
   Area of a circle = πr^2
   There are two circles, so their area is $2\pi r^2$

2 Find the area of the side of the cylinder, which when 'unrolled' is a rectangle.
   Area of a rectangle = width × height
   The width is the height of the cylinder (h)
   The length is the circumference of the end circles ($2\pi r$)
   The area of the rectangle = $2\pi rh$
   The surface area of a **cylinder** is
   $A = 2\pi r^2 + 2\pi rh$

The ability to calculate the volume of a part is useful as it can then be used to calculate the weight and cost of the material required. For example:
- the part uses 500 cm³ of aluminium
- aluminium weighs 2.7 grams per cm³
- the part weighs 1350 grams or 1.35 kg
- aluminium costs £3.00 per kg
- the cost of the aluminium is £3.00 × 1.35 = £4.05.

Worked example

The part shown in Figure 1 is a cylinder. Show all answers to two decimal places.

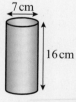

1 Calculate the cross-sectional area of the cylinder. **(4 marks)**

Area of circle = πr^2
= 3.142 × 3.5²
= 38.4895 = 38.49 cm²

Figure 1

2 Calculate the surface area of the cylinder. **(6 marks)**

Surface area of cylinder
= $2\pi r^2 + 2\pi rh$
= (2 × 3.142 × 3.5²) + (2 × 3.142 × 3.5 × 16)
= 76.979 + 351.904 = 428.883 cm²
= 428.88 cm²

3 Calculate the volume of the cylinder. **(3 marks)**
Volume of cylinder = $\pi r^2 h$
= 3.142 × 3.5² × 16
= 615.83 cm³

Now try this

Figure 2 shows the shape of an aluminium part to be used at the back of a sink and it has been made with a uniform cross section.

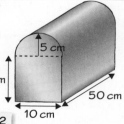

Figure 2

1 Calculate the cross-sectional area of the part. **(5 marks)**

2 Calculate the volume of the part. **(4 marks)**
Give all answers to four significant figures.

Maths skills 2

Decimal and standard form

Decimal places after a whole number signify the tenths, hundredths or thousandths of the whole number. Some calculations do not need such a high level of accuracy. For example, the volume of the cube might be 65.83756 cm^3. It is written as 65.84 cm^3 when expressed to two **decimal places**.

Standard form is a simple way of expressing large numbers. It is based on powers of 10.

For example:

$1{,}000 = 10 \times 10 \times 10$ or 10^3

$6{,}000{,}000 = 6 \times 10^6$

$9{,}000{,}000{,}000 = 9 \times 10^9$

$0.0071 = 7.1 \times 10^{-3}$

Significant figures and rounding

Significant figures are the level of accuracy needed in a calculation. For example, the volume of the cylinder might be 345.3247 cm^3. It is written as 345.3 cm^3 when expressed to four **significant figures**.

Rounding up or down for significant figures and decimal points expresses a number to the nearest 10, 100, 1000, etc.

If you are rounding to the nearest 10, and the last digit is 5, 6, 7, 8, or 9, round the number up. Example: 47 rounded to the nearest ten is 50. But, if the last digit is 0, 1, 2, 3, or 4, round the number down. Example: 43 rounded to the nearest 10 is 40.

Use ratios, scales, fractions and percentages

Ratios show how quantities are related to each other.

The 10 cm length of steel bar shown here is split in the ratio 2:3. This means that the material is divided by 5 (2 + 3) and then combined according to the ratios.

Fractions are a proportion of something. These can be less than 1, such as half (½), or larger than 1, such as $^5/_2$ (improper fraction).

Percentages are the ratios or fractions of 100 and are expressed as a %. For example, one half (½) or 1:2 is 50%.

Scales allow for items that are large to be drawn at a smaller size. The steel bar shown here is drawn at a scale of 2:1. On the page it is 5 cm long but will be two times larger (10 cm) when full scale. Any dimensions on the drawing will relate to the **full size** of the object.

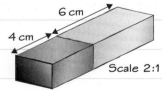

Scale 2:1

The shaded area of the steel bar can be expressed as:
* **Ratio** 2:3
* **Fraction** 2/5
* **Percentage** 40%

The **scale** indicates that it has been drawn half size.

Figure 1 shows a picture of liquid polyester resin and its liquid hardener.

The resin and hardener needs to be mixed in the ratio 100:3.

Figure 1

a) 50 litres of polyester resin is required. Calculate how much hardener will be required. **(2 marks)**

$50 \times \dfrac{100}{3} = 1.5$ litres

b) What percentage of the mixed solution is hardener? **(5 marks)**

51.5 litres = 100%

1 litre = $\dfrac{100}{51.5}$ = 1.941747

1.5 litres = 1.941747573 × 1.5

= 2.91621359%

c) Give your answer to 1 significant figure. **(1 mark)**

= 3%

d) Give your answer to 1 decimal place. **(1 mark)**

= 2.9%

a) The volume of a sphere is calculated to be 26.84987324 cm^3. Express this volume:

1 to two significant figures **(1 mark)**

2 to two decimal places **(1 mark)**

b) Multiply the volume by 10^6 **(2 marks)**

Maths skills 3

Present data, diagrams, bar charts, histograms

In many design activities, you need to identify and interpret data. Representing data in a visual way helps emphasise a point and usually helps to simplify the data.

Bar charts are used to show data that fits into categories.

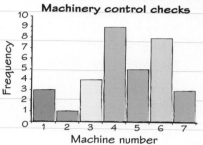
Machinery control checks

The number of errors from quality control checks for machinery in a factory to help identify problem areas.

Pie charts divide data into sectors that represent a portion of the whole.

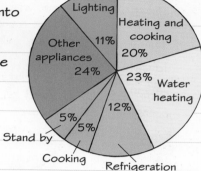

Typical energy consumption in a home. This could help identify how to make savings.

Histograms are used to show data that represents a measured quantity where the numbers can take on any value in a certain range.

Numbers of shoes owned

Worked example

Table 1 below shows the cost of replacing four AA size batteries in a children's toy. Using the information in the table, identify the point when it is more cost-effective to use rechargeable batteries. Show the calculations to justify your answer. **(4 marks)**

Table 1: Type of battery	Cost of 4 × AA	Cost per recharge	1 charge/ replacement	4 charges/ replacements	5 charges/ replacements	6 charges/ replacements
Rechargeable batteries	£17.50 with charger	£0.02	£17.52	£17.58	£17.60	£17.62
Alkaline batteries	£3.50	N/A	£3.50	£14.00	£17.50	£21.00

After replacing batteries five times, it is cheaper to use rechargeable batteries for the child's toy.

Plot, draw and interpret graphs

Line graphs are very good for comparing two pieces of information. Make sure you read the scales carefully, because they don't always start at 0. When drawing line graphs, use a sharp pencil and a ruler.

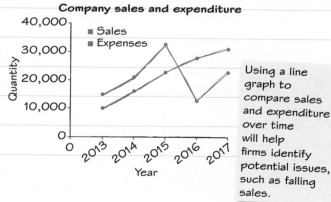
Company sales and expenditure

Using a line graph to compare sales and expenditure over time will help firms identify potential issues, such as falling sales.

Now try this

Using the information shown in Table 1, redraw the axis below then draw a line graph to show the relative costs of recharging the batteries in the children's toy for 1–10 times. Clearly indicate where it becomes more cost-effective to use rechargeable batteries.

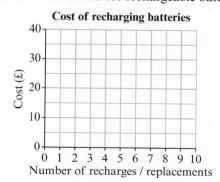
Cost of recharging batteries

(3 marks)

Maths skills 4

International system of units (SI units)

You need to know about the base SI units used in Design and Technology and their multiples or submultiples.

Name	Unit	Abbreviation
length	metre	m
mass	gram	g
current	ampere	A
capacity	litre	l
angle	degree	°

Converting units

1 metre (m) = 1000 millimetres (mm)
1000 metres (m) = 1 kilometre (km)

To convert from m to mm:

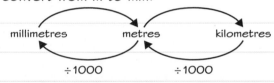

millimetres   metres   kilometres

÷1000   ÷1000

For example, 3200 m = 3.2 km or 3,200,000 mm.

Multiples and submultiples of SI units

Multiples and submultiples of SI units have special prefixes. For example:
1,000 grams (g) = 1 kilogram (kg)
1 Amp (A) = 1000 milliamps (mA)

Prefix	Symbol	Multiplier	Power of 10
terra	T	1,000,000,000,000	10^{12}
giga	G	1,000,000,000	10^{9}
mega	M	1,000,000	10^{6}
kilo	k	1000	10^{3}
none	none	1	10^{0}
centi	c	1/100	10^{-2}
milli	m	1/1000	10^{-3}
micro	μ	1/1,000,000	10^{-6}
nano	n	1/1,000,000,000	10^{-9}
pico	p	1/11,000,000,000,000	10^{-12}

When using units of measure, use the most appropriate measure for the situation. For example, the height of a table may be measured in cm while the length of a screw may be measured in mm.

Angular measure

Angles are used in geometry and are formed when two lines meet at one point. They are measured in degrees. A circle is divided into 360 degrees or 360°. A right angle is 90°.

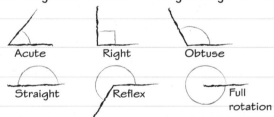

Acute   Right   Obtuse

Straight   Reflex   Full rotation

You need to recognise that angles have different names depending on their size.

Triangles

Angles in a triangle always add up to 180°:
A + B + C = 180°.
To help work out sides of a **right-angled triangle**, use Pythagoras' theorem:
$a^2 + b^2 = c^2$

Hypotenuse

Now try this

Figure 1 shows a cross section of a part to be used in a children's toy. The part is 500 mm long.

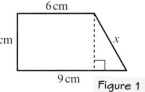

6 cm

4 cm   x

9 cm   Figure 1

1 Calculate the length of side x. **(4 marks)**

2 Calculate the area of the cross section. **(5 marks)**

3 Calculate the volume of the part. Show your workings. **(4 marks)**

Worked example

Convert the following units of measurement into the units given in brackets. **(3 marks)**

1 15340 g (kg)   15.34 kg

2 75 cl (ml)   750 ml

3 26805 mm (cm)   2680.5 cm

Exam skills 1

You will have two hours to complete the exam paper. The paper is worth 100 marks and there are three sections.

Section A (20 marks) – Core technical principles: multiple choice and short answer questions assessing a breadth of technical knowledge and understanding.

Section B (30 marks) – Specialist technical principles: several short answer questions (2–5 marks) and one extended response to assess more in-depth knowledge of technical principles.

Section C (50 marks) – Designing and making principles: short answer and extended response questions.

> Make sure you take an eraser, ruler, protractor, calculator, compass and pencils (including coloured pencils) to the examination.

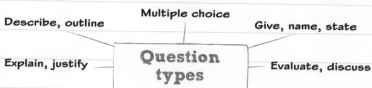

Context

Most questions will relate to a particular context and it is important that your answer relates to that context to get full marks. For example, a question which asked why aluminium is a suitable material for manufacturing outdoor furniture would have two contexts: **Furniture**, which requires properties such as strength, aesthetics and being easy to form and **Outdoor**, which requires answers such as corrosion resistant and weather proofing.

Understanding the question

- Read the question carefully.
- Identify 'command' words (give, describe, evaluate, etc.).
- Identify the context in which the question is set.
- Identify the number of marks. This will guide you as to the number of points required and the time you should spend on the answer.

Multiple choice questions

1. Read the question and think of an answer BEFORE looking at the possible answers, to prevent the options given from distracting or tricking you.
2. Read all choices and eliminate all answers you know are incorrect.
3. If you are unsure, give your best choice after removing the answers you know are incorrect.
4. If stuck, go to the next question and come back later, rather than waste time.

Short questions

You can give one-word answers or a simple statement. This requires you to recall information.

Give: Produce an answer from recall.

Name: Give the correct title or term.

State: Answer clearly and briefly.

> It can help to circle the key words.

Never leave multiple choice questions blank. You will not lose any extra marks if you answer the question incorrectly than if you leave it blank. Follow the steps above to give yourself the best chance of success.

Worked example

 1 Give the name of a suitable ferrous metal that could be used in the manufacture of workshop vices. **(1 mark)**

Cast iron

 2 Name the cam shape that causes a follower to gradually rise and fall in a sudden movement. **(1 mark)**

Drop (snail) cam

 3 State one reason why fossil fuels are non-renewable. **(1 mark)**

Once they have been burnt to release the energy, they are not replaced.

Now try this

 Give **one** reason why you would use an idler gear in a simple gear train. **(1 mark)**

Exam skills 2

Describe and outline

These questions require you to give the stages of a process or a list of points that will form a detailed answer to demonstrate an understanding.

You should also be able to list reasons, such as advantages or disadvantages relating to a specific question.

There are 3 marks available so you should try to identify three separate points.

'Using notes and sketches'

Some describe or outline questions may also ask you to use notes and / or sketches to explain a process or system in detail.

Always use notes **AND** sketches.

- **Focus** on the key features. The drawing does not need to be a work of art, but must be clear.
- **Label** all diagrams.
- **Simplify** diagrams, for example a power supply just needs to be a labelled box (time is limited in the exam.)
- **Equipment** must be appropriate. For example, a sharp pencil and ruler for straight lines. Draw lightly in pencil, so diagrams can be redrawn if needed.
- **Order** the stages correctly.

Describe or outline questions are often associated with manufacturing processes in your chosen material categories. You should practise drawing and labelling these processes.

Worked example

Outline **three** reasons why corrugated card is a suitable material for the packaging of television sets. **(3 marks)**

Corrugated card has excellent impact resistance.

Corrugated card is relatively lightweight and easy to carry.

Corrugated card is a relatively cheap material and will have a low impact on the cost of the product.

Worked example

Using notes and sketches, describe how a kinetic pumped storage system can consistently provide electrical energy. **(8 marks)**

When there is low demand for electricity, excess electricity can be used to drive a pump to move water from a low reservoir to a high reservoir. The water then becomes stored energy that can be used again as kinetic energy when the demand for electricity is high.

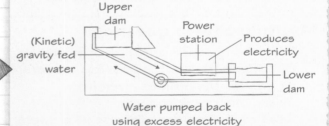

There are 8 marks available, so you should try to make eight points, using the combination of notes and sketches. The student answer shown here would not have gained full marks if they had only provided the text or the sketch on its own – they needed both.

Marks will not be awarded twice for the same information, but put relevant information in both the text and sketch to make sure your answer is clear.

Now try this

Describe using notes **and** sketches how a simple gear train can be used to drive a wheel when the drive gear is rotating at half the speed of the output gear but both gears are rotating in a clockwise direction. The wheel and driven gear is shown in Figure 1. **(6 marks)**

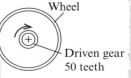

Figure 1

Exam skills 3

Extended answer questions require a number of points that are either justified or come together to give a final conclusion and show a detailed understanding.

Explain or justify

These extended response questions require you to give a two-part answer by stating a fact and justifying it in the context of the question.

> As there are **6** marks available, try to give **three** separate points and explain or justify each fully.

> When giving reasons for the statements, use linking words such as '**because**', or '**this means that**'.

Worked example

Companies are being encouraged to reduce waste in the design and manufacturing process. Explain how a designer can reduce the amount of waste generated in their product. **(6 marks)**

Designers can reduce the amount of waste by redesigning the product packaging by using card instead of bulky polystyrene. This means that less packaging is created and the card could also be recycled.

Designers could also design products that could be refilled, such as washing up liquid bottles. This means that fewer materials are needed in the packaging of the refills as the original bottle can be topped up from the liquid in a bag.

The designer could ensure that parts were labelled with the material that they are made from or that the product can be dismantled easily. This means that the product can be recycled.

> Always identify the context. In this case how changes in design and manufacturing can reduce waste.

> Take a look at the Sample Assessment materials and mark schemes on the AQA website for more practice.

Evaluate or discuss

You need to understand the advantages and disadvantages of a topic and form a conclusion.

> The use of '**however**' is a good way of moving to the disadvantages and '**overall**' leads into the conclusion.

Worked example

Countries are being encouraged to use renewable energy resources. **Evaluate** the use of hydro-electric power (HEP) as an energy source.

(10 marks)

One advantage of using HEP is that it is a renewable source of power that will not run out and power is provided when needed. It is also environmentally friendly as there are fewer CO_2 emissions created. The HEP plant, once set up, will last for a long time and gives a reliable supply of power 24/7 that is relatively cheap. The dams created can also be used as flood barriers and can create areas for water sports or tourism.

However, the dams created can cause ecological damage to animals, plants and humans. They are expensive to set up and rely on certain geographical conditions and there is a risk of dam failures.

Overall, HEP energy production is a good energy source of power. The ecological issues may be short-lived as areas will evolve and adapt, but it provides a reliable source of power that is relatively cheap to run (after its initial installation costs are paid). Although there may be low levels of further environmental damage when it is in service, it is a good method of producing energy as it has less long-term ecological effect than using fossil fuels, which contribute a great deal to global warming.

Now try this

Some companies are replacing the workforce with robot technology. Evaluate the use of robots in a company that uses a production line for high volume production.

(10 marks)

> The best answers, like this one, will include both advantages, disadvantages and a conclusion and always refer back to the context given in the question.

Exam skills 4

Some questions on the paper may ask you to interpret data and make conclusions from the information you are given.

Complete the table

These questions require you to finish a task by adding to the given information.

Always show your working.

Don't forget to bring your pencils, eraser, ruler, protractor, calculator, compass and coloured pencils to the examination

Worked example

A company has decided to change the hand dryers in the office from paper towels to electric blown air dryers as they are more environmentally-friendly. Complete the table below to show the costs of running the dryer for the first three years. **(5 marks)**

	Paper towels	Electric hand dryer
Running cost per month	£40	£15
Running costs for one year	£480	15 × 12 = £180
Running costs for two years	40 × 24 = £960	15 × 24 = £360
Running costs for three years	40 × 36 = £1440	15 × 36 = £540

Complete the graph

These questions require you to finish a task by adding to the given information.

- Use a ruler and be as accurate as possible.
- Draw graphs lightly (but legibly) in pencil.

Worked example

The initial cost of the paper towel dryer is £80 and the electric dryer is £550. Using the information from the table in the question above, complete the graph by drawing a line graph to identify when the electric hand dryer becomes more cost-effective than the hand dryer. **(5 marks)**

The electric dryer becomes cheaper after the 19th month.

Point where electric becomes cheaper than paper (after 19 months)

Cost for using paper towels

Cost for using electric hand dryer

(graph: Cost (pounds) vs Time (months))

Now try this

1 A developed country in Europe is producing 120 gigawatts (GW) of power from a range of different energy sources. The data in the table on the right shows the breakdown of the power mix for this country in 2018.

Complete the table by calculating the missing percentages for nuclear, coal and gas. You must show your calculations.

(6 marks)

Power source	Total energy consumption in gigawatts (GW)	Percentage of total
Renewables	30	25
Nuclear	24	
Coal	12	
Gas	48	
Oil and others	6	5
Total	120	100

2 Using the information in the table, complete the pie chart to represent the power mix in 2018. **(5 marks)**

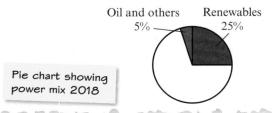

Oil and others 5%   Renewables 25%

Pie chart showing power mix 2018

Exam skills 5

Complete the drawing

These questions require you to interpret a drawing. This can be a conversion from 3D to 2D or to finish a drawing.

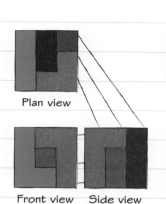

Plan view

Front view   Side view

Worked example

The diagram below shows the front and side views of a timber block that holds restaurant menus. Complete the third angle orthographic projection by adding a plan view of the shape in the box provided. Dimensions are not required. **(3 marks)**

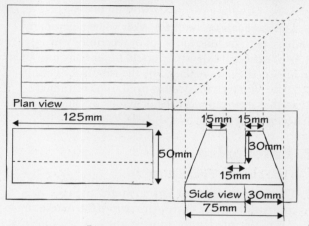

Plan view
125mm
50mm

15mm 15mm
30mm
15mm
Side view 30mm
75mm

Draw an isometric, perspective or orthographic drawing

These questions require you to produce a specified drawing. Use a ruler and be as accurate as possible.

Follow these steps to draw an isometric diagram:

1 Begin with a vertical edge – draw it as a straight line.
2 Draw construction lines at 30 degrees from this first line.
3 Fill in the next vertical lines.
4 Draw the next construction lines from these vertical lines.
5 Draw the product within your construction lines.

Worked example

The orthographic drawing in the question above shows a stand that holds restaurant menus. Using the isometric grid on the right, draw an isometric drawing of the shape. **(5 marks)**

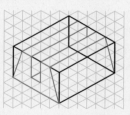

When using grid paper, draw the construction lines (in black here) to help you fill in the detail correctly.

Worked example

The menu holder shown above is going to be cut from a single block of timber with dimensions 125 mm × 50 mm × 75 mm. Calculate the amount of waste that is created from each menu holder. Give your answer in cm³. **(5 marks)**

Surface area of two triangular cuts (A):
$\frac{1}{2}b \times h \times 2 = 7.5 \times 50 \times 2 = 750\,mm^2$

Surface area of centre section (B):
$15 \times 30 = 450\,mm^2$

Volume of waste $= A + B \times L$
$= (750 + 450) \times 125$
$= 150000\,mm^3$
$= 150\,cm^3$

Now try this

The menu holder is going to be sold and packaged in a cardboard box with dimensions

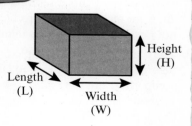

Height (H)
Length (L)
Width (W)

L = 125 mm
H = 50 mm
W = 75 mm

Calculate the surface area of the box. Give your answer in cm² and to one decimal place. **(5 marks)**

Answers

1. Industry

1 The advantages to the manufacturer for changing the design of the workplace to include more robot technology would be that the robots could easily carry out repetitive tasks without losing focus. They can carry out hazardous tasks so improve the safety within the factory for the company and workers. Productivity would increase as robots will be able to work for longer periods without a break.

2 The implications on the worker when a company decides to include more robot technology in production are that they could potentially lose their jobs as they are replaced by the robots for certain tasks. Workers would also need to be retrained so that they can meet the demands of the new technology as it is introduced.

2. Enterprise

1 The Fairtrade Foundation

2 The disadvantages of virtual marketing to a company are that customers ignore the marketing as it is not wanted at the time so it is not cost-effective. It may lose the company customers as they link the company to unsolicited communications.

3. Sustainability

To reduce the amount of waste by reducing the amount of packaging needed for the kettle.

The plastic waste from the injection moulding process could be re-used again in the manufacturing process.

The kettle could be designed so it is easily dismantled so that it could be repaired when broken or taken apart so that the materials can be recycled.

The waste heat generated from the production process can be used as a form of heating in areas of the factory, such as the wasted heat from injection moulding.

4. People

1 New materials with improved properties have allowed products to develop that were not possible with previous materials. New and improved manufacturing processes have been developed that allow for more complex product designs that were not possible with previous manufacturing processes.

2 The iPad® is a good example of push technology as before the iPad® people used laptops for portable computing, and were not aware of alternative methods. But as the technology improved, the development of a touch screen allowed for different integration with portable devices; the consumer demand was not there as it was a new product.

Once Apple developed the iPad®, they also introduced other similar devices, such as the iPad Mini®, as technology allowed for the development of smaller devices which essentially had the same purpose, but some consumers wanted both products.

5. Culture

As a trend develops the demand for a product will be low as there will be few trend setters or creators. Once the trend is established and is accepted in the mainstream the level of demand is maximised and manufacturers need to be able to respond to this level of output. As the trend declines, the late adopters or the more conservative people may buy the product but the level of demand is falling at this point.

6. Society

Blind people can take advantage of assistive technology such as the use of electronic book readers that can be used to read the text of newspapers or books, or devices that can convert text to a tactile braille pad which can be read by the user.

Other advances in technology are through the use of retinal implants or prosthetics that can restore partial sight to blind people which will help them perform functions that were not possible without any sight.

7. Environment

To improve efficiency, manufacturers can change their transport links by creating supply hubs where goods can be transported so that there is less movement of the products. The factory layout could be analysed to group machinery or bring machinery closer together to reduce the movement time of parts. The company could operate a just in time system (JIT) so that there is less storage required for parts and they arrive on the production line when needed and do not have to be double handled and moved twice.

8. Production techniques and systems

A JIT strategy aims to reduce the amount of stock that is being held at any time which reduces the amount of storage required and saves on costs.

Smaller batches of products can be made as the materials are only delivered when required which improves the cash flow.

There will be a high level of computer analytics being carried out to improve the efficiency and prevent any bottlenecks in the production line.

9. Critical evaluation

1 A company will examine the environmental impact of a product by analysing the distribution of the product and perhaps design it so that it is lighter to transport or takes up less space or has less packaging.

The company can look at the disposal of the product and make sure it is easy to disassemble.

They would analyse the manufacturing processes to reduce the amount of waste generated.

They would examine the materials used in the product to see if there are more environmentally-friendly materials that could be used to replace materials that are scarce.

2   A company may design products that cannot be easily repaired as it will mean that they will have to hold a lot of spare parts, which ties up a lot of money in parts.

It may also mean that they have to employ more staff to deal with the technical aspects of any repair and set up a distribution network.

10. Fossil fuels

1   The use of fossil fuels can be reduced if governments invest in a programme of using renewable resources. Countries can also give incentives to companies to be more energy efficient by the use of insulation for heating or using low energy lighting.

2   The use of coal as a power source is harmful to the environment as the extraction of coal from the ground causes damage to the landscape by digging from the ground or by creating quarries. It is also harmful when it is burnt as the carbon dioxide given off contributes to global warming.

11. Nuclear power

1   Coastal areas are good locations for building a nuclear plant because there is a regular supply of water that is needed to cool the reactors.

2   Risk of radiation leak through accidents, such as a natural disasters damaging the power plant.

There is a higher security risk through terrorism at the power plant or when the nuclear fuel is being transported around the country.

Nuclear fuel takes a long time to decay and when it is stored it may contaminate the land if it is not stored correctly.

12. Renewable energy

The advantages of using solar power are that it is a renewable energy source and environmentally friendly. Solar power can be used to heat water and to provide electricity. The energy is free once the initial set up costs have been paid for. However, as the company is in the north of England, the sunlight hours may be reduced, especially in the winter. Large areas of space will be needed to generate enough electricity. Solar power can be expensive to set up and it may take some time to recoup the costs, but once these costs are paid for the energy is at a very low cost. Overall, it is beneficial for a company to invest in the use of solar power as it is cost-effective to the company as long as it is a long-term investment and it is less harmful to the environment than using fossil fuels.

13. Energy and storage systems

Using an alkaline battery or a nickel-cadmium battery for a torch is useful as they are both a portable power source; they are also compact and will be easy to carry. The nickel-cadmium battery has added benefits because it can be re-charged a number of times, which means that it can be used many times, reducing the overall cost, despite them being more expensive in the first instance. Alkaline batteries tend to have more consistent power, but once they have run out they do not have any further use. For long-term use the nickel-cadmium will be better as it will cost less over time and can be used many times.

14. Modern materials

The titanium will be corrosion resistant as it will be exposed to elements such water moisture and other liquids. It has a good strength to weight ratio which will help the performance of the helicopter. It is also a very tough material that has an increased resistance to wear with a prolonged working life and increased reliability.

15. Smart materials

C   A material that responds to external stimuli.

16. Composite materials

1
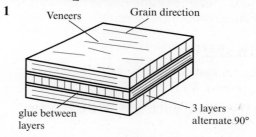

2   Glass reinforced plastic will be cheaper than carbon fibre for the manufacture of the kayak.

The strength of the glass fibres is good for a kayak as it does not need the extra rigidity or strength that you would get with carbon fibre.

17. Technical textiles

1   Fire resistant means that a fabric is non-flammable and will resist fire for a set period of time to prevent the risk of furniture catching fire.

2   Bandages can have microfibres incorporating micro encapsulation which will release medication to an injury throughout the day even when the injury is still covered with the bandage.

18. Systems approach to designing

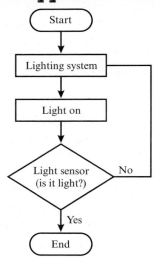

Start

↓

Lighting system

↓

Light on

↓

Light sensor (is it light?) — No

↓ Yes

End

19. Electronic systems – inputs

1 The light dependent resistor will have a high resistance when dark and low resistance in light.

2 The pressure sensor could be used in an alarm system where the pressure of a person standing on the pressure sensor would trigger an alarm.

20. Electronic systems – processes

Programmable microcontrollers are able to be given the specific commands that are needed from a basic programme and transferred by computer. This makes them much more cost-effective than a chip that may be specifically designed.

21. Electronic systems – outputs

1 A buzzer operates by using electromagnets that are switched on and off repeatedly to vibrate a metal disk between two magnetic poles.

2 LEDs would be used because they operate on lower voltages than filament bulbs, which mean they will be safer to use and they will also cost less to run. When filament bulbs break they have to be replaced as they will not work. With a cluster of LEDs, a single LED could be replaced and, before that happens, the rest of the LEDs in the cluster will still be operating.

22. Types of movement

D Oscillating

23. Levers

$$MA = \frac{load}{effort}$$
$$MA = \frac{160}{40} = 4$$

24. Linkages

The motion at B is moving at 90 degrees to A. Point B moves a shorter distance than point A and there is a greater force at point B relative to point A.

25. Simple gear trains 1

The rollers need to rotate in the same direction to move the paper through the printer. Without an idler gear, they would rotate in opposite directions. Therefore, an idler gear is needed to turn the rollers in the same direction.

26. Simple gear trains 2

1 $\frac{\text{Number of teeth on driven gear}}{\text{Number of teeth on driver gear}}$

Velocity ratio $= \frac{10}{44}$

This means that for every 10 revolutions of the driver gear, the driven gear will rotate 44 times.

2 Input speed of A = 100 RPM

Output speed $= \frac{\text{Input speed}}{\text{Velocity ratio}}$

Output speed = Input speed × Velocity ratio

$= \frac{100}{\frac{10}{44}} = 100 \times \frac{44}{10} = 440$ RPM

27. Specialist gears 1

D 9000 RPM

28. Specialist gears 2

Distance moved by rack

$= \frac{\text{Number of teeth on pinion gear}}{\text{number of teeth per metre on rack}}$

Distance moved by rack for 1 revolution $= \frac{80}{500}$

= 0.16 of a metre for one revolution

= 2 × 0.16 = 0.32 metres for 2 revolutions or 32 centimetres

29. Cams and followers

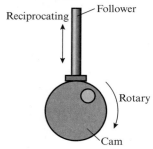

Reciprocating — Follower

Rotary

Cam

30. Pulleys and belts

In the pulley system in Figure 2 the user requires an output speed of 3200 RPM.

a Velocity ratio $= \frac{\text{Driven pulley diameter}}{\text{Driver pulley diameter}}$

$\frac{20}{80} = \frac{1}{4}$ or 1:4

b Input speed = output speed × velocity ratio

$= \frac{1}{4} \times 3200 = 800$ RPM

31. Papers and boards

1 Board is a paper-based material that is greater than 220 grams per square metre (gsm) or is made up of different layers.

2 A2

3 Paper is measured in grams per square metre.

32. Natural timbers

Hardwood trees will have broad leaves that they will lose in the winter. They also hold their seeds in a fruit and are usually slower growing than a softwood tree.

33. Manufactured boards

MDF is a suitable material for the table top because it is dense, which means that it will not mark when pupils use it as a writing surface. It is a very smooth flat surface that comes in wide sheets so there does not need to be a join. It is also cheap as it is made from waste wood and is therefore cost-effective for school use.

34. Metals and alloys

Stainless steel has been used for the kettle because it has good aesthetic qualities and will look good in the kitchen environment. It is also corrosion resistant so it will not be affected by the water in the kettle. Stainless steel is also tough and resists wear so that it can withstand the physical use in the kitchen environment.

35. Polymers

HIPS is suitable for the manufacture of the child's toy because it comes in a range of colours to attract the child to play with the toy. It can be easily injection moulded, which will keep the manufacturing costs low. HIPS is tough and impact resistant so that is not easily damaged by the child. HIPS is also hygienic so it does not pose a risk to the child and it can be easily cleaned.

36. Textiles 1

Wool fibres will be good insulators of heat, so the student will be kept warm in the winter. It is also a breathable material, so that the student will not get too hot. The wool can be dyed any colour to suit the school and it will be lightweight so it is comfortable for the student to wear. When the pullover is washed it will take a long time to dry and it must be washed carefully as it is prone to shrinking. Overall, the wool is a suitable material for the pullover as it will keep the student warm and it can be made any colour to suit the school.

37. Textiles 2

Knitting creates a flexible fabric which is important for a jumper so that the wearer can put it on easily, and it also allows the wearer to move about comfortably.

38. Materials properties

Domestic water pipes are often made from copper because they have good malleability so that they can be easily bent into shape when plumbing around a house, reducing the need for joints and fittings / thereby reducing costs. Copper also has good thermal conductivity which is good for distributing heat in a home heating system. In addition to these specific physical and working properties, copper does not rust in contact with water, which make it safe to use for drinking water and is also relatively easy to repair in the event of a leak.

39. Sources and origins

Stage 1   The timber for making the board will be de-barked and then chipped.

Stage 2   The chips will be mechanically broken down and mixed with water to produce a pulp.

Stage 3   The pulp will be treated to remove impurities and to prevent it from being too absorbent.

Stage 4   The pulp is then fed onto a wire mesh to dry out.

Stage 5   It is calendared with rollers and dried further until it reaches the thickness of board that is required.

40. Stock forms, types and sizes 1

500 microns = 0.5 mm

10 cm = 100 mm

$\frac{100}{0.5}$ = 200 sheets of card

41. Stock forms, types and sizes 2

Self-adhesive envelopes are more popular than gummed envelopes because to moisten the gum, the user may lick the gum and that may be unhygienic. Also, the self-seal envelopes will be easier to use as they will save time as you do not need to wait for the glue to cure.

42. Wastage

Any five of the following:

- Set the laser cutter with the correct feed rate for the thickness of board to be cut.
- Transfer the CAD file to the laser cutter.
- Place board in the correct position in the machine.
- Calibrate the cutter so that it is in the correct position to start.
- Ensure all doors are closed.
- Turn on extraction.
- Run the program to cut the board.

43. Addition

1 The poster will be encapsulated as it would seal the paper from any moisture as it is outside and the water cannot seep into the paper.

2

- A laminating pouch that fits an A4 sheet of paper is chosen.
- Place the paper into the laminating pouch and ensure that there is a clear edge all round.
- Switch on the laminating machine and heat up to the correct temperature.
- Place the pouch and A4 paper into the machine and the rollers will pull it through the heaters to seal.

44. Deforming and reforming

45. Surface treatments and finishes

The printed card will be fed by conveyor belt past the nozzles that will spray a fine spray of varnish over the surface of the card. The card then passes under UV lights where the light dries the varnish onto the card.

46. Commercial processes

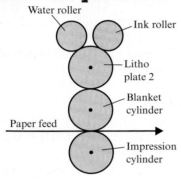

47. Selecting papers and boards

Two of:
- Function – The leaflet flyers can be made using standard sizes of paper which means they can easily fit in envelopes or through letterboxes.
- Aesthetics – The offset lithography process allows for bright and multiple colours to make the leaflet or flyer eye-catching.
- Scale of production – The offset lithography process suits the high volumes required for leaflets / flyers.
- Finishing – The offset lithography process allows for printing on both sides of the paper for maximum information.

48. Sources and origins

Kiln seasoning will have temperature regulation so there is more control over the level of moisture and the speed it is achieved and chemicals can be used to kill bacteria and pests. There will be a larger quantity of timber seasoned, it uses less space and it is a quicker process and will reduce costs.

49. Stock forms, types and sizes

Planks are available rough sawn or planed all round (PAR). Rough sawn wood is rough, has not been planed and is suitable for exterior work, for example fence panels. Planks which are PAR have been planed and are smooth to touch with more precise dimensions. They are suitable for interior work, such as skirting boards.

50. Standard components

Drill a pilot hole through both pieces of the timber.

Drill a clearance hole in part A to allow the shank of the screw to easily fit through.

Insert the round head screw and tighten to screw the two pieces of timber together.

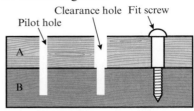

51. Wastage 1

The kerf should be wider than the blade because as the blade goes into the saw cut, it can bind in the groove and make it difficult to cut.

52. Wastage 2

Use a curved rasp or surform to roughly shape the back of the spoon.

Use the rasp or surform at roughly 45° to the wood grain.

Starting with a low grit abrasive paper, remove the scratches from the filing.

Gradually use finer grit (higher number) abrasive papers to remove the remaining marks.

53. Addition

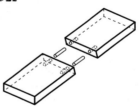

54. Deforming and reforming

1 Laminated wood will be stronger than solid wood for the legs of the chair. The natural faults of timber can be removed by selecting good laminates. Due to the layers, there is less chance of warping or twisting. There is a reduced chance of short grain in the laminated timber.

2 The lengths of timber are put into a steam box. Steam is then introduced to the box and it increases the moisture in the timber. Once there is enough moisture, the timber is removed and forced around a former and left until the moisture content goes back to the normal state.

55. Surface treatments and finishes

The pine to be treated will be placed into the tanalising tank. A vacuum will remove the moisture before the tank is flooded with a solution of copper sulphate. This is forced into the timber under pressure before the excess is removed. The timber is then dried out ready for use.

56.Commercial processes
- Mark the centre points of each end of the timber section.
- Drill a small hole in one end to locate the taper centre.
- Mark a cross on the second end from corner to corner for the drive centre.
- Cut a 'v' groove across the corners for a firm location of the drive centre.

57. Using and working with timbers
Any two of the following:
- Function – The MDF is available in wide sheets with a smooth flat surface which will take a decorative laminated layer.
- Aesthetics – Although the MDF is not attractive itself, it can be laminated with other timbers and polymer laminates.
- Scale of production – Suits high volume production and companies will make many thousands of these desks.
- Mechanical properties – The MDF has sufficient strength to support the weight of the construction and the weight of the objects placed on it.
- Environmental factors – The MDF is made from recycled or scrap timber which reduces the need for new timber to be processed
- Availability – MDF is readily available in standard forms such as thickness and sheet size to suit the different parts of the desk.
- Costs – MDF is relatively cheap and manufacturing costs are reduced further as the customer can assemble the product at home.

58. Sources and origins
To refine iron from iron ore, a blast furnace is used. The iron ore, coke, limestone and air is fed into the furnace and is heated up to 2000°C where the carbon burns and displaces the iron from the iron oxide to create carbon dioxide. The iron is then collected from the bottom of the furnace as a liquid. The limestone is used to remove any acidic impurities.

59. Stock forms, types and sizes
Cross-sectional area = Area of outer circle (A) − Area of inner circle (B)
Area of outer circle = $\pi r^2 = 3.142 \times 15 \times 15 = 706.95$
Area of inner circle = $\pi r^2 = 3.142 \times 10 \times 10 = 314.2$
A − B = 392.75 cm^2
$\qquad$ = 393 cm^2

60. Wastage 1
Piercing Saw or Abrafile

61. Wastage 2
- Fit the cylindrical bar into the chuck.
- Place left-hand turning tool in tool post.
- Face off the end of the bar to get it square.

- Put a roughing tool in tool holder.
- Set the cross slide to the correct angle and taper turn the bar to the 25 mm back along the length.
- Continue until the end diameter is 15 mm.
- Place left-hand turning tool in tool holder.
- Parallel turn the step back to 10 mm.
- Use parting tool to complete component.

62. Wastage 3
- Use a rough file and cross file the surface to remove the main marks from the hacksaw and check for accuracy using an engineer's square.
- Use a second or smooth file and draw file to remove the marks left by the rough file.
- Starting with a low grit number, use wet and dry or emery paper to remove the fine scratches from the filing.
- Gradually use finer grit abrasive papers to remove the remaining marks.

63. Addition
Brazing needs lower temperatures to join the metals and this will lower the cost and result in less thermal distortion.

Brazed joints will have sufficient strength for many applications and require less skill to produce.

The aesthetics of a brazed joint are better than the rippled effect of a welded joint. Welded joints may need additional finishing for aesthetic or assembly reasons.

The process is an easier process and because you are not melting the base metals it is less prone to error.

It is easier to join dissimilar metals by brazing rather than by welding.

64. Deforming and reforming
- A die made with the correct shaped cut-out is made, in this case it is an inverted 'T' shape.

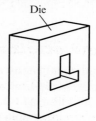
Die

- The die is fitted into the die holder of the extrusion machine.
- The billet of metal is brought to the die.
- The ram then pushes the billet through the die with great force (hot or cold).
- The extrusion is chopped to the desired length and cooled.

65. Modification of properties for specific purposes
The stages of hardening and tempering high carbon steel to be used in a screwdriver blade are as follows:
- Heat the steel to a defined temperature (900°C).
- Quench the steel in water.

- Clean the steel with emery cloth so the oxide colours can be seen.
- Heat the steel to a defined temperature (300–315°C) which is indicated by the colour of the steel as it turns dark purple.
- When the correct temperature is reached quench the steel in water.

66. Surface treatments and finishes
- The scissor handles need to be in two parts.
- The scissor handles will be sand blasted to remove any dirt.
- The metal part is heated to above the melting temperature of the polymer (230°C).
- Air is pumped into the powder tank causing the powder to rise and move around (fluidise)
- The handles are lowered into the liquidised polymer and the polymer sticks to the metal.
- The metal part is removed and allowed to cool.
- The polymer solidifies as it cools.
- The scissors can be assembled.

67. Commercial processes
The model car is made by die casting because there is very good dimensional accuracy on the model for a product this size. It is a repeatable process that allows for many cars to be made exactly the same size using the same mould. The process does not require much post finishing while sand casting needs waste metal to be cut off.

68. Using and working with metals
Two answers from the following:
- Function – The cast iron is corrosion resistant so that it will not decay if liquids are spilt on it.
- Physical properties – The cast iron is heavy so that it is more stable in use.
- Aesthetics – The cast iron can be painted which makes it suitable for workshop use.
- Scale of production – The cast iron can be easily cast into the shape of the body so it suits being made in large batches.
- Mechanical properties – The cast iron is strong so it can resist the compressive forces on it.
- Availability – The cast iron is readily available and can be melted so that it can be poured into the mould.
- Costs – Cast iron is a low cost metal that is readily available.
- Environmental factors – The cast iron can be easily recycled after use.

69. Sources and origins
Alkenes are produced in a fractioning tower. The process starts with the crude oil being heated until it boils and evaporates. This is around 400°C. The evaporated gas goes into the fractioning tower where it condenses at different temperatures. The fractions are then collected at different temperatures in the tower. Naphtha is used in chemical production to make polymers and different plastics

70. Stock forms, types and sizes
Diameter A − diameter B

25 − 20 = 5

$\frac{5}{2} = 2.5\,\text{mm}$

71. Wastage 1
- Set the laser cutter with the correct feed rate for the thickness of acrylic to be cut.
- Transfer the CAD file to the laser cutter.
- Place acrylic in the correct position in the machine.
- Calibrate the cutter so that it is in the correct position to start.
- Ensure all doors are closed.
- Turn on extraction.
- Run the program to cut the acrylic.

72. Wastage 2
Use a rough file.

Cross file the surface to remove the main marks from the band saw.

Use a second or smooth file.

Draw file to remove the marks left by the rough file.

73. Addition and deforming 1
- Place the former in the vacuum forming machine.
- Clamp the rigid polystyrene or polymer into the machine.
- Switch on heater.
- Wait until the rigid polystyrene is sufficiently flexible.
- Blow air in to raise the rigid polystyrene.
- Raise the base and lift the former to the rigid polystyrene.
- Use the vacuum to remove the air and the air pressure pulls the plastic around the former.
- Allow to cool and remove from machine.
- Trim waste material from the moulding.

74. Addition and deforming 2
The support material may be used at the arched hole at the front to stop the polymer collapsing into the hole.

The support material may also be used to support the piece at the top where it is wider (the cantilever).

75. Modification of properties
The use of expanded polymer means that the surfboard will be more buoyant and will float on the water. The foam will also be lighter, which makes the surfboard easier to carry. It will also reduce the costs as there is less material used as the expanded foam will have a lot of air pockets.

76. Surface treatments and finishes
The pattern will be printed onto a soluble film that is then placed in a tank of water. The paper will dissolve leaving the ink to float on the water's surface. The cycle helmet is then immersed in the water and the ink is transferred to the helmet and left to dry.

77. Commercial processes

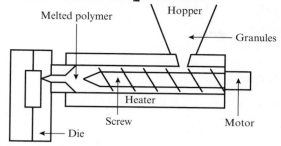

- The granules drop into the barrel.
- The screw thread moves them along the barrel.
- The heaters melt the polymer.
- The polymer collects and is injected into the die.
- The polymer is water cooled in the die.
- The moulded polymer is ejected by pins in the die.

78. Using and working with polymers

Any two of the following:
- Function – The UF is suitable because it is a safe material to use in this situation as it does not conduct electricity.
- Aesthetics – The bright white finish is suitable for all types of environment.
- Scale of production – The UF is easily moulded into shape which is suitable to large-scale production.
- Mechanical properties – The UF has good strength and is durable so it can resist the forces of the plugs being inserted and removed.
- Finishing – The UF is self-finishing and does not require any other finishes, which keeps costs low.
- Physical properties – The UF is an electrical insulator and is suitable for electronic products.
- Physical properties – The UF has heat resistance as it is a thermosetting plastic, and this means it will resist heat, if for example a socket is getting hot due to an electrical fault.

79. Sources and origins

1 Cotton seeds are dried and cleaned and the seeds and lint are separated from raw cotton. The lint is then carded to straighten the fibres before spinning.
2 The cocoon from the silkworm is put into hot water where the threads can be separated and unravelled into a fine fibre.

80. Stock forms, types and sizes

VELCRO® is suitable as you do not need any special skill to operate the fastening. The VELCRO® is also quick to fasten as it does not need precise lining up and is therefore adjustable. VELCRO® is also very quick to release in case of an emergency.

81. Wastage

1 Seam ripper
2 The saw tooth cut from pinking shears reduces the amount of fraying because it limits the length of the frayed thread and reduces the tendency to fray.

82. Addition 1

A basting stitch may be used on fabrics to secure a pattern to a fabric so that the material can be cut to the correct shape. It would also be used to tack a fabric with a temporary fixing so that it can then be put through a sewing machine and avoids the use of pins.

83. Addition 2

1 PVC is suitable for the sports bag because it is waterproof to protect the contents of the bag. The fabric lining is strong so that the bag can carry a good amount of weight. The PVC also comes in a range of colours to improve the aesthetics of the bag.
2 The piping around the edge gives the sports bag more strength as it is likely to be handled roughly. It also protects the edges of the bag when thrown on the floor. The piping also improves the aesthetics of the bag so that it is more likely to be bought by the customer.

84. Deforming and reforming

1 Pleating or tucking
2 Hems
3 Gathering

85. Surface treatments and finishes

A flame retardant protection would be used so it reduces the risk of the material catching fire if it is too close to a heat source. The fabric could also be given stain protection, to prevent the toy from becoming dirty, as it is important that children's toys are hygienic and can be kept clean easily.

86. Commercial processes

Chemical dyes will have a larger range of colours which can also be brighter to produce a wider range of designs. Chemical dyes can be made to exact specifications which mean that when a new batch needs to be made the colours will match exactly. However, chemicals are produced using chemicals from petroleum products that may be harmful to the environment or may be harmful to the people using the dyes. This means that for most applications the natural dyes will be much more environmentally friendly, but may not last as long or be as vibrant as the chemical dyes.

87. Using and working with textiles

Any two of the following:
- Function – The wool is very soft and comfortable to walk on in the home.
- Aesthetics – The wool can take dyes to be any colour to suit different people's tastes.
- Scale of production – The process of weaving is suitable to high volume production.
- Mechanical properties – Wool has good strength and wear properties and will resist being walked on.
- Finishing – Wool can have a range of finishes such as stain resistant so that it keeps its colour for longer.

- Environmental factors – Wool is a natural material and is very sustainable as it grows on sheep and other animals; it is also biodegradable.
- Availability – Wool is naturally occurring so it is readily available which keeps costs low.
- Physical properties – The wool is naturally fire resistant which is would prevent fire from spreading quickly.

88. Stock forms – circuit boards

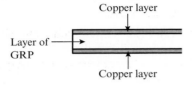

89. Stock forms – resistors

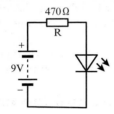

90. Stock forms – dual in-line packages and microcontrollers

The advantage of having flash memory in a digital radio alarm clock is that if there was a power cut the settings like the radio station will have been stored and will not have to be reprogrammed in.

91. Stock forms – mechanical

Pulley system A would be preferred because it has the same mechanical advantage but will take up less space. Pulley system A can also be suspended easily from a single point and be balanced.

92. Wastage

- Set the laser cutter with the correct feed rate for the thickness of acrylic to be cut.
- Transfer the CAD file to the laser cutter.
- Place acrylic in the correct position in the machine.
- Calibrate the cutter so that it is in the correct position to start.
- Ensure all doors are closed.
- Turn on extraction.
- Run the program to cut the acrylic.

93. Addition

To remove excess solder you need to heat the solder up until it has turned back into a liquid. You can then use the de-solder pump or braid to suck the liquid solder from the circuit board. The de-solder pump is similar to a bicycle pump and has a vacuum that sucks up the molten solder.

94. Modification of properties

The stages of case hardening steel to be used for gears are as follows:
- Heat the steel to around 950°C which is reached when the steel glows cherry red.
- Place the steel in a carbon rich bath of powdered carbon which hardens the outer surface.
- Repeating the process gives the added carbon layer greater depth.

95. Surface treatments and finishes

Grease is used in bearings as it has a high viscosity, which means it will stay in place when the bearings rotate, while oil lubrication will come out of the bearings as they spin fast.

96. Commercial processes

The advantages of re-flow soldering are that there does not need to be a secondary process to apply the flux for soldering and it is easier to add components to both sides of the circuit board than using wave flow soldering.

97. Using and working with electronic and mechanical systems

Any two from the following:
- Physical properties – The electronic system uses a minimum amount of space due to the microelectronics.
- Availability – The components used will be standard sizes and values which will reduce the cost of the system.
- Function – An electronic system will be able to control a wide range of functions and programs for the microwave.
- Scale of production – Suits high volume production and companies will make many thousands of these using commercial soldering techniques to reduce costs.
- Environmental factors – The materials used on the electronic system, such as solder and copper circuit board, can be recycled after use.
- Ethical sources – The materials used in the electrical system will be sourced from sustainable areas of the world and the factories assembling the systems will need to be ethically managed.
- Finishing – The circuit board will have a PCB lacquer applied so that it is not affected by the moisture present.
- Social factors – The electronic system will be made with quality parts that will last for the expected life of the microwave as there is more obsolescence in kitchen products as their life expectancy is shorter.

98. Selection of materials or components

A designer that is producing a child's toy that is being sold in a toy shop will need to ensure that the materials have good aesthetics, such as colour and texture so that they attract the child to the product. The materials need to be cost-effective as this will make the product cheaper and more can be sold. Finally, the materials need to be suitable for the needs of children and respond to their particular needs which could be the safety of the product or based on social factors such as fashion/trends.

99. Forces and stresses

1 A beam can be in tension because the underside of the beam is being stretched, while the top side of the beam is being compressed as it is being pushed into a smaller space.

2 Neutral axis

100. Ecological issues 1

1 The Life Cycle Assessment has identified that the greatest environmental impact in a family car is the use, as it will continually need fuel when it is in use. The manufacture of the mobile phone has the greatest impact due to the extraction and conversion of a large range of different materials.

2 The environmental impact of the car can be reduced if the family car was made more fuel efficient by making it more aerodynamic, or if it was made from thinner / lighter / recycled materials or used alternative energy resources such as hybrid technology for electrically power. The phone can be made more environmentally friendly by using more standard components, having more efficient recharge of the batteries, being constructed from thinner/ lighter/recycled materials or by reducing the size of the phone to use less materials.

101. Ecological issues 2

1 & 2

Any one from:

- Paper and boards
  Laminated board cookery book
  Avoid using laminated hard covers as it makes it difficult to separate the individual materials for recycling so there is less waste.
- Timber
  Oak bookcase
  Use timber that has been accredited by the Forest Stewardship Council as that means that it comes from a sustainable source where there is a replanting scheme.
- Systems
  AAA batteries in remote control
  The batteries could be made so that they are rechargeable, which will reduce the amount of materials needed for batteries over the life of the product.
- Metals
  Stainless steel pans
  Use recycled metals in the construction of the pans which reduces the amount of raw metals that have to be processed.

- Textiles
  Cotton curtains
  Use materials from eco-friendly resources, such as sustainably grown fibre crops or recycled fibres rather than using synthetic fibres.
- Polymers
  Electric food mixer
  Identify by labelling the different polymers used in the mixer so that they can be easily identified and separated.

102. Social issues

Companies will look after the welfare and health of workers in a number of ways:

- They will ensure that all health and safety regulations are being followed.
- Companies will ensure that there is adequate ventilation and lighting in the working environment.
- Companies will allow flexible working for employees and help with individual personal circumstances and ensure fair pay.
- Companies will provide welfare facilities for adequate breaks in the working day.

103. The six Rs and the environment

The designer has designed the bag to be reusable so that the customer can get maximum use out of it before it wears out. The designer has also refused to accept that plastic bags are suitable and has designed an alternative solution that is made from natural materials which make it sustainable.

104. Scales of production

Mass production methods will be used to produce the mouse because the mouse can be made more cheaply as the company will be able to buy the materials in bulk which increases the economies of scale. The mouse has a simple construction that is suited to assembly on a production line as it can be broken down into different stages. Many of the production methods can be automated which means that lower skilled workers can be employed at lower cost.

105. The use of production aids

Patterns can be used many times to mark out or form around. Patterns can be cost-effective as they are made from cheaper materials and can be easily remade if the design changes.

106. Quality control during manufacture

The colour of the inks to be printed on the surface of the radio may be visually checked against the original colour design to make sure it is the correct colour for the British flag. The PCB circuit boards may be monitored and timed when they are being etched to ensure that the copper tracks are accurate. The individual parts, such as the size of the circuit board or speakers, may be checked against a go/no go gauge to ensure that they fit the space within the carcases of the radio.

107. Investigation using primary and secondary data

One advantage of gathering primary data is that the researcher can target particular issues that are pertinent to the specific problem which will give valuable data that address the problem, such is individual preferences from the client or user. The data can then be interpreted better as there is no other information that is not required. The data are also very current as they are being sourced when needed rather than statistical data which may be sourced from government and out of date as surveys are completed infrequently.

108. Investigating using secondary data

- The office chair has a height adjustment so that it can fit a wide range of users from the 5th to the 95th percentile.
- The office chair has wheels at the base which means that it will be easy to move around the office.
- The chair is able to swivel on its base, which means that the user can turn the chair when sat at a desk to reach different areas.
- The chair has arm rests on which the user can rest their arms to prevent fatigue when working for long periods.

109. Investigation using secondary data

1 The materials are waterproof and the fabric protects the contents from getting wet in the rain or when in changing rooms. The bag has separate compartments for the convenience of the user to separate different items. The cost of the bag is relatively low so it will be within the price range of most users and readily available. The design is plain so it is pleasing to the eye with subtle colours that will not offend. However, depending on the textiles used, the bag may scuff when it is used. Overall the bag is very suitable for an athlete as it will be able to safely contain all the relevant items the user would need and be easy to carry.

2 The handles are a suitable size to fit the average user's hands. The shoulder straps on the bag have been designed to fit over the shoulder strap can be used to spread the weight being carried. The separate pockets make it easy for the user to access the contents, with a zip that will be within the strength range of the user. The materials are relatively lightweight so they do not compromise the bag when in use. Overall the bag is very good as it has specific features such as two types of handles, separate pockets and it is light enough to carry easily.

110. The work of other designers 1

Modernist designers were able to be more innovative because of the development of new materials, such as steel tubes and laminated wood, which were stronger than traditional materials. There was also the development of new manufacturing techniques that allowed for a wider range of construction processes, such as forming tubular steel or polymers.

111. The work of other designers 2

A model or prototype can be used to show a client how a design would look and feel as it can be physically handled and demonstrate actual features that may be in the finished design and used as part of the client questionnaire. A scale model or prototype allows the designer to test out construction methods and strength of joints and materials which cannot be tested fully on a computer. Making a model or prototype may identify design problems at an early stage before expensive tooling is set up for a long production run.

112. The work of other companies

Any two from:
- Alessi: Functional and visually appealing; mass produced.
- Apple: Cutting edge design; accessible to the user.
- Braun: Functional, simple designs; innovative.
- Dyson: Innovative designs; focus on improving efficiency.
- Gap: Ethical principles; everyday clothing.
- Primark: Quality products; economic for customers to buy.
- Under Armour: Innovative technical designs; enhance performance in sport.
- Zara: Customer-centred clothing design; manufacturing process embraces new technology.

113. Design strategies

Using the iterative design process you can produce a range of brainstormed sketches that can be shown to a client before focusing on a limited range as you will then be able to obtain the client's views at an early stage. In the development of a design, you could model an aspect of the design so that you can see whether it would work, such as modelling a container and fitting objects to be stored to ensure they fit. Testing can also be used on parts that are to be constructed to ensure that the construction method is strong enough. You also need to evaluate the design as it moves forward to ensure that it meets the criteria set down in the specification and make changes if certain aspects have not been covered.

114. Communication of design ideas 1

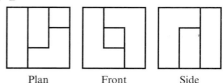

Plan   Front   Side

115. Communication of design ideas 2

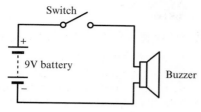

116. Marking out

As the blade is a straight line
$180° − 45° = 135°$

117. Material management

Surface area of the circles $= \pi r^2 \times 3$
$= 3.142 \times 3 \times 3 \times 3$
$= 84.834 \, \text{cm}^2$

Surface area of the square $= 12 \times 12$
$= 144 \, \text{cm}^2$

Waste $= 144 − 84.834$
$= 59.166 \, \text{cm}^2$
$= 59.2 \, \text{cm}^2$

118. Working safely

- All of the processes can be completed behind guards which mean that the workers are not close to moving parts or flying debris.
- The operations can be completed in sealed environments, which mean that the workers have less risk of exposure to toxic substances fumes and dust.
- The CAM machinery will be able to lift heavier weight for parts in the manufacturing process which could have caused injury if manually lifted.
- CAM machinery does not suffer from fatigue which could lead to a loss of concentration and mistakes being made when there is a human operator.

119. Maths skills 1

1 Area of square $= 10 \times 10 = 100 \, \text{cm}^2$
   Area of half circle $= \dfrac{(\pi r^2)}{2}$
   $= \dfrac{(3.142 \times 5 \times 5)}{2}$
   $= 39.275 \, \text{cm}^2$
   Total area $= 100 + 39.275 = 139.275 = 139.3 \, \text{cm}^2$

2 Volume $=$ total area $\times$ length
   $139.3 \times 50 = 6965 \, \text{cm}^3$ or $6.965 \, \text{m}^3$

120. Maths skills 2

a) 1. 27cm^3
    2. 26.85cm^3

b) $26.84987324 \times 1000000 = 26849873.24$

121. Maths skills 3

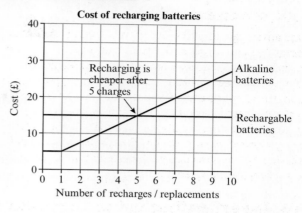

122. Maths skills 4

1 $A^2 + B^2 = C^2$
   $3 \times 3 + 4 \times 4 = X^2$
   $25 = X^2$
   $5 = X$

2 Area of triangle $= \frac{1}{2}$ base $\times$ height
   $1.5 \times 4 = 6 \, \text{cm}^2$
   Area of rectangle $=$ base $\times$ height
   $6 \times 4 = 24 \, \text{cm}^2$
   Total area $= 30 \, \text{cm}^2$

3 Volume $=$ cross-sectional area $\times$ length
   $500 \, \text{mm} = 50 \, \text{cm}$
   $30 \times 50 = 1500 \, \text{cm}^3$

123. Exam skills 1

An idler gear is used to reverse the direction of rotation of a simple gear train.

124. Exam skills 2

An idler gear is attached between the driver gear and the driven gear as this will keep the direction of rotation the same for the driver gear and wheel without affecting speed.

The driver gear will have twice the number of teeth than the driven gear as this will make the driven gear rotate at twice the speed.

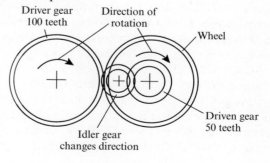

125. Exam skills 3

The advantages of using robot technology is that the robots will be ideal for repetitive tasks as they do not get tired and they will have a higher level of accuracy over humans. They will also be able to work much faster and will not need a break which means they complete more work. They will also be able to work in hazardous areas or lift heavier weights. They can be easily updated using software and can link to other automated systems such as quality control. However, robots do cost a lot of money to set up and they need to complete a lot of tasks to get a return. They could take away jobs from the traditional workforce and this may lower the morale of the workers. Overall, the robots will be beneficial because they will improve the safety in the factory and will be able to produce more units which in turn will help the company to be profitable. Some staff displaced by the robots will be able to be re-employed in different areas of the factory and will also be needed to operate or program the robots.

126. Exam skills 4

1 Convert the three amounts to percentage
- Nuclear $\frac{24}{120} \times 100 = 20\%$
- Coal $\frac{12}{120} \times 100 = 10\%$
- Gas $\frac{48}{120} \times 100 = 40\%$

Power source	Total energy consumption in gigawatts (GW)	Percentage of total
Renewables	30	25
Nuclear	24	20
Coal	12	10
Gas	48	40
Oil and others	6	5
Total	120	100

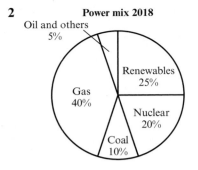

2 **Power mix 2018**

127. Exam skills 5

Area of ends = $75 \times 50 \times 2 = 7500 \, mm^2$

Area of front and back = $125 \times 50 \times 2 = 12\,500 \, mm^2$

Area of top and bottom = $125 \times 75 \times 2 = 18\,750 \, mm^2$

Total surface area = $7500 + 12\,500 + 18\,750$

$= 38\,750 \, mm^2$

To convert $mm^2 = cm^2$ divide by $100 = 387.5 \, cm^2$

Published by Pearson Education Limited, 80 Strand, London, WC2R 0RL.

www.pearsonschoolsandfecolleges.co.uk

Text and illustrations © Pearson Education Ltd 2018
Typeset and illustrated by Tech-Set Ltd, Gateshead
Produced by Hart McLeod Ltd, Cambridge
Cover illustration by Eoin Coveney

The right of Mark Wellington to be identified as author of this work has been asserted by him in accordance with the Copyright, Designs and Patents Act 1988.

First published 2018

21 20 19 18
10 9 8 7 6 5 4 3 2 1

British Library Cataloguing in Publication Data
A catalogue record for this book is available from the British Library

ISBN 978 1 292 19158 4

Printed in Slovakia by Neografia.

Acknowledgements
The authors and publisher would like to thank the following individuals and organisations for their kind permission to reproduce copyright material.

Photographs
(Key: b-bottom; c-centre; l-left; r-right; t-top)

123RF: 41, 67, 83t, 116, Tim@awe 19tl, Matteo69 19c, Kunertus 59, Ensup 95tl, Bialasiewicz 99, Bond80 104br, Vvoennyy 105t; **Alamy Stock Photo:** View Stock 16r, Dmytro Skorobogatov 19bc, Krys Bailey 21cl, Jakob Kamende 32br, Richard Hall 33b, Robert Convery 38r, Herbie Springer 41, Luminis 41, Tatiana Koroleva 41, FeedStock 41, ItsOnlyLight 41, PongsakPolbubpha 42tr, NielsPoulsenstd 42br, ZeynurBabayev 42b, Adrian Muttitt43t, David J. Green 43cl, 91, Chris Howes/Wild Places Photography 43b, Studiomode 44t, Gunter Kirsch 44c, LakovFilimonov 44bl, Johnanthony 50bcr, Olga Sapegina 51, Mint Images Limited 52b, Phovoir 56tr, 73, Jim Thompson/Albuquerque Journal/ZUMA Wire 56c, Phil Degginger 57bl, Olekcii Mach 59, 91, 70tr, Francesco Losenno/Zoonar GmbH 62cr, Ingram Publishing 75, Graeme Lamb 76t, Radka LinkovÃ¡/Profimedia.CZ a.s 79b, Ale Ventura/ PhotoAltosas 80tcl, Anton Starikov/Zoonar GmbH 80tcr, Vik_Y 81cbl, ArunasGabalis 82t, A-plus image bank 83cl, Cultura Creative 84tr, ZUMA Press, Inc. 85tl, Michael Rosenfeld/ Maximilian S/RGB Ventures/SuperStock 86, Mike Robinson 86, Wavebreak Media ltd 87cr, AndrzejTokarski 90cr, Igor Stevanovic 91, CheeKeong Lee 91, Rommma 91, Andrew Paterson 103t, IS2009-03/Image Source 103b, Goddard New Era 106, Ivan Smuk 110, V&A Images 110, CFimages 110, Amie/Mauritius images GmbH 110, PawelOpaska 110, National Motor Museum/Heritage Image Partnership Ltd 111, WENN Ltd 111, MaisantLudovic/Hemis 111, Pictorial Press Ltd 111, RiouJean-Christophe 111, Image Scotland 111, Duncan Snow 111, Malcolm Park editorial 111, SFM Press Reporter 112, Cyberstock 112, Hugh Threlfall 112, 112, KristofferTripplaar 112, Matthew Horwood 112, Roman Tiraspolsky 112, PhotoEdit 112, DmitriyShironosov 116, Will Burwell 116, Image Farm Inc 116; **Brand X Pictures:** Joe Atlas 42tl; **Carlisle Brass:** Image Courtesy of Carlisle Brass Ltd. 50br; **Getty Images:** J. B. Spector/ Museum of Science and Industry Chicago/Archive Photos 17tl, Víctor Del Pino/EyeEm 42bl, Coddy/iStock 59, Princessdlaf/iStock 64, Leemage/Universal Images Group 110; **Gold Eagle Co.:** Gold Eagle Co. 85b; **Imagemore:** 70tl; **Image Source:** 36; **Pearson Education Ltd:** Gareth Boden 27, 37c, 42cl, 42tbl, 50c, 51, 51, 51, 51, 52tr, 52cr, 60tr, 60c, 62b, 71tc, 71cl, 88b, 105b, 116, 116, 116, 116, Rob Judges 71cr; Trevor Clifford 32tl, 32tr, 32ctl, 32ctr, 32bl, 33tl, 33tr, 33c, 51, 51, 51, 51, 52tl, 62t, 71bl, 72t, 72bl, 116, 116, 116, 116; Studio 8 60tl, 68b, 71tl; Jules Selmes 62cl, 71bc, 71br, 90cl, 90b, 93cr, 116; Lisa Payne Photography 87b; Photodisc: C Squared Studios 78b, F. Schussler/Photolink 116; Photolibrary.com: Monty Rakusen/Cultura 104c; Sozaijiten: Sozaijiten 66t; **Science Photo Library:** Martyn F. Chillmaid 19tr; **Shutterstock:** DmytroZinkevych 1, Julia Ivantsova 4, Sportpoint 6, Pavel L Photo and Video 7, POM POM 9, Smallcreative11, Pukach 14, AlexandrBognat 15, Fabiodevilla 16l, Digital Storm 17tr, Fotokostic 17b, Hurst Photo 19bl, DmitrijSkorobogatov 19br, Monstar Studio 20l, Grasko 20r,

Note from the publisher

Pearson has robust editorial processes, including answer and fact checks, to ensure the accuracy of the content in this publication, and every effort is made to ensure this publication is free of errors. We are, however, only human, and occasionally errors do occur. Pearson is not liable for any misunderstandings that arise as a result of errors in this publication, but it is our priority to ensure that the content is accurate. If you spot an error, please do contact us at resourcescorrections@pearson.com so we can make sure it is corrected.